The

LAW

and the

LIBERAL ARTS

edited by

ALBERT BRODERICK, O. P.

The Catholic University of America Press

Washington, D. C. 20017

Table of Contents

Participating Personnel and Institutions

AMERICAN UNIVERSITY
Professor Lawrence W. Wadsworth, Associate Dean, Arts and Sciences, Political Science, International Law;
Professor Chester Earle, Government and Public Administration;
Professor Robert Goosetree, Law;
Professor Theodore Ratchak, Philosophy;
Professor Austin Vanderslice, Sociology.

AQUINAS INSTITUTE OF PHILOSOPHY AND THEOLOGY, River Forest, Ill.
Rev. John Corcoran, O.P., Philosophy and Theology;
Rev. Ralph Powell, O.P., Philosophy and Sociology.

UNIVERSITY OF CALIFORNIA, BERKELEY
Professor Philip Selznick, Sociology (Center for Study of Law and Society).

CARDINAL CUSHING COLLEGE, Brookline, Mass.,
Dr. Elizabeth J. Dolan, Social Science.

CARLETON UNIVERSITY, Ottawa, Canada
Professor Richard D. Abbott, Public Law.

THE CATHOLIC UNIVERSITY OF AMERICA
Graduate School of Arts and Sciences:
Professors Lang and Kenny, Anthropology; Farrell, History; Roberts and Beitzinger, Politics; Potvin, Sociology.
School of Philosophy:
Professor Nolan.
School of Theology:
Very Rev. Walter S. Schmitz, S.S., Dean,
School of Law:
Dean Miller, Associate Dean Garvey, Professors Arens, Broderick, English, Frankino, Granfield, Keeffe, Spark, Valeri.

CITY COLLEGE OF THE CITY UNIVERSITY OF NEW YORK
Dr. Reuben Frodin, Dean, College of Liberal Arts and Sciences.

COLUMBIA UNIVERSITY
Professor Adolf A. Berle, Law.

UNIVERSITY OF DENVER
Professor Robert B. Yegge, Law and Sociology (Program in Judicial Administration).

DE PAUL UNIVERSITY
Rev. John T. Richardson, C.M., Executive Vice-President, Theology.

GEORGETOWN UNIVERSITY
Rev. Richard McSorley, S.J., Economics and Theology.

GEORGE WASHINGTON UNIVERSITY
Professors Arthur Miller and Monroe Freedman, Law.

HOWARD UNIVERSITY
Dean Clyde C. Ferguson, Jr., Law.

COLLEGE OF MOUNT ST. VINCENT
Sister Marie Leonore, Social Science.

NORTHWESTERN UNIVERSITY
Professor Victor G. Rosenblum, Law and Political Science (Program in Law and the Social Sciences).

PROVIDENCE COLLEGE
Professors John F. Cunningham, O.P., Theology, Philosophy and Humanities; Thomas R. Peterson, O.P., Theology and Administration, Cornelius P. Forster, O.P., History.

UNIVERSITY OF PARIS, France
Professor Michel Villey, Faculté de Droit et des Sciences Economiques.

SETON HALL UNIVERSITY
Professor John Duff, History;
Professor Miriam T. Rooney, Law and Philosophy.

UNIVERSITY OF TOLEDO
Professor Francis E. Barkman, Law.
TRINITY COLLEGE, Washington, D.C.
Professor Edna R. Fluegel, Political Science.
TUSKEGEE INSTITUTE, Tuskegee, Ala.
Dean Richard Wasserstrom, Arts and Sciences, and Law.
VILLANOVA UNIVERSITY
Rev. Robert J. Walsh, O.S.A., Administration;
Professor Donald W. Dowd, Law;
Professor John E. Hughes, Sociology.
UNIVERSITY OF WISCONSIN
Professor Harry V. Ball, Sociology (Law and Sociology Program);
Professor Robert Alford, Sociology.
YESHIVA UNIVERSITY
Professor Emanuel Rackman, Political Science, Assistant to President.

OBSERVERS

ANCILLA DOMINI COLLEGE, Donaldson, Indiana
Sister Mary Florian Weber, R.H.J.C.
BRENTWOOD COLLEGE, Long Island, N. Y.
Sister James Eugene Madden, C.S.J.;
Sister Maria Eucharia Meehan, C.S.J.
CALDWELL COLLEGE FOR WOMEN, Caldwell, N. J.
Sister M. Regina McEntee, Chairman, Social Science.
MARYKNOLL SISTERS MOTHERHOUSE, Maryknoll, N. Y.
Sister Marie Gabriel Hobler.
CONVENT OF MOUNT ST. VINCENT, New York
Sister Miriam Ellen.
COLLEGE OF ST. ELIZABETH
Sister Frances Augustine Rickey, Philosophy.
ST. MARY'S COLLEGE, Winona, Minn.
Brother K. Basil O'Leary, F.S.C.
COLLEGE OF ST. ROSE, Albany, New York
Sister Catherine Therese Knoop, C.S.J.;
Sister Felice Shumway, C.S.J.
NORTHWESTERN UNIVERSITY
Michael Barkun, Program in Law and the Social Sciences, Political Science.

SPECIAL GUESTS

Mark S. Massel, Senior Associate, Brookings Institution, *Conference Chairman*.
Dr. Gustave A. Arlt, President, Council of Graduate Schools in the United States.
Gary Bellow, Legal Aid Society, Washington, D.C.; consultant, Ford Foundation.
Edgar S. Cahn, Office of Economic Opportunity, Washington, D.C.
Gerald M. Caplan, Assistant United States Attorney, District of Columbia; Young
Lawyers' Committee, District of Columbia Bar Association.
Matthew Clarke, Religion and Labor Council, Washingon, D.C.
Zona Hostetler, attorney, Legal Aid Society, Washington, D.C.
Earl Johnson, Jr., Neighborhood Legal Services Project, Washington, D.C.
John Kenna, National Catholic Welfare Conference, Washington, D.C.
Virginia Lehmann, attorney, Washington, D.C., formerly Attorney-in-Charge,
Family and Probate Division, Legal Aid Bureau of United Charities of Chicago.
Robert J. McDonald, attorney, Sullivan and Cromwell, New York.
Rev. Alban A. Maguire, O.F.M., Holy Name College, Washington, D.C.
Rev. Richard Murphy, O.M.I., Seminary of Oblates of Mary Immaculate, Wash-
ington, D.C.
Very Rev. E. Ferrer Smith, O.P., Regent of Studies, Dominican Province of St.
Joseph, Washington, D.C.
Charles Vihon, Washington Planning and Housing Association.

Preface

This book is the joint product of educators from American colleges and universities (and two colleagues from Canada and France), and some practical educators now active in governmental and private institutions. They gathered at a conference that they called "Law in the Liberal Arts: the Social Dimension," which was held on the campus of The Catholic University of America in Washington, D.C., on December 2-4, 1964.[1] This conference was funded by no outside group; it was supported by the participants themselves, who had things they wanted to say and to learn, that centered, it developed, on three intersecting propositions: (1) Law is everybody's business; (2) the rigid disciplinary categories of America's higher educational structure are out of tune with some urgent needs of contemporary life; (3) faculty training and creation of course materials for interdisciplinary courses in Law-Society are needed for colleges and universities across the land, regardless of size and orientation, if American education is to produce men and women equipped to participate in the decision-making and policy formulation of an advanced nuclear-industrial age democracy.

The conferees included educators from large universities like California (Berkeley), Columbia, Northwestern and Wisconsin, and from small ones like Trinity and Providence and Howard; from public institutions such as the City College of the City University of New York and the University of Toledo, and from private ones with differing religious and cultural orientation such as, for example, American University, Yeshiva, Tuskegee Institute, and colleges for women run by orders of Catholic sisters.

The disagreement at the meeting did not turn on the differences in size or in religious orientation. Although the disciplines represented included anthropology, economics, history, law, political science, philosophy, sociology, and theology, divisions loomed among representatives of a single discipline as often as along disciplinary lines. The overwhelming view took the affirmative of the three propositions enumerated above. The concentration of effort was on first corrective steps to be taken. Considerable discussion turned on the place of values in education, and readers of these passages may, perhaps, be reassured of the vitality of American pluralism and be piqued anew at those still too timid to admit to the dialog points of view differing from their own.

If the power of ideas is more far-reaching than the power of the transient men who possess them, it is none the less true that power in the men moved is necessary to translate ideas into reality. In America this power in higher education has rested largely in private hands, in the educational leadership (or "power elite") of the largest universities and of a few large foundations. Some read in current signs an impending, and not universally welcomed, federal governmental catalyst.

The ideas and the concern of the educators from colleges and universities in many diverse strands of the nation's intellectual life who gathered on the campus of a university in Washington, D.C., in December, 1964, are passed on in this summary of their proceedings. The hope is that this publication of their discussions and proposals may serve colleges and universities that are open to change, and able to change. But since such openness and ability are often dependent upon availability of funds and trained personnel, notably in the smaller institutions that afford education to the bulk of college-trained Americans, an early and significant response undoubtedly depends upon the educational leadership.

More enduring than any specific comments or programs advanced by these educators may be the undercurrent of their discussions, which calls in question some inherited dogmas that encrust much of American higher education:

> That disciplinary simplicity, and atomization, afford the best educational preparation for dealing with the complex realities of life;
> That undergraduate education is purely a training of minds, and not of the whole man;
> That values are not a fruitful, or proper, subject for educational discourse;
> That dialog and interchange among social disciplines, professions, philosophies and faiths, is not a function of education in a nuclear-scientific age.

These dogmas proved no obstacle to the Washington discussions. Still, they are not dead. To experiment in sensitive areas requires courage in educational leadership, as in any other. It is "safer" to wait for the "consensus" to form. But is there time?

Acknowledgements are too numerous to exhaust. The first must be to Mark S. Massel of the Brookings Institution, the distinguished lawyer-economist[2] whose effective chairmanship gave the meetings pace and grace. More than an historical bow is due to Professor Harold S. Berman of Harvard University. His splendidly organized and reported conference of ten years ago, although more exclusively devoted than this one to law and lawyers,[3] was a direct inspiration of this meeting. And, although he is not to be charged with the form this conference finally took, his encouragement and permission to use extracts from his Harvard conference report[4] as pre-conference materials were generous in the extreme. The present conference owes its program principally to the members of the steering committee that included: the Conference Chairman, Mr. Massel, and Professors Harry V. Ball of Wisconsin, Arthur S. Miller of George Washington, Howard Mann of Indiana, Victor G. Rosenblum of Northwestern, Richard Wasserstrom of Tuskegee Institute, and Robert G. Yegge of Denver. Thanks are also due to Dr. Leonard Cottrell of Russell Sage Foundation for encouraging the participation of the four projects in law and the social sciences now being conducted under the auspices of that foundation at California (Berkeley), Denver, Northwestern and Wisconsin,

and to Mr. Christopher Edley of the Ford Foundation for a continuing
interest in the development of the conference. A partial list of educators
interested in interdisciplinary activity in the Law-Society field, who by
letters or conversations encouraged and, perhaps more than they realized,
guided the conference to the format it took, would include: Dean J.
Douglas Brown of Princeton University, Professors Jerome Hall of Indiana University, Willard Hurst of the University of Wisconsin, Harry Jones
of Columbia Law School, and former Dean Carl Spaeth of Stanford University Law School. Without the hospitality of the Rector of The Catholic
University of America, Bishop William J. McDonald, and the University's Director of Workshops, Very Reverend Robert P. Mohan, S.S.,
the conference could not have been held here. A persistent interest expressed in the work of the conference and the gracious sponsorship of
Monsignor James A. Magner, Director of The Catholic University of
America Press, has led to this publication of these proceedings.

The Proceedings have been edited from a transcript of 556 pages. The
dialog has, where possible, been reported as delivered. The participants,
in general availed themselves of the opportunity to edit their principal statements. The workshop on Law and Poverty (in Chapter V) was edited by
Mr. Gerald M. Caplan, formerly Assistant United States Attorney for the
District of Columbia and now an attorney with the President's Commission
on Crime. The workshop on Social Studies in Religious Education (in
Chapter VII) was edited by Reverend Anthony D. Lee, O.P., editor of
The Thomist. To each of these scholars acknowledgement is gratefully extended. The Law and Poverty workshop moved from tape to transcript
thanks to the kindness of Mrs. Earl Johnson, Jr.

Albert Broderick, O.P.

September 28, 1965.

School of Law
The Catholic University of America
Washington, D.C.

INTRODUCTORY PART

Welcoming remarks by Bishop William J. McDonald, Rector of The Catholic University of America, and by Very Rev. Robert P. Mohan, S.S., executive director of the University's Diamond Jubilee and Dean Vernon X. Miller of the Law School, under whose local auspices the conference was held, opened the conference on *Law in the Liberal Arts: the Social Dimension,* on Wednesday evening, December 2, 1964.

This introductory part[1] has three components: (1) The opening statement of the Conference Chairman, Mark S. Massel of Brookings Institution, which serves as the Introduction to this volume, "Law and Society in the Mid-Sixties"; (2) The "Historical Survey of Interdisciplinary Studies," which Dr. Gustave A. Arlt, President of the Council of Graduate Schools in the United States, presented at a later session; and (3) The dialog on "Interdisciplinary Difficulties in Law-Society" to which the opening meeting was chiefly devoted.

1. *Introduction:*

Law and Society in the Mid-Sixties

MARK S. MASSEL*

This conference involves some of the most profound problems of modern times. The role of law affects many of the emerging issues of public policy: the relationship between the individual and society; the proliferating functions of government; the posture of the United States in international affairs; economic development in our country and in others; and the social and economic relationships among individuals.

A public understanding of the issues affecting the legal system and the role of government has particular significance today because of the rapidity of change—technological, economic and social. Therefore, the premise of this conference has a deep significance. The development of a university tradition that promotes an appreciation of the role of law can help the body politic to accommodate the many new developments without losing the underlying values and principles of a democratic society. Indeed, such an understanding can make it possible to apply the changes to further implementation of these underlying values and principles.

Progress in this direction requires a deep-seated appreciation of the various intellectual disciplines.

In recent years it has become clearer and clearer that the social sciences have something to do with the law, and the law has something to do with the social sciences. The notion that the law and the social sciences stemmed from the same philosophical background is a rather interesting historical, philosophical speculation, but it fails to meet the substantial problems of today. The increasing interest in these interdisciplinary relationships rests not so much on the background as it does on the many vital problems which affect the operations of our legal system, as well as the newer applications of economics, political science, sociology and psychology.

The pertinent problems, both public and private, are manifestations of the substantial revolutionary development of our times. The combination of technological advances, the additional crowding of population, problems of natural resource use, and of urban transportation would be sufficiently important, in themselves, to provide the underpinning for these

---

* Senior Associate, Brookings Institution (law, economics).

developments. Moreover, this combination has been supplemented by a growing public recognition of the importance of interdependence within our society. This realization of interdependence has brought with it a profound increase in social awareness, an awareness which has stimulated new conceptions about the relationship between the individual and society. We are witnessing a novel rethinking about the responsibilities of the individual *to* society, and, even more importantly, the responsibilities of society to the individual.

These revolutionary developments are affecting many issues of public policy. The passage of the Full Employment Act of 1946 has created the need to inject specific content into these brave words. We have been forced into basic consideration of our social and political responsibilities to minority groups. We are faced with practical need to breathe life into the general concepts, concepts which we have discoursed on in somewhat vague terms. Never has a society had to give serious consideration to the practical implementation of so many public goals at one time—goals expressed in terms of civil liberties, in terms of minimum housing, in terms of minimum purchasing power and adequate living standards, and in terms of the opportunities offered to each individual to better his life.

On another front we have to contend with a whole new set of international problems. We are forced to give up the refuge of our old clichés about international relations. A combination of forces compels new thinking about the developing countries: the new social awareness; rivalry among types of economic and social systems; and among countries. We have been thrust, almost unwillingly, into serious national reconsideration of many problems: regarding foreign and international law; regarding practical stimulation of economic and social development; and regarding new forms of international cooperation. In brief, the international situation has forced us to develop the flow of radically new ideas to pour into some of the old vessels that held the clichés of yesterday.

All of these societal pressures have been affected by the remarkable emotional impact of atomic fission. The Bomb challenges the conventional security of the nation and of the individual. The prospect of harnessing nuclear energy for the benefit of mankind, together with the accelerating pace of technological change, presents us with a serious quandary. On the one hand, we visualize technological developments raising standards of living, of education, of housing, and of medical care. On the other hand, these same developments reduce the need for human work and produce the spectre of sustained unemployment for many. How do we reconcile these technological developments with our new social awareness, with the growing interdependence of a more complex society and with the increasing crowding of the earth's surface?

The pattern of these changes offers many opportunities for promoting further breadth in our understanding of the world. Such breadth calls for a breaking-down of the pigeon-holes which separate the various social science disciplines from each other and from the legal discipline. This need is analogous to recent developments in other scientific areas, notably in those that have been stimulated by atomic developments. The people working in the physical and the natural sciences have learned in recent years that substantial progress requires breaking down the conventional walls between physics, chemistry, biology, mathematics.

Unfortunately, the participants in the social sciences, the liberal arts, and the law have not yet learned the lessons that have affected development in the physical and natural sciences. We have not kept pace with these other disciplines in finding major areas of coordination. We must achieve a greater awareness of the tremendous necessity for an improved coordination in order to retain the basic institutional frameworks of our society.

It seems to me, therefore, that the program we will follow for the next several days responds to a substantial continuing sociological need The issues do not require radical intellectual and philosophical break-throughs. They call for a consideration of what practical means can be found to narrow the cultural lag between current developments and the progress in the intellectual disciplines which are represented at the conference.

We should recognize the practical orientation of our conference. There is no need to consider these interdisciplinary areas in a self-conscious way. We are trying to see what can be done to satisfy the tremendous need for an educated citizenry that is prepared to consider, to analyze, and to weigh the emerging social problems, in the United States and elsewhere.

The organization of the conference fits into several blocks. We shall start with a dialog about the interdisciplinary difficulties. Why does the lawyer have so much trouble in understanding the problems and the methodology of the social scientist? Why do the social sciences—anthropology, sociology, political science, history, and economics—theology and the humanities have so much trouble in understanding the problems of the law and of lawyers? Do these difficulties rest on the disciplines or on the values of the practitioners in the disciplines? Why do so many practitioners nurture their arrogant feelings of superiority about the other disciplines? We do not propose this dialog to amuse those people who are in the audience, or to encourage interdisciplinary mayhem. The purpose of the discussion is to attempt to clarify the nature of the intellectual fences which retard cooperation and understanding.

The conference program calls for a second set of discussions concerning several experiments in relating the law and the social disciplines in the intellectual world. We hope that a review of several university efforts at coordination will provide some clues to future development.

The third session considers what advances can be made at the undergraduate level. What courses will give the student informed preparation for citizenship, through a firm understanding of our legal system? This discussion includes a consideration of course structure. Is there a need for one or two courses which would cover the legal framework of our society and its underlying values? Would it be desirable to offer a major or minor dealing with the subject?

The fourth block of discussion deals with graduate courses. The separation of the discussions of graduate and undergraduate work rests on a basic difference in the objectives of the two levels. The undergraduate level tends to accentuate the liberal arts tradition and education for citizenship. Graduate school, on the other hand, tends to concentrate more on professional preparation for specialized careers. For example, graduate departments in economics are interested in turning out economists who are professional in the same sense as lawyers are professional, with all of the advantages and disadvantages in the breadth or narrowness of their professional education.

There will be no effort to develop a consensus. If one should emerge, it might be useful. However, the conference was constructed to improve our appreciation of the pertinent issues, achieved through interchange of ideas, rather than for the promotion of a specific program.

2. Historical Survey of Interdisciplinary Studies

GUSTAVE A. ARLT*

I'm still surprised to be here as Saul among the prophets, so to speak, for I am not a lawyer and my acquaintance with the law leaves much to be desired. But perhaps I can contribute something in the way of historical background with respect to interdisciplinary studies. I have the good fortune, or misfortune, to be spearheading a movement started here a few months ago for the establishment of a National Humanities Foundation,[2] and for the reestablishment, the rehabilitation of the humanities as a respectable part of the academic curriculum and as a respected feature of our modern life.

Since the objectives of this conference can hardly be achieved without a very substantial degree of interdisciplinary cooperation in the fields which, in the past, have been somewhat less than amenable to it, it may be profitable to review briefly the history of previous efforts in that direction.

The structure of the American university from its beginnings on has been along strictly departmental lines. Teachers were assigned, and students assigned themselves to self-contained and self-centered academic departments, each of which presided over a so-called discipline and field of study. Knowledge was neatly compartmentalized, like goods on the shelves of a grocery store, and to put a can of beans among the cans of

---

* President, Council of Graduate Schools in the United States (humanities).

corn was regarded, if not as heresy, at least as bad housekeeping. As knowledge increased, departments and disciplines divided and subdivided, like the famous amoeba, and each new subdivision again became a self-contained entity. In 1920 even the largest universities listed no more than thirty-five departments; in 1960 no self-respecting university listed less than sixty-five. One large—and great—university awards Ph.D. degrees in 114 different fields.

The first breaking down of departmental lines came, as might be expected, in the natural sciences. With new insights and new knowledge, disciplinary dividing lines dissolved of their volition. Today biochemistry and biophysics, geochemistry and geophysics, and fifty other interdisciplinary fields in the natural sciences are recognized and respected.

In the humanities the first feeble attempts to secure recognition for programs leading to degrees in comparative literature were made some twenty-five or thirty years ago. These attempts were generally impeded by the rigidity of departmental lines and departmental requirements. Departments of English, French, German, or Italian professed willingness to entertain dissertations in comparative literature but each insisted upon its pound of flesh in the form of the full requirements of its own Ph.D program. The few hardy individuals who survived this ordeal found themselves at the end with a degree for which there was no ready market.

During World War II a sudden need developed for persons with at least a nodding acquaintance with the regions in which the armed forces were engaged. This need was met by the establishment of so-called "area programs," in which the language, geography, history, economics and even a little literature of a country or a region were intensively studied. Area studies, all on the undergraduate level, mushroomed on large and small campuses chiefly subsidized by federal funds. Their graduates proved the worth of these programs and showed up their weaknesses—in many countries of Europe, Asia, and Africa.

It is interesting to note that a war-time exigency achieved what years of peaceful discussions in faculty meetings had not done. It proved that sacrosanct departmental lines could be crossed without destroying their integrity and that reasonable breadth and reasonable depth were not necessarily incompatible. After the war many of these programs became fixtures, adjusted to a less frenetic pace. Cautious experiments were made to expand them to the master's level. By the mid-1950s a number of them had grown into "study centers" or "institutes." Some now have programs leading to the Ph.D. and a few are even sought by post-doctoral scholars. Moreover, their graduates find a ready market for their degrees. Specialists in African studies, for example, are in such short supply and long demand that it is hard to keep track of them as they move from one high bidder to another. Doctoral degree holders in American studies are in greater demand at the moment than doctors in conventional American literature.

After World War II, in the wake of area studies, a few of the leading universities timidly initiated interdepartmental programs leading to the master's degree in folklore. These generally involved at most the departments of English, various foreign languages, anthropology, and perhaps archaeology. It was not until the late 1950s that the first folklore institutes were established. There are still not many today but a few have already achieved high distinction. Best of all, they now cut across the lines of a dozen or more departments, typically including, besides those previously mentioned, art, history, linguistics, music, philosophy, psychology, and theater arts.

In the field of history the trend toward interdisciplinary collaboration is also apparent. In recent years, in some of the major universities, doctoral dissertations on the history of law, medicine, science, and technology have appeared with some frequency. At least two universities have made joint appointments in their Schools of Medicine and history departments to facilitate research in medical history. Joint appointments between law and history or law and political science are also not uncommon.

To conclude, this gradual loosening of the structure of strict departmentalization will be increasingly advantageous, not only for the humanistic and social science fields, but also for the learned professions, law and medicine.

RICHARDSON*—Would Dr. Arlt explain just how broad is the context of the humanities. We've been talking mostly in terms of the social sciences in relation to law. But we have crossed over to such areas as history, which touches both the social sciences and the humanities.

ARLT—I'm glad you asked that because I can talk all the rest of the evening about that, if you like. But I won't. In my book, the social sciences are humanistic subjects. And of course if you go into this historically you find that the so-called social sciences are rather recent inventions, or rather recent areas of study and that, like the humanities, they descended from the area that was known in the Renaissance and before the Renaissance as moral philosophy. And moral philosophy at the beginning of the 19th century began to disintegrate into various areas, and the first one that broke off was the area of economics, followed pretty soon by what was called political economy which became political science. The curious thing is that these new disciplines that the 19th century produced were not called social philosophy (as you might think they should be coming from moral philosophy), but were called social sciences, perhaps in order to indicate their consanguinity with the natural sciences. Because they did learn to use some of the techniques of the natural sciences. I think the areas of political science, of economics, of anthropology, even of sociology, belong in the humanistic orbit especially where they use humanistic techniques of approach for research. I don't mean to say that

---

* Rev. John T. Richardson, C.M. Executive Vice President, DePaul University (theology).

econometrics, for example, is a humanistic subject: econometrics is a more specialized mathematical discipline. And where sociology uses statistical and mathematical methods, there it also goes outside the area of the humanities.

To make the distinction as practical as possible: The American Council of Learned Societies announces its support program in the fields of the humanities, and includes in the fields of the humanities history, first of all (because if history isn't a humanistic subject, I don't know what is). Then of course, languages, literature, philosophy, the history of science, law, medicine and religion, those areas of the social sciences which use humanistic methods, and the fine, creative and performing arts. Now that language has been taken over pretty fully in the bill which is now before the Congress for the establishment of a National Humanities Foundation. In other words, it provides for support by the federal government in practically all areas which today are not supported by the National Science Foundation or the National Institutes of Health. The National Science Foundation has adopted a few areas of the social sciences with great misgivings. It has had authorization from the beginning to do so but it did not until the year before last adopt a few of the social sciences into its program. The Humanities Foundation proposes to integrate within that foundation all those areas which are not now supported by the National Science Foundation and that includes practically the entire spectrum of social science disciplines.

SISTER MARIE LEONORE*—Are you making any distinctions, now that they are using the terms "behavioral sciences" and "social sciences" in this area?

ARLT—Now this is another one of these fragmentations, fractionalizings of knowledge. The behavioral sciences are certainly social sciences, aren't they? It is really quite difficult to find definitions that cover everything. We think of philosophy as perhaps the oldest of the humanities—philosophy must be a humanistic field. Well, is ethics a humanistic field? Ethics deals with the relation of the individual to his fellow man. Doesn't that make it a social science? Thus, you have a field of philosophy that could very well be classified as a social science. What about the semantic philosophy that we are developing nowadays and the philosophy of mathematics, are they humanistic or are they sciences? You see we begin to get into grey areas that you can't very well define.

ROONEY**—Just how free are our faculties in innovating? In other words, are the accrediting agencies that are concerned with standardization still so limiting in their departmentalization that innovation is going to be difficult? Or are we more or less free to innovate?

ARLT—I think it must be said that nothing is quite as conservative as an educational system. Innovations in the educational system are always

---

* College of Mount St. Vincent (social science).
** Professor Miriam Theresa Rooney, Seton Hall University Law School (law, philosophy).

difficult, are not accepted for a long time. Just look back 50 years in history. Today the natural sciences are the pride of higher education. It took a hundred years to get the natural sciences even to be recognized as a respectable area of study in the American university. This is how slow a process it is. Now when you talk about the accrediting agencies, the accrediting agencies will do only what their constituent members, that is, the universities, want them to do. The accrediting agencies are not independent agencies that set up standards. We in the universities set up standards and we *will* the accrediting agencies. We would like them to look at these institutions to see if they are doing what *we* want them to do, not what the accrediting agency wants them to do. Therefore, the responsibility and the power for innovation lies within the universities. The accrediting agencies aren't going to stop anything the universities want to do. The accrediting agencies will merely see that the standards— I use the word standards as distinct from standardization—that the standards which the universities want maintained are maintained. God protect us from standardization in our educational system. This is the greatest thing that we have to fear—any attempt to make everybody alike, to make everbody teach and study the same thing.

GOOSETREE*—One eminently practical question from my point of view, Dr. Arlt. Since law is being rapidly redefined this afternoon as either folklore or social science, is law included in the Humanities Foundation legislation?

ARLT—Law is not specifically included by name. There were long discussions in the commission which wrote the report, which I hope some of you have read, and where law was very ably represented by Kingman Brewster of Yale as a member of that commission. Law was discussed for a long time, and it was decided not to mention law specifically but to let nature take its course. And if law is to be regarded as a social science or as a humanistic science, it is naturally included.[3]

MASSEL—Was this on the assumption that if the subject matter covered included folkore, law would have a very easy entrance?

ARLT—We can't be too certain of that because folklore along with church music, theology and classical history were particularly condemned in 1961 by the United States Congress and were put in a category all by themselves for *no* aid from the Federal government.

---

* Professor Robert Goosetree, American University (law).

3. Interdisciplinary Difficulties in Law-Society: A Dialog

Participants in the interdisciplinary dialog were invited by the Chairman to frankly air obstacles to interdisciplinary cooperation, as they saw them. The discussion opened with some general observations by a few participants from various disciplines, but soon moved into specifics: physical and intellectual distance of law schools from the university community, communication problems (concepts, language, meaning), difficulty of defining disciplinary areas, academic competitiveness, each discipline's fostering its own mystique and ascribing reduced roles to the others:

Dean Lawrence Wadsworth of American University, a political scientist, saw an obstacle to interdisciplinary cooperation in law-society in the law schools' steadily professionalizing themselves in isolation from the rest of the academic community:

WADSWORTH—In the first place, I think difficulties in viewing the law as a whole, in relation to the liberal arts, arise from the increasing separateness and autonomy within divergent communities, of law schools and legal education. This I think is imposed, not necessarily by the desire of the law schools; it is imposed by the desire of society that there shall be increasingly better training of men who are officers of the court, who are attorneys, and, therefore, it desired to withdraw this training from other aspects of the teaching of related subjects. It is imposed by strengthened professional standards which are imposed upon the law schools by the laws of the states within which they operate. It is imposed, not least of all, however, by the development of financially and academically powerful units within universities which are called law schools. Along with this, I think, goes an increasing crowding of curricula—in the law school, by the very increasing separateness and greater concentration and specialization, in political science, on the other hand, by an exactly opposite development. Political science is a sprawling discipline which is burgeoning in all directions, and which is putting out pseudopods in all sorts of areas.

Now in this situation here on the one hand the law school in narrowing its focus of attention to training officers of the court, and on the other hand political scientists are spreading out in many different directions; the subject of law in relation to social control, law in relation to philosophy of government and similar areas of inquiry fall in between these two schools. Neither the political scientists nor the law schools have time within crowded curricula to take up these matters in sufficient detail and weight. The political scientist is likely to say this is the domain of the law school. If the political scientists attempt to move into this domain, the law schools will disregard it or discount it. The law schools say training in these areas is not part of the problem of training of officers of the court.

An anthropologist from Catholic University, Dr. Godfrey Lang, emphasized the difficulty presented by the conceptual estrangement of one social discipline from another, and the resultant problem of finding focus for interdisciplinary discussion:

LANG—I think that I would like to talk about this rather in terms of an experience that we have had in talking not so much to lawyers but among different disciplines. Some anthropologists, sociologists, economists, philosophers, even moral theologians participated in an experiment that we have been conducting the past few years here on this campus. We list it in the catalog as an interdisciplinary seminar.

The main purpose is to exchange ideas and to bring our thinking together, and perhaps to clarify our own thinking. It hasn't always been very successful, and I would like rather to point out some of the difficulties we have had in achieving some success. First of all, I think it has not always been very easy to agree upon concepts. We all use similar words but we frequently discover, over a period of time, and over much discussion, that we are talking about two different things, or three or four different things, depending on how many people are talking, all at the same time. This is a very difficult problem for me because English is, by the way, not my native language, but I discover that it is even difficult for people who come from different subcultures such as economics, or political science. This makes it difficult for us to understand each other, and we develop considerable heat occasionally only to discover later on that we really didn't mean it quite this way. This is then the problem of meaning. The problem of meaning is much more complicated than we usually think. Because even if we look up the words in a dictionary, some standard dictionary hopefully, we discover that actually in the course of events, in the course of the development of a concept, in a particular discipline it has taken on entirely a highly specific meaning, and occasionally, not too often, but occasionally, a highly private meaning. And the meaning is not communicated because we do not know each other's disciplines well enough in which a particular concept developed.

Perhaps the most difficult problem that we have experienced in the interdisciplinary seminar is finding a focus for discussion. Those of us who are interested in the study of man have a focus in that, but we have very quickly discovered that this focus is much too broad.

We have also suffered from an historical development in the academic disciplines in that we believe on the one hand that each discipline has its own body of knowledge, that each discipline has its own conceptual tool kit, so to speak; that each discipline is very much interested in knowing more about a specific problem. And at the same time we also have discovered that we need to know something about what the other man is thinking, what the other man is doing, and more important, to discover the relationships between these various ways of thinking about sometimes very similar behavior. Psychologists look at the same kind of data that anthropologists and sociologists, and occasionally economists and political scientists, do. Yet, when we get together, we come to interpret all of these things in quite diverse ways, and we finally, as a result of not being able to get in agreement, say, Well, what I know, I know, and what you know, you may know, but we got apart, and there has not been any integration.

And this is my last problem which I would like to suggest. It is the problem of integrating our various ways of thinking about the behavior of man. I do not want to make a plea for behaviorism, but I think these are our basic data and we look at them. Yet, at the same time, it is a little bit like looking at a statue or looking at a building. If you look at the Shrine coming from the west, you see you get one perspective. If you look at the Shrine from this side, you get another perspective. Nevertheless, we both see the Shrine. How can we bring these diverse views together? This is our big problem. I do not mean to suggest that we have found a solution to the problem. The fact is that we continue talking, and in fact, we continue these discussions late into the night. I can only suggest problems at this time, and the reason why I am here, for instance, is in order to discover, perhaps through this dialog, how to solve some of these problems that I have suggested, which I think are fairly real (I am told other people have had similar problems), and how we can go beyond this stage of our development.

Professor John F. Cunningham, O.P., a philosopher from Providence College, emphasized that difficulties in interdisciplinary cooperation derive both from the personalities of the would-be cooperators, and from the nature of the disciplines themselves:

CUNNINGHAM—We must, I think, divide these difficulties of interdisciplinary approach, as has already been suggested, into two general groupings. There is always, of course, the personal difficulty. The humanities program in which I have been working is precisely an interdisciplinary program in which the chairman must deal with the head of just about every department of the university. This personal difficulty, I have discovered, can be minimized with a little bit of prudence, some diplomacy and a modicum of intelligent compromise. I think sometimes that we are so jealous of the prerogatives of our own particular disciplines that we want to stand firm and not move. At this early stage of our project, however, I do not think we can afford to be intransigent. These personal difficulties exist, of course, in the business world and indeed at every level of human enterprise. And we learn to deal satisfactorily with them only through experience.

The other difficulties are, I would say, disciplinary themselves. They evolve not so much from the personality of the chairman of a department as from the discipline of which he is in charge. Specialization, as has already been pointed out to us, has made individual disciplines far more extensive and all-embracing. It seems that as new problems arise, each discipline wants to get in on the ground floor and deal with them. So, for example, we have the philosophy of eastern cultures, the study of the economic structures of eastern countries, far eastern international relations, and the like. As soon as something new develops on the intellectual hori-zon every department wants to incorporate a couple of courses in its curriculum. And any suggestion that these might be treated in any other department is, of course, treated as sheer heresy.

There is also, of course, the basic tension between the rationalistic and empirical approach. There will always be those philosophers and theolo-gians who will claim that problems are solved by definitions. I can remember a stimulating educator mentioning that the whole notion of natural law is very difficult to put across at any level. During the question period which followed his lecture, a professor of political philosophy rose and said that he simply could not see that there was any difficulty. After all, hadn't Aquinas defined natural law once and for all in the 13th century? Then, of course, there is the other extreme represented by the mentality which states that if you cannot compute data, feed it into a machine, and arrive at mathematical certainty, then any conclusion you draw is *ipso facto* suspect. We are always going to have this collision of interests and out-looks. Each science is going to think that its area of investigation is being invaded by the mathematical, by the statistical, by the physical, even by the biological approach.

An attack mounted upon the lawyers. Professor John Farrell, an historian from Catholic University, suggested that lawyers were simply "quasi-busi-ness men", and Dean Wadsworth returned to his theme:

WADSWORTH—The professionalization of the law schools has resulted in a great loss to American education in which important topics are not being discussed by anybody. One of the forces that has brought this about is this attempt to make the law school all encompassing with respect to law.

MASSEL—Well, I think the evidence is overwhelming that without the law being represented here we can all have a great deal of fun beating a dead horse.

At this juncture, Dean Vernon Miller of Catholic University Law School, President of the Association of American Law Schools, took up the cudgel with a lawyer's "professional" point of view:

MILLER—I am not sure that it is a language difficulty. It can be that we get so old in this business, we people who are teaching law, that we just can't think unless we are dealing with specifics. And yet I am not sure that this isn't the way it should be with everyone in every one of these disciplines. Why are we worried about anything unless we have something right in our laps? If you call it a conflict, if you call it a claim that we have to settle, if you call it a decision that we have to make—we just don't go and draft a statute because we want a statute—we draft a statute because there have been some experiences in the community that people talk about, and we think through some projects, if you will, for helping adjustments to be effected. Adjustments to be effected how? Through the judicial process? Yes, because that's one—I won't say the only way, but it is one of the important ways where conflicts, whether they have to do with plumbers or railroad operators, are going to be solved and settled. Now I grant you that some law teachers want to be economists, sociologists, and historians. I'm that way. I have to be an historian, a sociologist, an economist. There isn't any one of these little problems, whether it has to do with a collision at an intersection or something else, that I don't have to bring to it my analyzing and my thinking. Everything I think I know about people is a combination of experiences from the community. The personal injury lawyer certainly has to be a sociologist. Now I don't know how we are going to talk with sociologists, with economists, with philosophers, if we aren't dealing in concretes. I don't want to be boxed in by propositions and logic. I want to be flexible, to be able to adjust to the things that will land right in my lap.

Now let us suppose that somebody thinks through a concrete case and generalizes beyond what he has to consider and comes up with a proposition that lends itself to some logic. I may be crippled in the next little case. I think in all of our disciplines we have got to get back to the specifics. If we think as people of experience, we've got to be concrete about it. The generalizations may stymie us. I think most of our problem is that we talk bigger than our little problems justify. We are constantly talking as if an event is more profound than it is. I don't want to minimize the significance of these little problems, and how they are to be related to the community structure. I've got myself so tied down to specifics such as what happened, who was there, how many of them, how fast were they going, that I can become lost in detail, but I think it all leads to supposing that we can spell out from these specifics what we should do about traffic codes or housing. Every case is a fragment. Our problem is certainly to appreciate that it is a fragment, that there is a whole elephant, that this isn't just one of the hairs. We have to share experiences, we have to know what the sociologists have to offer—not in the way they talk about it, but from the facts they find for us.

The sociologists did not warm to the underlaborer role suggested for the social sciences by Dean Miller's "the facts they find for us":

SELZNICK*—I myself don't have a very strong commitment to serving lawyers or the legal profession.

YEGGE**—Yes, the lawyers always ask the question, what can social science do for us? How may it be our handyman? Without considering that the social scientist may be interested in a greater problem. On the other hand, the social scientist is interested in the theoretical framework in which the problem that the lawyer presents to him is only a very small part, and he finds very little interest in just examining a little piece.

Now where do we go from here? Well, maybe an understanding of the subject matter of each of the disciplines is the place to begin, and in the Russell Sage projects, of which I am the director of one, we are trying to

* Professor Philip Selznick, Center for the Study of Law and Society, University of California, Berkeley (sociology).
** Professor Robert B. Yegge, Program in Judicial Administration, University of Denver (law, sociology).

create on the graduate level an understanding of the subject matter of law by the social scientist, and of social science by the lawyer, as a discipline and not trying to put two disinterested pieces together on a fragmentary basis.

This question of subject matter provoked lively debate:

BARKUN*—We happen to be here discussing law and the liberal arts. I suggest that another group might just as easily get together to discuss medicine and the liberal arts and for similar reasons. Because of a whole complex of factors, it seems less likely that this will come to pass in the near future, but in principle many of the problems are the same. One of these is the problem, or at least the assumption, usually unstated, that there is an insuperable barrier erected by the nature of the subject matter; that consequently it is impossible to bring about a proper connection between law or medicine and the liberal arts tradition; that somehow the subject matter is much too esoteric. And this I think goes back to the observation made earlier that the law schools and legal education have gained increasing autonomy. As they move farther and farther outside the ambit of the liberal arts, institutional distance reinforces substantive distances. In fact, I think that we might state as a hypothesis that the development of the scholarly study of a subject area varies inversely with the degree of professionalization, that one is less likely to find some kind of liberal arts study of law and medicine than one is likely to find a liberal arts study of music, or English or any other field within the liberal arts tradition; that as professionalization increases, the belief increases that the profession contains esoteric material inherently too difficult to be brought within the limited resources necessarily available to a liberal arts college. I think it is at this point that the generalizing abilities of the social sciences can be brought to bear together with the position of the social scientist as an outside observer. It is precisely an external perspective that is required in order to break down the beliefs that we are dealing with something for initiates only and something that cannot be communicated to the general student body.

WADSWORTH—It seems to me that we are right back at the point I was trying to make at the outset—that in law school you train officers of the court; in the political science department you are burgeoning off in a dozen different directions.

DOWD**—In both the undergraduate liberal arts or social science curriculum it seems that when the law is an element of a problem, that the legal determination should be taken into consideration. I do not suppose that our social scientists or political scientists shy away whenever they see something "legal" in a problem.

---

* Dr. Michael Barkun, Program in Law and the Social Sciences, Northwestern University (political science).
** Professor Donald W. Dowd, Villanova University (law).

ABBOTT*—I feel political scientists will shy away from this sort of judgment. I suggest that there is a necessity of providing this basis for criticism to students, and if the political scientists themselves feel shy and will not provide it, it is up to the legally trained man to do so.

DOWD—It seems to me that a non-lawyer is rightfully reticent when it comes to problems of giving legal advice. In other words, college professors should not be discussing what to do if someone breaks his leg in an automobile accident. But it seems to me perfectly within the competence of the political scientist to criticize what, in fact, is the legal procedure. He cannot advise us as to how, within the legal system, a particular case will or will not be decided, but I assume he is perfectly free to criticize the role assumed by the courts or the role assumed by the lawyers as part of the general decision making process in society.

ROSENBLUM**—I hate to leave this on the note of the shyness of political scientists. Political scientists are about as shy as Brigitte Bardot in a bedroom scene. Would that there were some shyness in my esteemed profession on this score, but there are two sides to the manifestation of incompetence in this area: On the one hand, there is total avoidance of all of the issues including the issues expressed already; on the other side there is the political scientist who tries to out-lawyer the lawyer and says, "Never mind the principle, never mind what ought to be. I have read what the court said and I tell you what the law is." And these are two sides of the coin which seem to me equally wrong.

A former law professor, now the Dean of a College of Arts and Sciences, found fault with the mystique of social scientists:
WASSERSTROM***—The social scientists have developed the aura of mystery around the social sciences that has made difficulty. They have set up barriers and said "Let no one who isn't thoroughly conversant with our mysteries enter here." Certainly the social sciences aren't as complicated or as mystical as our academic structures have made them.

An historian complained of the arcana of the law:

DUFF****—There is a tendency to try to veil the law in mystery, to make it something people don't understand. When you enter a lawyer's office to have a discussion on a particular legal problem with him, you have to be in the position of being a complete supplicant to the lawyer.

And a lawyer-political scientist saw justice in both complaints:

ROSENBLUM—What I think we are doing today through programs like this is restoring the natural opportunities for exchange of information, re-

---

* Professor Richard D. Abbott, Carleton University, Ottawa, Canada (public law).
** Professor Victor G. Rosenblum, Program in Law and the Social Sciences, Northwestern University (law, political science).
*** Dean Richard Wasserstrom, College of Arts and Sciences, Tuskegee Institute (administration, law).
**** Professor John Duff, Seton Hall University (history).

moving some of the forbidden and foreboding aspects of the law. It's just as appropriate for social scientists to rip the law, as it is for the law occasionally to rip what the social sciences are doing.

If no clear cut rules of the road are available between law and the social sciences from the standpoint of the subject matter, can an understanding be achieved from the standpoint of recognizing differing methodologies? MASSEL—Some interdisciplinary differences develop because of differences in orientation. One group may be interested in treating specific problems, while another is occupied with the interpretation of broad trends. Other differences may depend on analytical methodology. Lawyers and social scientists may not use data in the same way.

YEGGE—Donald Young, a former president of Russell Sage Foundation and a sociologist of renown, made this very simple observation to Walter Gellhorn, professor of law at Columbia University, at a conference in connection with one of our programs: "The trouble with you, Walter, is that you always find some remote case. Now we social scientists look at data on an actuarial basis rather than at an isolated case." I think this is the problem between the lawyer and the social scientist. Their frame of reference is a bit different. A lawyer looks at cases, and can find a case to support a position, while the social scientist is interested rather on an actuarial basis.

The dialog persistently returned to three central difficulties: the consequences flowing from the "fragmentation" of law that Dean Wadsworth had signalled at the outset; the misunderstandings deriving from failing to distinguish academic men from practitioners, within law and within each of the social disciplines; and the factor of values (which is reserved for the next chapter).
WADSWORTH—You are faced with a real vacuum here with respect to law as a major means of social control in our society. We have business to be done here by the philosophers—who can say where we should be going in this social control—and we have business to be done here by the sociologists—who say what effect this increasing use of law as the principal means of social control is having upon our society. Nobody is doing a lot of this intellectual business that needs to be done.

ROSENBLUM—I think this points up the need to restore the natural place that law had in the liberal arts before we insisted on removing it through artificial creation of academic structures, and on clothing it with a mumbo-jumboesque tradition that said social scientists or philosophers or historians couldn't look at it, that you had to be admitted to the cult before you could properly know what law was. And I think this is one of the great charlatan victories of the century—being able to convince a large section of the society that this was so. Social science is now, and has always been, a part of the law. The conflict, perhaps, has been that social scientists have not been a part of it.

DOWD—I think one of the most unfortunate things is that in some areas of the social sciences there are some people who really feel that the decision making is to be socially determined and not legally determined, and that when there are legal rights involved that conflict with their idea of what is just or unjust everybody should ignore them. And when you start to introduce the legal question, they accuse you of trying to tie up everything, and threaten to throw the book at you.

SELZNICK—There is a difference between what one might call the pure social sciences—scholarly studies in sociology and political science and so on—and the applied work of the social work practitioner and others in those areas. It is certainly true that the emphasis on therapy, on getting the job done in some way that seems helpful to the client—the child or what have you—does produce among these solid practitioners a distrust of legal intervention, a feeling that law introduces criteria that interfere with the kind of decisions that they want to make. On the other hand, I think you will find that among research people, professors, graduate students— people who are interested in the relation of law and social science as a scholarly enterprise—there is a very strong feeling that precisely one of the things to be considered is the way the values of legality do get extinguished, and are threatened, in just such situations.

SISTER CATHERINE THERESE*—Look at the lawyers' attitude toward right to work laws, compared to social scientists on the whole. This is because lawyers, I think, have been trained so much on the individual rights of man and haven't had so much training on social relationships, especially in industrial relations. Arbitration and mediation have been too often handled by those who have had training only in individual rights.

MASSEL—In examining the interdisciplinary differences we may tend to bring a strategic unstated variable into consideration. Usually we think about the attitude of academic people when we discuss social scientists, and practicing lawyers when we discuss lawyers. Now, if we compare law teachers of social sciences, the differences are not nearly as great as our discussions seem to imply. At the same time, if we compare practitioners of law with those in the social sciences, the differences may not seem to be so great.

* Sr. Catherine Therese Knoop, C.S.J., College of St. Rose, Albany (social science).

Part One
VALUES: THE SOCIAL DIMENSION

CHAPTER I
LAW, SOCIETY AND VALUES

Discussion of the place of values continued throughout the conference. Three main papers dealt with the general theme of values as related to law: Professor Adolf Berle of Columbia University spoke on "The Processes of Creation in the Great Society", Professor Michel Villey of the Faculté de Droit et des Sciences Economiques of the University of Paris addressed himself to "Law and Values—a French View", and Robert J. McDonald, a New York legal practitioner, discussed "The Importance of Values to the Practicing Lawyer." These statements, some questions and answers and commentaries that followed them, and selections from the conference dialog on the subject of values are grouped in this chapter.[1]

1. The Processes of Creation in the Great Society

ADOLF A. BERLE*

THE YEAR 1964 SAW the culmination of an old era and the announced intent to open a new. The old era recognizably brought to high development the potential elaborated in 1933.

That year laid the foundations of a socially-guided economic system. Politically it was called "the New Deal." This short-phrase meant that the federal government assumed responsibility for the functioning of the American economy. It undertook to direct that economy so that it should produce enough to provide comfort for everyone and should so distribute the product that everyone was provided for. Section by section, a social-economic structure was erected.

Policy and purpose were finally codified in the Employment Act of 1946. By that law, the Congress enacted as national policy, use of "all the resources of the United States to achieve maximum employment, maximum production and maximum purchasing power." I attempted a description of this

* Professor of Law, Columbia University.

1

structure in a recent book, *The American Economic Republic*,[2] and need not repeat it here.

The economic effects of the measures, institutions and procedures, now become part of the legal and economic structure of the United States, imperfectly but in substantial measure have achieved their intended end. By 1964, rather more than one-third of the whole population of the United States has been moved out of proletarian poverty and into middle class comfort. Poverty, previously assumed by Malthusian economics to be the inevitable lot of the great majority, has been reduced to about 15% of the population. Of that number, 5% or 6% probably have available to them, and have capacity to use, tools by which they can lift themselves out. The remaining 10% is a standing challenge to American social-economic engineering. Already it is the declared policy of the incoming Administration of President Lyndon B. Johnson to seek abolition of poverty in that sector also. Meantime, the relative "affluence" of the large majority of our people continues to increase. Every individual worker in this group can expect his real wages and purchasing power to go up about 3% a year. The economic machine as we now have it thus provides a present material base from which the next major advance can be made. Not only is that base now present, but it clearly can be expanded to meet any demands we are likely to make on it in the future.

Against that background, proposal has been made to lift sights and steer toward organization of what is called "the Great Society." The Administration to be inaugurated next month is pledged to undertake the task. Here, we are consciously crossing a great divide in American history. It is essential that we recognize it. For a solid century, all proposals for a better society have been merely economic. No philosopher was needed to prove that hunger was bad. Social thinkers from the early nineteenth century on have assumed that, once problems of production and distribution were solved, men would automatically become honest and unselfish, and Utopia would result. (Marx thought the State itself would then become unnecessary.) But an affluent society was assumed to be an almost impossible ideal. Now (though it has not yet been attained) we are on the threshold of a society offering material comfort to substantially everyone, to an extent undreamed of by our grandfathers. Simultaneously it becomes clear that the driving force from here out will not be primarily economic. It will not be primarily the profit-motive—though that will not disappear. It will be the desire, not merely to have a good living, but even more to make a good life. Developing that set of desires—and offering resources to satisfy them—becomes the precise task for the creators of a great society. That task will involve elements transcending economics. We are therefore bound now to examine techniques and objectives outside the business and economic field. We must examine how these other disciplines can be used as America now seeks to make an affluent society into a great society.

The White House has assembled a large number of working committees or task-forces. In the past few days they have quietly been reporting. Their conclusions will eventually be reflected in legislation proposed to the Congress. All the subjects under study are important though they will have to be supplemented, since they are still primarily economic in character. Reportedly these task-forces have investigated these problems of the national economy: (a) sustaining prosperity; (b) intergovernmental fiscal cooperation (a highly complex and technical subject); (c) reorganization of the Executive branch of the government; (d) foreign economic policy; (e) cost of production; (f) maintenance of income; (g) agriculture; (h) transportation; (i) natural resources.

In addition, task-forces have been reporting on fields outside the economic area. These include (a) education; (b) preservation of natural beauty; (c) health; (d) metropolitan and urban problems.

The first group deal with the improvement of economic and governmental machinery—as indeed they should.

The second group go more into the content of life. In a deep sense they are more important than the economic committees. An economic structure is only a means to an end—not the end itself. Men do not exist to eat and consume. They exist to attain life. If they desired only to survive, the brute levels of primitive life would have been enough; but in that case economic advance would be unnecessary. Man's desire to live above the survival level—first, to live at a level of mere comfort, but eventually to have a life of meaning and significance—has been the driving force requiring economic development.

We can put this in a number of ways. Sordidly, men and women are not customers unless they have two qualifications: educated desires and purchasing power to satisfy them. Without educated desires, they would not be consumers beyond the survival level. Ultimately, the driving power behind economics—indeed behind any advance in civilization—is the desire of men and women to have a good life as they conceive it. The business of economics is to provide both purchasing power and production so that men and women can carry on that quest.

Now desires for the "good life" whose aggregate creates a society do not occur spontaneously. They are the product of what we call "a value system," whose values transcend the elementary value of survival or even of comfort. If a society seeks greatness, it must call out, sustain and develop, greater values and more splendid desires. Once accepted, satisfaction of these become imperatives.

At this point those social sciences which decline to make value judgments must necessarily seek guidance from and find common ground with those other branches of learning in which values are essential. Economists do not undertake to say what men ought to want, or what wants are most important. Rather, they record what men did in response to whatever wants they had. Their predictions are based on the theory that tomorrow's wants will be similar to yesterday's. Sociologists do not say that the structures they describe are "good" or "bad." They say they exist. Sociologists of the school of the late C. Wright Mills insist that the structure they describe is "amoral." But they decline to define "moral." As individuals, of course, economists and sociologists have their private value system and value judgments but they rigidly separate these from their scientific conclusions. These social sciences endeavor to present data, processes and probable consequences on whose basis statesmen, politicians, managers and others can make reasoned choice of measures. A value system, on the other hand, precisely involves judgments that some results are better than others. Criteria of these judgments are essentially philosophical. The operative value system of a great society is essentially philosophy in action.

Other social sciences do acknowledge and endeavor to give effect to value systems. My own profession—law—explicitly endeavors (however imperfectly and unsuccessfully) to make effective the values involved in public peace and in justice, as each generation conceives and defines these values. The medical profession, in theory, endeavors to forward the values involved in health—as health is conceived and defined. Architecture, in theory, gives effect to combined values of usefulness and beauty, as these are conceived in contemporary life.

Statecraft, planning, in its great or small aspects now must make use of a combination of these disciplines. It can not work merely with the non-value making disciplines. Socially creative politics automatically involve value choices. Either the politicians must make these themselves or they must draw on medicine, philosophy, law and the arts. This highlights the importance of inter-disciplinary studies, as social development goes forward.

Let us apply these considerations to the great affair going forward—the impulse towards "the Great Society."

It must make some great assumptions about human values, and must lay out the lines along which the struggle should be directed. Rushing in where angels fear to tread, let us attempt the outline of that dream. It will be based, I think, on two majestic values: first the value of truth, always unattainable but always pursued, and second the companion value of beauty, never finally crystallized and always expanding. Neither, as we shall see, is abstract. Both call for concrete, direct, though frighteningly difficult measures.

The value of truth demands attention to education, learning and research. The range runs all the way from primary schools to top scholarship in great universities. Adequately realized, this value requires that no child shall fail to go to school up to the limit of his capacity and will. It requires that no school anywhere shall fail to give him the greatest possible stimulus and training. A "Great Society" will thus insist on school reform from the bottom to the top. It will seek to organize a primary school system in which there shall be a teacher for every 15 students instead of for every 30 or 40. It will require that teachers shall be of the kind and quality President Conant of Harvard has been demanding in his recent books. It will mean that our great universities—some of which are in danger of becoming frauds on the public—shall assure to every student continuous contact with good minds—instead of telescopic views of a professor on a lecture platform, while teaching and contact are left to junior apprentices.

This in turn connotes that education everywhere shall be quite adequately financed: and that no student shall be forced to forego education for economic reasons. It calls for continuing the unparalleled support which society now gives to research, but would emphasize pure research and teaching as effectively as it now engenders applied research.

The cost will run into billions, and raising the money will be the least part of the problem. The value of beauty, once accepted, is no less drastic in its demands. A great society would seek, perhaps impose, higher social standards of community construction and management than American life now exacts. It would ask that every city or town shall cease to tolerate ugliness —and that their architecture, their planning, their streets, their residence sections, shall be distinguished. (This might mean shooting a considerable proportion of advertisers or—more humanely—putting an end to the aesthetic scavenging and blackmail which now insult our eyes and ears at every turn.) It would mean that no home should be constructed which did not evidence its occupant's dignity. It ought to include arrangements giving to every town and every region access to drama, to music, to painting, and to the greater manifestations of the fine arts. It would assume as a necessity far greater support and diffusion of music, of literature, and of the arts.

Acceptance of these values in the sense here contemplated would almost immediately create—and also tend to solve—certain economic and social problems. Techniques of a number of social disciplines would have to be combined to indicate ways by which our great and growing production of goods and services could be channeled towards realizing the newly recognized values. Already we are fairly well advanced in the techniques of national economy. That is demonstrated by the effectiveness of the Council of Economic Advisers, working in conjunction with the Federal Reserve Board, the Treasury and the Bureau of the Budget. Our new conception involves working also with state and local governments, as the nascent war on poverty has already shown. Here, economics must work with political science, and both with the emerging discipline of public administration. The three disciplines have to understand each other so thoroughly that they can come up with valid plans.

Again it is already certain that public education will be a major factor at all levels. This means that to the three disciplines just mentioned, educational theorists and administrative methods have been chosen; the lawyer becomes indispensable. He must overcome existing legal hurdles involved in the American federal system. He must give form and procedures to the administrative institutions and the supporting financial machinery. And he must assure continuing regard for civil rights and civil liberties as the movement rolls forward.

All this sounds obvious, but is not easily realized. Thirty years ago, with Dr. Gardiner C. Means, I made one of the early inter-disciplinary studies. Its result was the volume called *The Modern Corporation and Private Property*,[3] in which a lawyer teamed with an economist in studying one phase of our economic system. Our aim was not to have an economic study paralleling a legal study. We intended to integrate the two techniques, coming up with a result. Neither the lawyer nor the economist quite cared to surrender his unique position, so integration was not easy; but was nevertheless attained. It will not be easy for the economist, with his data, and the scholar of public finance, with his technique, to integrate their thinking with, let us say, an educational administrator or the city planner who must set the concrete objective for each project. Yet there is no escape. The educational administrator must set objectives capable of being reached—abandoning some of his hopes. The economist must relinquish some of his rigidities and preconceptions, even some of his "conventional wisdom" in Professor J. K. Galbraith's phrase. Out of this common thinking, plans can emerge in shape to be handed to politicians, legislators, and government officers.

Even the most modest start in this process directly engages the talents of further disciplines. Even at outset, it becomes clear that method—that is, how the problems are to be met—is itself of supreme importance. A huge centralized bureaucratic machine could be constructed—as the Emperor Napoleon I constructed a civil service for France which governs France to this day. Or the method might be selected of reliance on local units—a classic American choice which today may be impractical. Intermediate state government might be relied on and local responsibilities stimulated, perhaps with agreed standards of performance worked out for the entire nation—a solution President Conant has recently proposed in his suggestion for educational reform. The possibilities and probable results of these various methods have been, or can be, determined by political scientists and their subordinate discipline of public administration.

Academically we shall probably wind up with a sort of hierarchy. At the top there must be—in fact, there certainly will be—a continuing philosophical debate on values, and their development. Closely allied would be historians: they could be charged (among other things) with attempting to define the impact of thought-currents on events. Presumably their results would be illuminated by sociologists attempting to describe the existing social structure and its roots and causes. Next would come the economists, statisticians and econometric specialists, recording present capacities, and making predictions. At the engineering level, we would find lawyers attempting to elaborate institutions and set up the relevant rules. In sum, we should have a process of describing what exists, of setting it against the assumed value system, of seeking to repair present omissions and of laying out means of forward movement. This is the rationale of interdisciplinary work in its current phase.

It is not mysterious. There is no mystery when architects work with financiers and construction engineers and get their projects built. These have learned to work together though sometimes uneasily. Architects have already discovered how to work with artists. In wider context, the process is not different when a town, a city, or a social structure, is under discussion.

There remains the great question of impetus—that drive which will impel men to seek a good life, whose aggregate requires a community or a nation to seek a good society. Unquestionably the State can assist—but the American State is not a philosopher or a church. Americans must rely on the ceaseless beat of individual idealists in press or in pulpit, in classroom or in conference, in universities or in local societies, in literature of perception and poetry, in literature of reform and of revolt. All these, leading a society to transcend itself, are the life-force of expanding civilization.

Following Professor Berle's talk, a series of questions was directed to him from the floor. Some of the more significant appear below.

MOHAN*—I gather, Professor Berle, you think it is more relevant that the lawyer be trained in humanistic values than that the average person be trained in legal values. Would you agree to that?

BERLE—In the main, yes. There is always the *"déformation professionelle"* of the lawyer. I think the layman has to know what the lawyer's difficulty is and what his job is, not asking him for the impossible, and I do not see how the lawyer, being himself the professional in the transaction, can do his job without knowing the humanistic result desired by his peers. I don't see how we can avoid having him know what *they* are trying to do.

MOHAN—Since you seem to suggest that the esthetic aspirations of a people will have to articulate themselves in some kind of a legal structure, it would also seem to indicate the necessity, too, of some kind of legal knowledge, would it not, for those who were furthering these things?

BERLE—I think non-lawyers must know what they are up against. Of course I was there drawing a good deal on some studies made at the Yale Law School with which you are familiar—land use, that grim, unpleasant term which involves the possibility of erecting the framework of a living, pulsating fragment of society. That is a humanistic job. What's involved if you zone an area so that no plot may be less than, say, four acres? What's involved if you zone the same area so that no lot shall be less than, say, three hundred feet square, or something of the kind? Translating these restrictions into a picture of who lives here, how he will live and what will happen, is a humanist's job.

I sat in on a fascinating conference in Puerto Rico the other day. Governor Munoz Marin was dealing with the proliferation of super-markets there. It's a small island and its economy could be easily wrecked. The group was trying to see whether they could not work out zoning arrangements so that super-markets should recreate to some extent the old Spanish plazas—these in the old days were not only places of exchange but also by reason of their beauty, places of meeting. Now I can't imagine how any lawyer working at that could do an intelligent job unless he knew what a Spanish plaza had been, what it was, had at least looked at photographs and understood what the actual necessities were.

---

* Very Rev. Robert P. Mohan, S.S., Catholic University (philosophy).

SELZNICK*—One of the questions about the Great Society that bears upon your own work, Mr. Berle, has to do with the significance of affluence in the achievement of the ideals we want. I have been much impressed by your own suggestions that in the modern corporation we can see the development—that is, in the private corporation, in the private sector —of some sense of conscience, and reasonable self-restraint, and so on. Now I have a question about that, that is of great importance to the whole pattern of development in society. First of all, can we see in the private institution not only the possibilities of minimal self-restraint, but also the possibilities of more positive social responsibilities? I can see pretty clearly the forces that limit some of the large private groups in modern society, some of the more outrageous things they did in earlier times. Can we see in the private sector the possibility of a positive commitment, for example, to the reconstruction of our urban life in cooperation with government? It seems to me, that is the one basic issue we are going to have to face. How much can we rely upon private organizations and private enterprise for this kind of social commitment?

BERLE—Bluntly, not too much. Only up to a point. I don't know anything I have said that was more attacked and, I like to think, more misunderstood than that observation. Actually that book was retranslated in France and because this was picked up it was called *La Société Anonyme et le Conscience du Roi*. (*The Modern Corporation and the Conscience of the King.*)

What is called "the corporate conscience" is no news to lawyers. We're familiar, of course, with the fact that a corporation is an artificial entity, therefore has no soul, can't take an oath, and so forth and so on. And yet we also know that inside corporations there are men. Actually the conscience of a corporation represents in large measure a rather lively appreciation that if they do not restrain themselves from violating community standards, there will be an intervention by the state. These will follow almost automatically. Any sane public relations department will tell them to be ahead instead of behind such situations. Every corporation lawyer knows that his client will ask him, "*Can* I do this?" and the lawyer will say, "You *can* but you certainly had better *not*, because the next thing is you'll be investigated by the Senate, or the New York legislature, or you'll be in a row with these and these groups in the community." In this way, there is a lively appreciation of the working of a public consensus which limits or guides the technical and legal powers of the corporation.

In some things it is working fairly well. For example, building of factories essentially decent to look at instead of hideous has almost become second nature to the corporations that are "affluent" enough to do it. Those of you who ride on the trains from New York to Wash-

* Philip G. Selznick, Director, Center for the Study of Law and Society, University of California, Berkeley (sociology).

ington have seen the line of factories that Johnson & Johnson have constructed. That is some of the best commercial architecture in the United States. Anyone can look at them with pleasure. If you take out the advertising matter (in fairness to them, it is reduced to a minimum), you have a beautiful piece of work.

Your private corporation today is essentially a statist instrument. It is left to private enterprise because the state chooses to do so and not for any other reason. We have made that work well in terms of product. We take some losses in terms of what some of these private enterprise people will do. I note with some interest that the Russians are just beginning to move their productive units more nearly into that frame although it is only a tiny advance.

You *can not* expect corporations to do your humanistic work for you. They do not create humanist standards. The work of making standards is fundamentally the job of the teacher, the priest in the pulpit, of the press and of you and me and all of us. In a democracy, all this produces a political result, if the level does not move up towards the standards on which consensus is reached.

Dean Reuben Frodin of the College of Arts and Sciences of the City College of the City University of New York introduced Professor Villey and Mr. McDonald and commented on their remarks.These comments are included here directly after each main text, and are followed (in Section 4) by Mr. Massel's reflections on the views of Professor Villey and Mr. McDonald.

2.   Law and Values—A French View[4]

MICHEL VILLEY*

I should like to begin with a brief look at the title of my report: "Law and Values—A French View." Let me take the second part first.

The organizers of our conference wanted an echo to be heard here of the thought of the other side of the Atlantic, of continental Europe, and among the countries of continental Europe their choice fell upon France. Personally I am very happy for it.

However, the task of representing France, or worse still the continent, is a bit heavy for my shoulders.

---

* Professor of Law, Faculté de droit et des sciences économiques, University of Paris.

French I am—you have already noticed it! I am afraid that my poor English will make it difficult for you to understand me. But despite my Frenchness, I cannot pretend to *represent* continental European juridical thought, nor even French juridical thought. As you know, theoretic studies, studies in the *philosophy of law,* abound in Europe. It is impossible for a single person to represent all these contradictory doctrines.

My whole ambition, then, is simply to represent one sector of the European doctrines. To sum up my position: Perhaps because I am an historian I find it useful to know the ancient doctrines, including the doctrines of the Greeks and of the Middle Ages; I am not content with collecting a lot of current opinions. I know that the progress of physical sciences and techniques is gigantic; I am aware of the atomic developments and the giant planes and the television all around us. But it is much more dubious that there has been any true progress in philosophy, especially in the philosophy of law, since the Greeks. Or if you prefer, I do not believe that progress can be achieved unless we use the help of ancient teachings. Well, that is a commonplace; please forgive me for making it.

Now I'd like to turn to the first and most important part of my title: "Law and Values." I must confess that these are three terrible words for me.

First of all, does your Anglo-Saxon word *law* mean the same thing as the French word *droit,* the German *Recht,* the Italian *diritto,* or the Latin *jus?* I am afraid that it does not. You Anglo-Saxons and we Europeans have very different types of law, and this is another reason for me to fear that I shall be obscure for you.

But the most difficult word of all is this word *and.* It is a dangerous word. What sort of *relationship* do you want me to find between law and values? I racked my brain for a long time to try to understand my subject.

Is it possible that anyone could doubt that there is a relationship between law and the values of common life? No, not seriously. There are legal technicians who perform their task like machines and who do not consider what they are serving. But anyone who thinks just a little perceives that juridical activity serves all kinds of values, serves liberty, serves the common peace, etc., and that it protects all these values.

And that *everyone* is concerned with law. If you enjoy the liberty to travel about, to speak your opinion, to gain wealth by your work—if, on the contrary, you are now in a state of misery—it is due to the laws of your country; things would not be the same in other juridical regimes. We historians of law, who compare the laws of diverse societies, know this fact well. The choice of values of a society is embodied in its laws.

I think that these truths have no need of demonstration.

And so I concluded that my subject might be conceived in the following way:

What is the end of juridical activity? What are the values that law serves? Or better, what is the proper specific value of law?

I think this question is an important one because you cannot seriously define the proper domains of law, as compared to those of political economy, moral science, etc., unless you reflect a little about the aim of law. If we want to examine the programs, the organization, and the sphere of influence of legal teaching, legal studies, I think we must first reflect upon the aims, the values of law.

Unfortunately this question is also a very philosophical one. It is the first question of what we call the philosophy of law and what you call jurisprudence. It is a typical philosophical question because the answer to it really depends on general philosophy and, I think, on metaphysics.

In Europe you Americans have the reputation—true or not, I do not know; they say many things about Americans in the world that are not true —of disliking metaphysics. I am sorry, but for my part I am convinced that if we think that we can dispense ourselves from metaphysics, it is only that we are servilely and blindly following the conclusions of a single school of metaphysics.

In my opinion there are chiefly two kinds of philosophies of the value of law. The first I call the nominalist philosophy, and this is the most modern, in a certain sense of the word. The second I call the classical philosophy. It is more ancient and I shall look for it in the juridical philosophies of Aristotle and St. Thomas. But I find it tends to appear again in many contemporary doctrines. I should like to compare these two sorts of philosophies of the value of law—and to try to choose between them.

I. Let us begin, then, by considering (this will be a critical consideration) the answers offered to our problem by nominalism, or, if you prefer, by modern thought, if you let me take this word "modern" in the French sense. In France when we speak of modern thought, we mean the thought that is derived from the 16th and 17th centuries. We still depend on this philosophy. We are educated under its influence. It dominates our thinking.

I do not like the theory of juridical values that has come from *modern* philosophy in this French sense of the word. The reason for my doubt is this: most of the philosophers of the modern period, even if they have written on law, have had very little practical knowledge of law.

This is still true today, at least in Europe. Our professors or our students of philosophy often have some training in mathematics, in the experimental sciences, in psychology, occasionally in medicine, sometimes in sociology, in political science, in religion, and in moral science: no one is completely ignorant of moral problems. But they hardly ever have any training in law. For example, the most famous, such as Husserl, Heidegger, Sartre, do not seem to have had any experience in law. (So I am a little disturbed when I see some of our colleagues intent upon drawing *juridical* applications from these philosophies.)

But the same observation could have been made apropos of the great thinkers of the 16th to the 18th centuries.

Well this modern philosophy was built up under the empire of *nominalism*. We can say that modern thought—and this is especially true of Anglo-Saxon thought, which is still developing this way today—developed along the way opened up by William of Occam, founder in the 14th century of the *via moderna* (from which we get the word "modern"), that is, of nominalism.

And to summarize: Nominalism, as you know, attributes reality only to individuals—John or James—and not to universals or to groups, such as humanity, the state, the city, which are only conceptual instruments of our minds.

As for values, the result of this philosophy is a tendency to recognize individuals or at least singular beings as the only possible support or subjects of values. Because only these singular beings are real; therefore only to them can a value be *definitively* attached. Values will be, then, the objects of *interest* of individuals.

This is the logical consequence of nominalism. If, for example, the family is not a reality, there is no sense in looking for the good, the value, of the family. But in the final analysis we look for the good of John, Mary, and of their different children. These we can call individual values. To put it more generally: Nominalism knows only singular values.

But this will appear more clearly if we examine the catalog of values that the modern philosophies have drawn up in our domain and proposed to juridical thought. We see first that there are diverse ways of conceiving of the good of individuals; from this point of view you can already distinguish a wide assortment of juridical values.

The good of the individual can be taken to be the moral value, the moral religious value of the individual (for example, in the doctrine of Calvin, when he wrote about law). But more often it was taken to be his temporal happiness; a happiness that has often been conceived as chiefly material. Instead of seeking the *virtue* of the individual, his material *well being* was considered to be the end of law. This is the tendency of the great English school of the 18th and 19th centuries, of Hobbes, of Locke, of Hume, of Bentham, whose ideas have spread widely in France and over the whole continent—and I think even more over America.

You all know that in Bentham's thought the end of juridical activity (in the broad sense) is the happiness of the individual; the happiness defined, according to Bentham, by the criterion of *pleasure.* The objective, at least of *legislation,* is then, for Bentham the greatest possible pleasure for the greatest possible number of individuals.

Or, instead of insisting upon man's economic well-being and upon his pleasure, you can put the accent upon his liberty, conceived not so much as the condition of his pleasure but as a condition of his *moral dignity,* according to the philosophy of Kant. Or you can stress the development of his being and of his *power* after the fashion of Nietzsche.

Or again you can seek—with another school—the *future* goods of individuals, that perfect liberty, which it is impossible to give men at the present time, but which one hopes at least to give to future generations. This is Marx's position, on a way opened up by Kant. It ranks in the first place the value of progress, in view of the *future* generations of individuals.

And now I should like to note that I don't think it makes much difference that many thinkers have made a place for the interests of *corporations* alongside of the interests of individuals. We know that strictly individualist positions have not been tenable for a long time. And that alongside of the values attached to the individual, a place has been made for the interest of collections of individuals: the interest of the social class, or of the enterprise, or of the state (which had first been confused with the service of the person of the king). Our values will be the *wealth,* or the *power,* or the *independence* of a *group.* We all know that this tendency has been carried very far—in Marxism, for example—or among certain sociologists—or in the thought of the German National Socialist jurists. The task of law for a German National Socialist theorist of law was to serve the power of the German community.

However, modern thought conceives of these collectivities as fictitious persons or "moral persons" as we say in French law. This does not get us out of nominalism. In the last analysis, law is still at the service of *interests* and of *particular interests,* whether these interests be of the state, of the social class, or of the enterprise—or of flesh and blood men.

There you have a summary list of the ends that modern thought proposes to law. This list is very incomplete—extremely incomplete. It is partial, even a bit of a caricature. Even in the 17th and 18th centuries it is very certain that no serious theorist of law was able to evade the fact that the objective of law was more complex; that law had, as they say—but the term is very confused—a social character; that its task was *not* to serve the interest of *one* individual or of *one* social body, but, as Bentham says, to serve the interest of *all* individuals or of the greatest number possible of them.

It is also certain that many legal theorists did not fail to mention *justice* in the catalog of juridical values: we shall come back to it in a moment. However, in the framework of nominalism they could not give justice much consistency. Most often they reduced it to a *form* empty of content, to a sort of vague or remote ideal. And they could give it no more than a secondary place, a place *among* other values

Well, if I wanted to draw a complete picture of the values that modern juridical thought proposes to juridical art, we would be here till midnight! I just wanted to point out the *principal values that a nominalist inspired vision of the world leads to*: those values that recent legal philosophers invite us to choose from or to combine—security, liberty, well-being of individuals or of groups.

Before leaving this first point, allow me a few words of discussion.

I do not like this way of describing the values of law:

1) It seems to me a false description, a false analysis of the objectives of juridical activity. It proposes that we serve the particular interests of individuals or of groups, or at the most a combination of particular interests.

I do not think that this is a true description of the end of the activity of the jurist. Perhaps the description fits some lawyers, but it does not fit the barrister. Nor is it correct for the judge, nor for the legislator who guides the judge, nor for juridical doctrine and the legal theorist that also guide the judge. For example, when a judge settles a case concerning the custody of children—in connection with a divorce—he is not really at the service of the interest of the child (this is the function of the social worker), nor at the service of the interest of the father or the mother. His aim, the value he serves, is something different.

2) This incorrect description of the objectives of law—which was thrust upon jurists by modern philosophy, a philosophy of non-jurists—has brought about certain *deviations* in juridical practice.

It tends to make the jurist *partial,* the servant of particular interests or of particular values, which seems to me to be contrary to his vocation.

How disastrous it was, for example, for Locke and Bentham to have made law the servant of the interest of "individuals," who are in fact often only the rich property owners!

Or another example: in French criminal law there is a movement called "social defense"; it proposes to reform penal law, on the premise that the objective of penal law is the defense of *public tranquillity.* Well, I say again: The aim of penal law is something different. The judge neither pursues the interest of social tranquility nor that of the culprit. Whose interest does he pursue then?

You will answer: The interest of *all* men; *all* the interests of *all* men: this is his aim.

I am afraid that it is impossible to pursue at once the infinite interests of *all* men. This aim is too vast to be realized! If you take this doctrine as your guide, you risk arriving at juridical formulas that are completely impracticable—formulas such as the solemn declaration of the rights of man made by the United Nations. You wind up proclaiming that *all* men have a *"right* to health, to culture, and to ease." This is a marvelous ideal; but I do not think this sort of talk should please jurists. For, alas! it is impossible in the present or in the near future to give all men culture, health, even enough bread. These are *false credits,* which cannot be paid and which risk giving rise to illusory dreams. This has nothing to do with law.

When you give law the objective of serving particular interests, you either make the judge *partial,* or you sink into *utopia.*

3) My third remark concerns the *place that is made for law in education,* which is one of the objects of our conference.

I do not think that this place can be very great if you consider the end of law to be the service of the interests of individuals or of groups: whether these interests be the moral value of the individual, or his economic wealth, or the power of the state. For these values principally depend on other disciplines: moral philosophy, economics, the political sciences.

In this philosophy, law plays only an auxiliary and a rather sordid role. It is simply an instrument of *sanction* in the service of morality or of state politics—or else it is given the task of protecting the *security* of individual riches. The jurist is only the servant or policeman of the moralist, the economist, or the politician. Law is nothing but a *technique.* It consists in a certain number of tools, which are laws, charters, or other juridical rules, and which are used in the service of economics, morality, or politics.

Of course there is a place for the specialized study of these tools, just as there is a place for the study of the instruments and recipes of agriculture, subordinate to the *science* of economics. There is a place for a *technology* and for technical schools of law. But in them one risks shutting oneself up in this technique and forgetting the ends, the values that law serves—values that are studied theoretically *elsewhere.*

And if law schools are like this, why would they interest the general public? The public has no more need to understand this specialized technique than I have to know the latest specialized techniques of agricultural production.

(True, we might recommend that our fellow citizens study law because of the quality of juridical reasoning, because of its precision, because of the certitude of its method, etc. Frankly, from this point of view, I prefer mathematics.)

If our current legal writings do not interest many readers outside of jurists properly so-called, you see that it is perhaps our own fault. Modern philosophy has deceived us in its analysis of the objective of law and of the content of legal studies. But there is another way of conceiving of law and legal studies to which I shall now turn.

II. Now I invite you to a quick trip into the past, to the doctrines of Aristotle and of St. Thomas Aquinas, doctrines that I call *classical.* For a long time they reigned over the thought of jurists: over Roman jurists and over the learned jurists of the European Middle Ages. And truly they have never been entirely forgotten in Europe, but they have been combined in a more or less confused way with the modern philosophies of which I have just spoken. Moreover, there is a remarkable likeness between these ancient doctrines and some of our most recent thinking.

Personally, I repeat, I am very fond of these classical philosophies, as philosophies of law. It seems to me that Aristotle and St. Thomas Aquinas have analyzed juridical activity very well; they have understood its meaning and its values. Perhaps it was easier to do this in the microcosm of an ancient city or a medieval seignory. In a democratic Greek city like Athens especially, every citizen was involved in the administration of justice and had a chance to be judge, whereas in our great modern states the administration of justice is a very specialized affair, and the general public knows nothing about it. As I said, Descartes, Hume, or Kant did not know much about law. But it was quite different with Socrates, Plato, or Aristotle.

What answer does the philosophy that I call classical—the philosophy of Aristotle and St. Thomas—offer to our problem of the values that preside over law?

An extremely simple answer: that law is not at the service of particular interests, whether they be of individuals, of the state, or of social class. Classical philosophy said: Law is at the service of *justice:* "the *just*" is the value of law. This conception seems to have been generally accepted in antiquity, as the languages of Greece and Rome testify. In Greek there is only one word, the word *dikaion,* to designate law and just. And the same thing is nearly true in Latin: *jus* is almost the same word as *justum,* just.

So we have to speak a bit about justice. The word alone, I confess, certainly does not give us much light. Because (under the influence of modern philosophy) we have completely lost the ancient sense of this word. Generally, justice has become something very utopian for us: an ideal in the future, an idyllic state of things where all men would be perfectly free and equal, where all the interests of all men would be equally realized—because we tend to think of everything in terms of these interests. Justice is a pole of political action, but nothing that can be realized in the present. This common idea of justice is very vague.

Justice was nothing like this for Aristole and St. Thomas. It was not at all idealistic. We need to rediscover the *content* that this notion had in classical philosophy.

Well, I take out my Aristotle: Book V of the *Nicomachean Ethics*. It deals with justice precisely and it used to be famous among jurists. In this text Aristotle gives us a very realistic and very positive study of the sense of the word justice. I have heard it compared to the most current studies of the phenomenologists.

(It is a pity that this text is almost unknown today by most jurists. Of course, not by all. After I had denounced this ignorance in an article, my colleague from Manchester, Mr. Wortley, sent me the program of required reading for all the students at Manchester: on it was Book V of the *Nichomachean Ethics*.)

In the strictest sense, what St. Thomas, following Aristotle, calls *particular justice* is an effort to realize, in concrete circumstances, in the present, in the life of such-and-such a time and such-and-such a society, a *fair distribution* among citizens of goods, of honors, of responsibilities—a fair distribution, which is however necessarily unequal in the present life. As Aristotle puts it, a proportional distribution.

In scholastic language, as you know, the principal kind of particular justice is what is called *distributive* justice. For example, the task of distributive justice, for a French jurist, is to try to share the powers fairly between our President and the French parliament—or in a divorce suit, to work to share equitably between the father and the mother the rights over the child and the corresponding obligations.

To try to give each one his share: *jus suum cuique tribuere,* as the Roman jurists said precisely to define the objective of the juridical profession. And in fact, the analysis of the value of justice that Aristotle gives us is simply a description of the objective of the jurist's task, and nothing else.

So we see that this objective of juridical activity is by no means to serve particular interests or particular values: for example, in a divorce case, the particular value that is the good education of the child, or the maternal love of the mother, or the financial ease of the father. The task before the jurist is, knowing all these values, to arbitrate among them, to choose among them, to put each one in its proper place.

The end of law is none of these singular and disconnected values that are the objects of particular interests. Justice, the value of law, is a sort of supervalue. Justice seems to be that value which consists in the harmonization of all other values.

You see, I have certainly not made any great discovery! All this is childish! Yet I do not think it is really easy for us to grasp again this old notion of justice.

We live under the influence of modern thought, I mean under the influence of nominalism. (If the only realities are individuals, or social groups conceived as individuals, then the only subjects of values are individuals, or these groups conceived as fictitious persons, and every value is the object of their interest.) Somehow it is difficult for us to admit, on the contrary, that the human individual is an abstraction. We are an *ensemble,* if I may use this French word; or, as Aristotle said, man is a political animal. And secondly it is difficult for us to admit that this ensemble can also be the subject, the support of a value and that this value can consist in a harmony.

Beauty is also a value, and the subject of this value is an ensemble— whether it be a person or the cosmos. Beauty is a harmony.

The same thing is true of justice. But we cannot seem to grasp this classical notion. We cannot seem to break out of the web of nominalism.

There is also a difficulty from the theological point of view.

It seems to me that the *Protestant Reform,* following the *Augustinian* tradition of the Middle Ages, has played the greatest part since the 16th century in dispelling the classical notion of justice. Luther and Calvin conceived of justice exclusively as the justice of the Bible, the justice of the kingdom of heaven: a perfect justice that would be characterized by the *equality* of all men and the perfect liberty of all men. They have helped to make justice a utopia that is too ideal to be realized today on this earth.

But to accept the classical notion of justice, we must, on the contrary, recognize with St. Thomas that there can be a value even in the *natural* harmony of human societies, despite the fact that the order of these societies is based on the *inequality* of men, for the distribution in question is an unequal and proportional distribution: for instance, you cannot grant the child the same number of hours to the father and to the mother once they are divorced; and despite the fact that this order is changing, since human societies are changing and historic, just like the laws of harmony in music —despite all this—there would be a value in the fair distribution of goods as it would be realized on earth.

I do not think that this difficulty is insurmountable, for in this time of Council, there are many Catholics who think more like Protestants on this point; and perhaps there are Protestants who would think more like St. Thomas.

Still, there are difficulties. It will certainly take more than an hour to recapture the classical notion of justice as the value of law.

However, before closing, allow me a few critical remarks. But this time they will be favorable.

I repeat that this description of the objective of the juridical profession (in the broad sense) appears correct. It has the merit of not confusing the task of the judge and his auxiliaries with the task of the social worker, or with that of the policeman, or with that of the moralist; and of not confusing the office of the legislator (in drawing up laws to guide the judge) with that of the economist or the financial adviser.

Moreover, Aristotle's analysis more or less coincides with certain contemporary theories; you have recognized its kinship, for instance, with certain recent sociological doctrines. Perhaps it is almost the same thing as what they wish to signify today in a more or less confused way when they speak about "social justice," about social control, about the interest that society function well, and so on.

And, of course, it matters little to us where the analysis comes from. I love Aristotle and St. Thomas; I do not idolize them. It just seems to me that their doctrines have an interest for us because their analysis is undoubtedly more clear and more solidly founded.

And there can be a certain practical advantage in thus having a good analysis at our disposal: it can keep us from errors. I repeat, our juridical science or art has been deceived by modern legal philosophy with respect to values. For example, Bentham tells us that the objective of law is enrichment, the greatest possible pleasure: this is not our proper task. Or Calvin considers the purpose of law to be the protection of the moral value of the individual. For him, this is the reason the individual does not steal (it could also be for economic reasons); for the Decalog says: You shall not steal—even if the distribution of goods is unjust. But we also have the obligation of providing for a just distribution of goods.

I think I am laboring the obvious when I say that the great mistake of modern occidental law is, it seems to me, to have neglected this *distributive justice,* to have neglected the problem of the just division of goods among peoples—I mean among the developed and the under-developed, the colonizers and the colonized, the rich and the poor—to have neglected what we call today, more or less clearly, *social justice.* This is not the only value. There are others—power, wealth—that the occidental world has very happily cultivated. There is the moral value of the individual. But justice, as we have defined it, is the proper value of law, and a false philosophy should not lead jurists to sacrifice it. It is indeed serious for modern law to have forgotten the value of justice.

Now I come to my conclusion, which concerns the topic of our conference: juridical education and the place of law in general education.

I think that this very simple philosophy of the value of law that I have just presented to you could help to elevate law studies, and consequently to restore them to a place of honor in general education. For in this philosophy law ceases to be a mere *technique.* It ceases to be simply a collection of *tools* designed to serve extrinsic ends, such as economic well-being, the moral value of the individual, or the power of the state. It ceases to be subordinated to economics, moral science, or political science, which have other objectives, other viewpoints upon the world. Law is itself a distinct and autonomous art: the art of seeking this special value, the value of the just.

Let me look again into the past, into the European system of juridical education of the late Middle Ages. The medieval university was not, as you know, divided into departments, but into faculties. The faculty of law took its place beside the faculties of arts, medicine, and theology—as it still does today in Europe. It was on the same level as these other faculties, it had the same dignity, nearly the same importance, and perhaps the same amplitude. For in seeking a value, you can consider nearly all of reality from the point of view of this value. For instance, in the faculty of arts you study many diverse subjects from the point of view of the value of beauty; in the faculty of science, from the point of view of the value of truth; in the faculty of theology, from the point of view of the religious value. Each of these faculties contains an ensemble of very different subjects that are ordered in view of the specific value pursued. To take another example, in the faculty of economics you cultivate the value of wealth and you consider everything from the point of view of wealth. Or again, in the faculty of the political sciences you take the view of the power of the state, or of public tranquillity, or of progress. In the very same way, in the faculty of law you can also gather together many diverse subjects, you can consider nearly all of reality from the point of view of the specific value of justice.

In the schools of the Roman jurists and of the medieval jurists (which I consider not for the purpose of slavish imitation, but for inspiration) certainly they studied positive rules; because in every country the existent positive laws are a major factor of the problem of justice. But they had a different way of studying these texts than we have today. They had a more liberal way: they studied positive laws in terms of justice, because laws are for one thing a resumé of the results of the anterior search for justice, because this search for justice is the meaning of the laws.

Furthermore, such a search requires not only the study of the rules of positive law, but also a proper study of all interests and all other values; and it requires history, and psychology, and moral philosophy, and some sociology as we now call it, some study of societies. You know, before writing his *Politics* Aristotle with his School studied more than 100 contemporary social constitutions of the diverse cities of Greece and of the Oriental empire. He believed that we draw our knowledge of the concrete content of justice, that is, of the just distribution of goods and values among men in such-and-such an historic or geographic condition, from an internal *observation* of social groups, and from a special consideration of those that appear most harmoniously organized and that can serve as models.

This was the method of natural law. I mean of the *classical* natural law of Aristotle and St. Thomas, which is not at all the same thing as—which indeed is the exact opposite of—the natural law of the moderns, or what is generally understood today by natural law. But it is too late to speak about natural law.

I suppose that you are very skeptical about the possibility of such a science of justice. You doubt that it is possible to find the concrete content of justice in a scientific way. You think that this is simply a matter of one's subjective choice. For this is the way modern philosophy has taught us to think. The effort of modern philosophy has been to deny this ancient notion of justice; to reduce it to the value of pleasure, as Hume has done, or to deform it. Well, I grant you that this science of justice is difficult and fluctuating, that it cannot be a science in the same way as mathematics or physics. But it can be a well-ordered ensemble of knowledge. To take up my comparison: It is also very difficult to understand the science of beauty and its rules also vary. *All* values are *mysterious*. But, for me, the proof that this science of justice is possible is that it has existed, and that it still exists. This was the science of the Roman jurisconsults, and it is also the science of many modern jurists. It is only our philosophical prejudices that make us deny that such a science is possible.

Perhaps I too am utopian, but I think that our programs of legal studies could be even richer and nobler than they used to be, thanks to the steady contributions of many other sciences (because the subjects studied are often the same, only the viewpoints differ). But this would presuppose that we conceive of law not as a mere technique at the service of external values, of particular interests, but as an autonomous science, the autonomous search for the specific value of the just.

And finally, I think that if legal studies were renewed in this way, they would interest a large public. Because in the kingdom of earth nothing is perhaps so necessary as the harmonization of all other values—which is the proper task of justice and of law. If legal studies fulfilled this vocation I do not think they would leave the general public so indifferent. We know that in antiquity and in the Middle Ages they interested *all* educated men. As I said before, the great philosophers of ancient Greece, for example, were well versed in law. The same result *should* be obtained today if we would draw our inspiration from the same principle, while adapting it to the circumstances of our time.

But I have been much too long. I thank you for your patience in listening to my awkward English. I thank the organizers of this conference for giving me the pleasure of crossing the Atlantic to participate in it.

FRODIN*—Our speaker has reminded us, I believe, that the search for justice is the search for the *sense* of the law, and he said the search requires, besides the history of juridical art, sociology, the study of societies, a concern for philosophical inquiries which we have had in the classical studies of Aristotle, Thomas, Augustine and—as an American I would add—Locke. We have in our Constitution the statement that all men are created free and equal and that we are looking for liberty of the individual, and that we have a concept of the uniformity of justice under the Constitution. Now these are glosses out of the Protestant tradition, which in part springs from the great heritage of Aristotle and Thomas. They also help get us over some problems with respect to slavery; we have not solved all of them—we seek to. Restraints on man's activity under our government, as well as protection of freedom, may be attributed to the flexibility and practicality of the American Constitution. I think that it is useful not to regard justice as an utopian idea but as something that can be achieved in a society in

---

* Dean Reuben Frodin, College of Arts and Sciences, City College of the City University of New York (administration, law).

which the equality of men is the aim of all people. We are indebted to our speaker for presenting the appeal to the classical approach, to the philosophy that comes to us from Plato, Aristotle, Thomas and Augustine, and to remind us of the problems of the modern society.

3.   The Importance of Values to the Practicing Lawyer

ROBERT J. McDONALD*

This conference, at least the portion which I have been privileged to hear, and this address tonight,[5] have been wide-ranging and most learned. In these discussions, I understand there have been allusions to the continuing deterioration of communications among the various disciplines. The case is at least partially proved because there has certainly been a failure at times to communicate with me. I would hasten to add, however, that this failure is not in the transmitting but in the receiving. My mission here tonight is obscure. I have been far away from the academic atmosphere for so long, and even if I had kept such ties close, I think I would feel ill-equipped to play a harmonious counterpoint to M. Villey's beautiful philosophical music. I therefore concluded that my mission tonight is to render a myopic review of M. Villey's speech from the point of view of a practicing lawyer.

It has always been my view as a practicing lawyer that law seeks justice. Here, of course, I am using justice in a broader sense than "justice according to the law" which, as Roscoe Pound put it, means the decision of disputes by adjudicators, judicial or administrative, who apply rules and principles of law—or lawyer's law. In this broader sense I include also structural law that sets through legislation and administrative rules the framework of government and which must also seek justice.

But then it occurs to me as one who practices law—and isn't that a wonderful way to put it in a discussion such as this—that the philosophical distinctions between the nominalists and the classicists have little day to day reality. Whether the end of law be the auxiliary, or even parasitic, role of servicing individual groups, their economic wealth, or the state, or whether the law has its separate, independent grail, in operation the law and the individuals who practice it must have ethical and moral values. Whether these values have their existence only in the limited area of the techniques

* Member, New York bar.

of law or a separate existence in a recognized discipline, they seem to me to come out the same. I assume then that law seeks justice.

In using a word such as justice, I assume like Humpty Dumpty that it means what I mean it to mean. To rationalize for me the conflicting philosophical views of law to an acceptable common denominator for daily practical application I mean "justice" to mean the fairest compromise which weighs and reconciles at a particular time and place the conflicting positions among individuals, groups or governments. I do not ask perfection of justice at a particular time or place; it is fallible. I expect only to strive hard for perfection.

To effect this compromise in the fairest possible way in this most complicated of modern worlds the practitioner of "lawyers law," whether by *avocat, avoué,* barrister, solicitor, attorney or judge, and of structural law, whether by a legislator, governmental administrator or community leader, must have the tools with which to fashion this fairest compromise. Thus, for example, if he be a lawyer acting as a legislator fashioning the law with respect to the dissemination of birth control information or a practicing lawyer commenting thereon in a bar association committee, he must understand—or before he reaches a solution to his problem he must learn—the economic, political and sociological impact of the population explosion; he must, especially in states such as in New York or Connecticut, appreciate certain theologians' position including the predicted deterioration of the family as the basic unit of society. He must, of course, have a sense of history and at least an intuition of philosophy. Whether the legislator in equipping himself to deal with such a problem be a lawyer who studies various aspects of the problem when confronted with it, or whether the political scientist follows the same course, learning also the legal techniques, it comes down to a question of choice.

Whatever the approach, the lawyer, including the lawyer acting as a legislator, must be able to break down, or crawl over, the walls built between the various disciplines so that in his quest for this fairest compromise of a problem he can bring the necessary knowledge and values to bear upon the problem. This can, in my opinion, best be accomplished by a person who has the general training, experience and education to be able to communicate among the various disciplines.

Two choices in the solution of this problem immediately suggest themselves. Either teach the other disciplines the tools of law or teach the lawyers the other disciplines. The first is probably impossible because practitioners of each discipline before they learned the tools of law would first have to learn to communicate among the other disciplines and they may not really care to communicate; the second is likewise impossible because the lawyer obviously cannot be a philosopher, an economist, a political scientist or various other things. It would seem, therefore, that I have created for myself an insoluble dilemma.

I do not think so. I believe the answer lies—in this narrow area to which I am confining myself of seeking justice—in striving to educate generalists who will then learn law with a generalist's approach. In this connection,

I would like to read you from the remarks, at times facetious, of Sir Eric Ashby, Master of Clare College, Cambridge, in a recent address. He said:

> But the world needs generalists as well as specialists. Indeed you have only to read the newspapers to know that the big decisions on which the fate of nations depends are in the hands of generalists. I do not believe that universities, American or British, are satisfied with the education they give to the man who is to become a generalist. Some believe he should have a rigorously specialist's training in some field which he then abandons for life. Others believe he should have a synoptic acquaintance with the ways of thinking of humanists, social scientists, and natural scientists. And I suppose there are still a few antique persons who cling to the view that generalists need no higher education at all. We can with some confidence prescribe the minutiae of curriculum for doctors, physicists, and lawyers. The unpalatable fact is that we have no such confidence in prescribing curricula for men who become Congressmen, presidents of industries, newspaper editors, or senior civil servants. This shortcoming in universities is part of a larger deficiency which universities will have to remedy without awaiting pressures from society.

I would put lawyers in this generalist category.

Would I be presumptuous to suggest that lawyers who practice, sit as judges, teach and become legislators, because of their basic mission of seeking "justice" or, as I put it, of seeking the fairest moral compromise for the most complicated disputes involving finance, economics, government and human rights and a host of other problems, would be among the best of the generalists? But, if lawyers are to be generalists in this sense, they must assume the burdens of the generalists. Thus, as legislators, teachers, community and governmental leaders in every day practice of their art, they not only must have the ability to communicate with the various disciplines but they should lead the moral values parade; they should like Caesar's wife be above suspicion because they are the arbitrators of justice which must be based upon moral solutions.

These moral values and ethical standards must be honed, sharpened and brightened by lawyers and those who practice law in every area in which law is practiced or taught. If not, lawyers deserve to become no more than bail bondsmen. Thus, in the university both at the undergraduate and especially at the law school level, where much of the training of lawyers is done, it is painful and erosive, for example, that values are such that examinations must be proctored and that the potential seekers of justice do not have sufficient ethical standards to police themselves; or that writings are published that are not original work, or at least represent the collective work of many, without proper acknowledgment; or that objective examinations are given in subjects that defy fragmentation because it is easier to correct them; or when a professor is tempted by payola, the student body of his university rises up in sympathy and blames the tempter.

At the practicing law level, it is unforgivable that justice can be delayed or defeated by legal gymnastics or even by crowded calendars; or that community morality has reached a point where the almost universal avoidance of the tax law is not considered a moral issue, only the Spartan concept of being caught is offensive. In this area, ethical standards are so eroded that they are close to collapse.

At the community level, for example, it is imperative that a solution be found to the political bartering of judgeships, and to the filling of important policy posts of government as a political reward. Otherwise, the dispensing of justice in this area becomes a mockery.

But most of all, the legislative level where structural law is practiced needs a reassessment of its own morality since it too is a purveyor of justice. Thus, for example, the use of public funds for political patronage only, or the lack of thrift in public office is immoral. A double standard of conflict of interest, one for the public and a separate and looser one for the legislators, is rather hard to stomach. The legislator who is uninformed or who fails regularly to attend legislative deliberations erodes ethical standards. And finally, special legislation for the benefit of the few at the expense of the many, usually as a result of political backscratching, is reprehensible.

My examples are perhaps too simple. In the face of these and the myriad of urgent problems in the law area which need a moral approach (meaning conforming to a standard of what is right and good) for their solution I can state categorically—and like all lawyers I am always categorical even though I am not always right—that the undergraduate and law schools cannot forget morals and ethics and smugly conclude that their teaching cannot affirmatively be taken over by the university but should be left to parents and churches, as the president of one large university said to me several months ago, because as he noted—if they don't have these values when we get them it is too late to teach them. If this is right, then I say at the very least don't tolerate the lack thereof.

Thus, the teaching of law or the teaching of a person who will practice law in this broad sense must be concerned not only with what the law is as an aid to proper advocacy, but what it ought to be, not as a pragmatic exercise in which the professor's views are expounded, but by instilling an approach which recognizes with a sense of urgency that justice is essential in lawyers' law and structural law. Thus, the student should be urged and taught that when he as a lawyer becomes a legislator or speaks for his community, or is in governmental office, or urges legislative reform individually or through bar associations, he must be equipped to bring moral and ethical values to bear upon the particular problem and not take a rigid position which represents a particular client's or particular political group's special interest, whether it be economic or political. And even when he is acting as an advocate, he should never do it in a manner which erodes justice or, to be trite, the shining image of the law. Lawyers pretend they practice this way; let's hope some day that they actually do.

FRODIN*—One of the advantages of education is that it is not dogmatic.

---

* Dean Reuben Frodin, College of Arts and Sciences, City College of the City University of New York (administration, law).

To hear the practicing lawyer from New York was to me, an academic, very rewarding. We have by the citation of Sir Eric Ashby a plea for the generalist, and a suggestion, that it may be that a call for general education comes both in the concern with the classics suggested by Mr. Villey, and from the dedication to the search for justice and righteousness of Mr. McDonald. In general, I think well of the education of the lawyer. Of course, some bad men are lawyers, but great good has been done by lawyers throughout history. As Adolf Berle pointed out earlier today in somewhat a reminiscent way, the fact that there have always been lawyers writing the minutes of meetings is a consideration not to be despised. And the scribe who was taking down the material that the thinkers and the actors and the doers were producing probably was, as Mr. Berle suggested, a lawyer. This is not to say that the lawyer has a monopoly on wisdom. On the contrary, as all of our diverse discussion of last evening and today suggests, a lawyer is, in large measure, a middleman. He is not without morals, he is not without a sense of justice, and he is not without the intellectual capacity to seek out a method which will do good. So I want to close what was for me a very exciting evening with the suggestion that the relationship between the search for the good life and the search for justice and means of achieving it are not only to be found in the "professional" way but in the application of the many disciplines: philosophy and law, political science, economics, sociology and history. The role of the generalist in today's educational world is like that of the lawyer in the professional world—that of the middleman.

4. Reflections on the Papers of Messrs. Villey and McDonald

MARK S. MASSEL

It seems to me that some of the basic issues emerged in the two interesting papers given by Professor Villey and Mr. McDonald. Both speakers dealt with the influences of values on the concept of justice. The practicing lawyer gave us a rather succinct and forceful description of the need for justice; of the areas in which justice was not being done; and of the need for developing programs for the restoration and the improvement of justice. The theoretician was not preoccupied with the question of whether there *should* be justice; he was interested in exploring *what kind* of justice. He asked, "What is our focus? Is the concept of justice to be considered in its relation to the individual, or should we strive for collective justice?"

One of the outstanding features of the discussion during the last day and one half was the recurring preoccupation with values and the significance of values. We have heard many references: to justice for the individual; to truth; to beauty; and to the dignity of the individual. One factor emerges particularly from Professor Villey's statement about distributive justice and the differences between considering justice from the viewpoint of the individual and from the viewpoint of society: that much of our discussion has concentrated on the direct problems of the individual. Professor Villey's statement seems to imply that it would be distinctly worth while to consider —along with the problems of the individual—some of the broader aspects of society. Such an analysis requires considering the broader aspects of our social, political, and economic system, and the basic relationships between law and society.

The problems of the individual are clearly affected by general conditions in our society which, in turn, are intimately linked up with the legal problems under discussion. However, they are affected also by economic problems.

Following Profesor Villey's suggestions, our interest should go beyond furnishing legal aid for people on the poverty level in order to give them dignity. We should strive to avoid poverty conditions so that all individuals can maintain their basic dignity without dependence on charity to protect their rights.

Looking at the problem still more broadly, should we nurture a preoccupation with the problems of the citizens of the United States? Or should we consider the influence of our own and other legal systems on the development of standards of living, on human dignity, and on the values that dominate the lives of people in other countries? How much consideration should we give to international and comparative problems?

What I think emerges from Professor Villey's statement is that in the consideration of the relationships between law and society, we would do well to broaden our perspective, to consider the social sciences on a somewhat broader basis than we have. We should go beyond sociology (particularly an individual-oriented sociology) and give renewed attention to issues of political science, and economics and anthropology in order to avoid being limited to the problems of the individual.

5. Value Problems Among the Social Disciplines—A Dialog

Most of the discussion on values which is included here, but by no means all of it, took place during the opening dialog.

SISTER CATHERINE THERESE*—I got so interested in this program here because of what I saw happening with the word values—the use of it by political scientists, economists, and myself. One philosopher we had in our program preferred to use the labor theory of value, rather than propose a public philosophy based upon the relation of man and society. Each one of us must develop his own philosophy, he told us.

MASSEL—Value in philosophy and value in economics, for instance, have totally different meaning. And we all use accounting concepts. However, I know of no accounting concept that means the same thing to accountants, to economists, and to lawyers. The ranges in meaning are just tremendous.

YEGGE**—Are the sociologists interested in how the law should be? The answer to that question is unanimously, "No." Because the sociologists aren't interested at all in values as values. But they are interested in values as data. And they are interested in a social system and how it operates, which social systems may be substitutable—not any one system, but a variety of substitutable systems.

ARENS***—What struck me as central about the stirring statement we have heard was that social scientists were not interested in values but that we lawyers were. Primarily that makes us moralists and social scientists immoralists or amoralists. Now I cannot claim to speak with any authority whatsoever for the social scientists. I have, however, had occasion to observe them, both in interdisciplinary work financed by the National Institutes of Health, and in the courts. What struck me as significant about almost all of them was that in most instances they pronounced moral, political, economic, yes, and legal judgments, without any awareness whatsoever as to what they were about.

YEGGE—The people you call social scientists weren't social scientists. They were sentimental social workers.

MASSEL—Now we are really in a semantic mantrap. As long as a so-called social scientist has no value judgment whatsoever, he is a social scientist,

---

* Sister Catherine Therese Knoop, C.S.J., College of St. Rose, Albany (social science).

** Professor Robert B. Yegge, Program in Judicial Administration, University of Denver (law, sociology).

*** Professor Richard Arens, Catholic University Law School.

according to Professor Yegge, but if he makes any judgment at all, indeed if he does any work on any social problem, trying to make some contribution, then he is no longer a social scientist. I would like to raise the question: here we have a range of important and significant public policy problems. A range of problems which are getting to be quite pressing, with regard to the way in which our government operates and our entire economy operates, a range of problems which move in such directions that it affects our economy and it affects human rights, affects the relationship between the individual and society.

Are the other social scientists here willing to support Professor Yegge's position, that the social scientist has no contribution to make to this, that the function of the social scientist is merely to observe, and to make studies, but that it is really up to the lawyers to see what can be done about solving these problems, without the help of the social scientists, because the poor lawyers don't know enough about social science, about the theories that the social scientists work with, to be able to impress the sociologists or the economists or the political scientists with the notion that these are interesting problems to work in. And if so, is it possible that we are beginning to touch upon some of the basic conflicts among the disciplines?

LANG*—I don't know whether the sociologists include the anthropologists among the social scientists or not. I do feel that we are talking about two kinds of problems nevertheless. One is the problem of training people in the humanistic tradition, and this is nothing new that I am saying. I was trained as an anthropologist by a man whom I consider very much a social scientist, as well as a humanist, that is, Professor Wakefield at Chicago, who was also trained as a lawyer. In fact, that was his first love. But before he died he made a very strong pitch in the direction of the fact that the social scientists also have a responsibility, which should not detract from their objective studies, that is, to act as scientists in the sense in which Professor Yegge spoke about this. But these are two separate problems, one of which is forming a person, developing a personality as a responsible human being, anywhere, in the United States or abroad; and the other one is forming a scientist, in the broad sense. And these are two separate problems, and I think we ought to keep this clear.

BEITZINGER**—Anybody who is concerned with politics, if he is worth his salt, has to be concerned with the question of policy—what *should* be done. I don't know how anyone can be a responsible political scientist and divorce himself from the subject of the ends of society and the end of man. Consequently, I think that when you talk of a social science which is divorced ultimately from these fundamental norms, you are talking about something which is floating in air, and I disagree wholeheartedly with my eminent colleague, Professor Lang, on that point. I don't think that there is anybody who can at this date contend that there is such a thing as a

---

* Professor Godfrey Lang, Catholic University (anthropology).
** Professor Henry Beitzinger, Catholic University (political science).

wirtlos social science. I think we should consciously face up to the fact that we have to be concerned with goals, with policies, and with ends, and that we cannot talk about something which is insulated therefrom. Because we do study man we must be concerned about what man does, and thus concerned about what he should do.

But all political scientists are not of the same breed, the conference was reminded by Dr. Edna Fluegel, chairman of the political science department at Trinity College:

FLUEGEL*—We have been talking about the social scientist as though there were not 57 varieties of social scientists, too. I think the same problem we have between the lawyer and the ethical social scientist also exists within departments of political science. It is true that the old type political scientist was just as you said the old type lawyer was. Today it is very, very difficult to get a recent political scientist who is also a liberal arts person. Some of the behaviorists in political science would have more in common with the mathematics department, actually, than with the lawyer. If you had a behavioral department in political science, you might find a lawyer who is more the old type of political scientist—and the only one around.

POWELL**—Professor Yegge maintained that the social sciences are by their nature value-free and that the legal sciences are, of course, concerned with making value and especially policy decisions at the highest level, and it seems to me that this is very true. I don't see how you can escape this. And it seems, at least if we believe the social scientists, they are explicitly attempting to exclude value judgment. And this is perfectly legitimate, because they are studying what is socially determined in human action. In brief, the whole cultural and structural aspect of society is put into a person in a half-conscious way during his formation, especially his early formation, and this he never critically examines, and yet it is always an important component in all human action, whether social or individual. This is a very classical idea I am giving you, none other than the old idea of the *hostes voluntarii:* that in all human action you have two dimensions. You have the dimension of determinism, the unreflected part, the assumptions which aren't examined; on the other hand you have the responsible part, that which has been considered by the subject, where he knows what he is doing. And it seems to me that in contemporary anthropology this sort of consideration is coming much to the fore. People like Raymond Firth[6] and David Bidney[7] are saying just this:that in analysis of any social system you must look for these two components: the cultural determinism on the one hand; and, on the other hand, a certain area of freedom, however small, where man, the individual or the group, is able to come to

---

* Professor Edna R. Fluegel, Chairman, Department of Political Science, Trinity College, Washington, D.C.
** Rev. Ralph Powell, O.P., Aquinas Institute of Philosophy and Theology, River Forest, Ill. (philosophy, sociology).

responsible decisions. And it seems to me that it is in this area that the social sciences and the law come together.

MASSEL—I wonder whether we are all in agreement and clear on what we mean by value and by value judgment. Is Professor Yegge's point that the social scientist does not come up with an ultimate value judgment about what policy shall be at all, or is his point that the social scientist shall not participate in policy formation? Because the role of the social scientist, as he has described it, and as we have just heard it described by Father Powell, could be the role of understanding and explaining what is taking place, not merely for the esoteric purpose of describing past history, but for purposes of setting up some basis for predictions with regard to the future. If this is so, it is possible that the social scientist, instead of taking the position that this is what we should do, may be in the position of saying, "Here are several courses that are open for public policy, and on the basis of what we know about man's behavior or what we know about economics, we can set up some predictions about what will happen under each of the various alternatives." The social scientist then may not have value judgments in the sense of saying, "This is what we shall do," but may be in the position of making a substantial contribution to the formulation of public policy. In this case also there may be a basis for making suggestions about the ways in which the social scientists and the lawyers can come together because in good part the legal discipline involves prediction, and as a matter of fact I'd like to suggest that part of the conflict that comes about turns essentially on the issue of prediction. About two years ago, I heard a statement made by a highly placed government lawyer that he was waiting for the time when he could have the pleasure of working with some one-armed economists because he was getting sick and tired of hearing economists say, "On the one hand this."

Now, Mr. Keeffe,* I was just as impressed with that statement as you, until, in the course of meandering around through some of the so-called legal literature, I found that about 40 years ago a prominent businessman talking to a group of lawyers said he was sick and tired and he was waiting for a one-armed lawyer.

It is possible that the social scientist gets sort of fed up with the lawyer because the lawyer ought to be able to make a specific prediction about what the outcome will be in some specific litigation, or what the result will be of some specific legislation, or some regulation which is being contemplated, and the social scientist thinks the lawyer really isn't too sure of himself because he doesn't come through with a specific prediction. On the other hand, the lawyer thinks to himself, "What disciplines are the sociologists talking about, and the economists and such. You ask them a simple question, and do they tell you 'This is what will happen.' Oh, no, they've got to use both hands."

---

* Professor Arthur J. Keeffe, Catholic University Law School.

Is it possible that part of the problem rests upon this tremendous drive and desire for certainty in the areas in which one does not work? Because if you could have certainty with regard to certain variables, the variables you work on would be a whale of a lot more manageable.

LANG—We anthropologists don't know the answer to this one any more, I am afraid, than the lawyers do, partially because I think that we also talk with both hands. But when social scientists try to generalize upon human behavior, that is, ultimately in policy decisions, there is always a judgment involved which usually the social scientist refuses to make unless he is personally involved. But at the same time, the range of judgment or the validity of the judgment can be closed as a result of experience. It seems to me that systematic experience is a little better than unsystematic experience, and this involves, when you make policy judgments, not only courage, but a considerable amount of insight. I think if we have experience, this is where the anthropologist can show his experience, and probably most of us are very happy to leave the ultimate judgment to somebody else. We are a little bit chicken sometimes.

RICHARDSON*—The question regarding values that we have been discussing with Professor Yegge and others points to the necessity of establishing some relationship between law and other disciplines. It also points to some of the problems of integrating an undergraduate curriculum. It is my hypothesis that law does not have values of its own; rather it adopts the values of society which may or may not depend in turn upon the organized knowledge of various disciplines. The law, moreover, is very reluctant to move from traditional ways. It is more comfortable when it expresses the consensus of society.

The problem arises in that the social sciences, which have a closer relation to the law, attempt to be empirical and free from value systems.

It is to philosophy and theology that we must turn for value systems. Without them society and the social sciences will be hardpressed to establish or maintain values. Law, therefore, seems to acquire its values through society or through the social sciences which in turn receive their values from theology and philosophy. Little practical recognition seems to be given to these interrelations. To cite an example: one of Chicago's papers today stated that the City's Public Health Service would definitely be distributing birth control material on a very broad scale by the end of the present year or the beginning of next year. The law will undoubtedly support this decision, but there are few lawyers who will be able to explain the sociological and moral implications upon which a decision should ultimately rest.

Lawyers seem more prepared to talk to sociologists than sociologists to moralists. They may be of the opinion that their investigations into crime and into human depravations that result from unwanted children

---

* Rev. John T. Richardson. C.M., Executive Vice President, De Paul University (theology).

would be stifled by attempting to fit these problems into the framework of a very rigid moral system. If moral theology and ethics are open to new ideas, I believe that their influence can be reestablished in the social sciences. Those who are interpreting public policy in writing the law can profit much from an understanding of social sciences which have been influenced by moral principles. Perhaps the greatest demand will be made upon moral theology and ethics to prove once again that they are valid disciplines today, not conclusions simply handed down from theologians and philosophers who lived centuries ago.

It is not easy to integrate law, the social sciences, and morality in an undergraduate curriculum. It is my hope that at least these three disciplines will be integrated, particularly in the minds of the lawyers. It is not easy to convince lawyers that their profession is fundamentally blind, that is, it depends upon other disciplines to give it a sense of direction. We expect lawyers as educated persons to be familiar with the values of philosophy and theology. We expect them to be committed to these values. On the other hand, we expect them to be practitioners and leave the moralizing to others. We would like to integrate the knowledge that maintains the distinctions between the professions.

ARENS—In discussing the value orientation of social scientists, or perhaps the lack of value orientation of the social scientists, one thing appears to have been left out of account. Are the social scientists to participate in the decision-making process of the community, or are they to be drawn upon as perhaps accountants or mechanics for a non-original piece of work? I believe that the social scientists have indicated clearly and consistently their desire to participate in the decision-making process of the community, and I believe that we lawyers have clearly indicated a willingness to work with them. If there is to be joint work of any profitable sort, there has, of course, to be consensus as to basic values, as it is elementary that any decision has consequences upon the shaping and sharing of values by those affected. The more important the decision, the wider the ramifications of the consequences in the economic, political, and moral realm, to take just these examples. There may be differences of opinion as to whether consequences stemming from particular decisions are desirable, but one cannot deny that these consequences exist. And any social scientist who would leave consideration of these consequences completely out of his thinking would strike me as failing to perform his work, and more significantly, as rendering collaboration with lawyers who do tend to think of broader consequences difficult if not impossible.

MASSEL—May I suggest that there are some fields in which the positions are reversed. Shall we consider for a moment the antitrust field? Shall we in connection with the antitrust field consider why there are antagonisms between the academic economists and the lawyers? The academic economists start off with some ideas about how the economy shall operate, and they have fairly strong feelings about what the economy should do, based upon a series of value judgments. And the quarrel of many of them with the lawyer runs along the lines that the lawyers are not concerned about value judgments, that the lawyers are concerned only with the practical question, the practical problem of winning cases, regardless of whether they represent the government as plaintiff or private parties as plaintiffs in treble damage actions, or whether they represent defendants and respondents in such actions. Now it seems to me that when one looks at one group of social scientists, namely the economists (and I must say many of the political scientists share this feeling), and their reactions and feelings with regard to the lawyers, our discussion here with regard to the differences based upon value judgment are completely reversed. Then, do we move along lines of a clear, rational, simplified pattern which says: lawyers are interested in value judgments, and social scientists are not interested in value judgments? Do we then proceed from that simple, straightforward premise to the notion that most of the economists, the academic economists working in the antitrust field, are not social scientists because they feel this way, and on to the further premise that the lawyers who are involved in antitrust litigation are not lawyers because they aren't occupied with value judgments but are simply occupied with winning cases?

KEEFFE*—I attempted to teach antitrust with an economist at one end of the table and myself at the other, and I had a graphic illustration of what we are talking about here tonight. And I couldn't agree with you more that there's plenty of fault with the lawyers; on the other hand, there's plenty of fault with the economists.

The economists talk about pure competition which hasn't existed in America in 50 years—two people make our cans, three people make our automobiles—until the government finally put the Democrats in the business, we only had Alcoa making aluminum.

The trouble here is both ways. The law is moribund, and it's moribund in whole fields, and I would start with antitrust because we haven't had the help from the other disciplines. It is clear that they haven't been interested in helping us, that is, those of us who are crusading for some type of law reform in whole areas. Take torts. Nothing is more moribund than tort litigation in America. Airplanes go down; people can't sue. If you are so unfortunate as to be a nonbreeder and you and your wife die, most of the states won't allow any suit, unless you have a dependent relative, so that airplanes, automobiles, and missiles, and everything, are free to kill anybody who doesn't have a dependent. It's open season on nonbreeders.

And in every field it seems to me that the law is woefully behind the times, and it's behind the times for real reform because we aren't making the use of social science developments that we should, and we have somehow or other brainwashed the other disciplines into thinking that we know what we are doing.

MASSEL—I would like to point out to you that Professor Keeffe has made a rather telling point. I have heard on several occasions that one of the

---

* Professor Arthur J. Keeffe, Catholic University Law School.

troubles with the interdisciplinary meeting is that people get together and exchange jargon with each other, and go back home satisfied because they can throw the other fellow's jargon around. Here is a fine illustration of it. Professor Keeffe was unfortunate enough to give a course together with an economist who talked about perfect competition, and who accomplished the remarkable task of persuading Professor Keeffe that we did have perfect competition 50 years ago, when as a matter of fact perfect competition is simply a theoretical idea in somebody's mind, and we have never had anything that could be called perfect competition. John Stuart Mill indeed wrote a most interesting passage in which he warned his colleagues not to take too seriously this fine theoretical treatment of theirs, but apparently an economist who cannot persuade other economists that perfect competition operates today, can sit on the other end of a table from a lawyer and persuade him not that it exists today but that it did 50 years ago.

SISTER CATHERINE THERESE—I am just wondering if there isn't another dimension to the problem of Catholic colleges. We expect to develop values through philosophy courses, especially I think in more recent years in social philosophy courses. Is this whole interest of Mr. Ball[8] especially, and those who are working in programs to teach values through legislative law, through court cases and so on, because they have no other way? I am just thinking maybe we have a different way of approaching this and that some colleges do need a course in law-society as such, because they have no other way.

BALL*—First of all, I think American society has a very high level of consensus at the most fundamental level of values, and an almost complete lack of consensus on how to get there, and on the problem of how to implement these values. In fact I can't find any major shift in what you can call the fundamental American values except probably, if we can judge by the studies, a little more concern by the newer generations with something that is called abstract principle. And I think that no one works in the area of law and society without getting concerned with the problems of value; the law and society context is ideal for discussions of values. It separates all kinds of things that philosophers keep trying to separate in rather abstract context in the class, that is, problems of motivation, as distinguished from collective intent, as distinguished from the consequences of the act. You have all these things in the legal area. What is the significance as an ethical problem of the relationship between the motives of the judge or the legislature, and the intent, as a matter of fact, meaning here the state of affairs he hopes to achieve, as distinguished from the state of affairs which are actually achieved. I don't really comprehend anything more fundamental. Questions of value are basically those questions to me. I remember one study I did where the major classification, the major division between the students, and it was much related to their religious con-

---

*Professor Harry V. Ball, Program in Sociology and Law, University of Wisconsin (sociology).

victions by the way, was a split between them on the question of which was more important in evaluating the ethical rightness of an act—the motive of the act or the consequences of the act. This is very much related to the split that exists in our society in terms of how you evaluate patterns of conduct. Suppose your consequences are disastrous but your intentions are good. Is this all right?

What I am really objecting to is, again, that our studies of law and our considerations of law tend to stop at questions of intention. Now let's get on to try to find out what is the relationship between matters of intent, matters of motive, matters of consequences. This presents some very concrete situations in which to raise very major questions of values. As I said, there may be other contexts in which values can be raised, but I don't really understand them except from the perspective of individual motives of actors, collective intentions of group action, and the consequences of acts. And they are all there in the law.

Part Two

SOME RECENT INTERDISCIPLINARY EXPERIENCE IN LAW-SOCIETY

CHAPTER II
RESEARCH AND GRADUATE STUDIES—
THE RUSSELL SAGE FOUNDATION PROJECTS

Evidence of considerable recent experience in interdisciplinary cooperation in the Law-Society area was brought before the conference by the
directors of four projects currently sponsored by the Russell Sage Foundation: Northwestern University's Program in Law and the Social Sciences,
the University of Denver's Program in Judicial Administration, the University of Wisconsin's Program in Sociology and Law, and the University
of California (Berkeley) Center for the Study of Law and Society.[1]

1. The Northwestern Experience

VICTOR G. ROSENBLUM*

What we think we have in our Northwestern project is a community of
scholars. The community was established first and a program was developed
second to try to embody that sense of community rather than create it. We
have a set made up of sociologists, of political scientists, of one or two
economists, of a visiting philosopher, and of several members of the law
school, who had a series of interests stemming from work in their own
respective disciplines that involved them in the work of the others. When
a series of questions arose in the minds of some of the law faculty and
some of the political science and sociology faculties that required us to go
beyond the lines of our own disciplines, we found ourselves meeting together, talking together, conflicting together, exchanging some ideas that
seemed useful, some ideas that seemed not at all useful. And after doing
this for several years we thought the time had come for us to embody this
exchange in a more precise training program. After beginning the program
on our own, we asked the Russell Sage Foundation last year to provide
assistance for its implementation. This they very graciously and generously
did.

---

* Director, Program in Law and the Social Sciences, Northwestern University
(law, political science).

What this involves is a program in law and the social sciences which is administered by three faculty people, Jack Coons of our law school, Red Schwartz of our sociology department, and myself in political science. And we have this year ten fellows, four who are being put through their LL.B. training; three who are working toward the Ph.D. in political science; three who are working toward the Ph.D in sociology. We were surprised to have several fringe benefits along the line in that we had two other law students, one other political scientist and a graduate student in philosophy join the program—through joint funds participation we found it possible to incorporate them.

As a part of the training we have a series of interlocking seminars which receive joint credit so that all of those within the program participate in the Law and Society seminar, which on occasion is housed in the sociology department and on occasion is housed down at the law school. It involves a joint credit arrangement which I think is somewhat unique in view of the fact that the law school runs on a semester system and the sociology and political science schools run on the quarter system. The law school is in Chicago and philosophy, political science and sociology are in Evanston. In a sense we faced these obstacles by ignoring them instead of trying to knock them down: we simply pretended that they weren't there, and behold they weren't. Problems in dealing with registrars, dealing with allocations of credit, have somehow been resolved. And the unifying seminar of all this is a non-credit seminar that meets every second week and involves all of the faculty with interests in the program. Some of them participate once every four to six weeks; the core group of Red Schwartz and Jack Coons and myself is there each time. We have put into this unit all of those who have begun their training, as well as those who are advanced in their training, in the hope that we will be establishing lines of permanent communication and that even for the first year freshman law student there is a dimension of time and commitment which enables him to begin to communicate with the beginning students in sociology and political science and philosophy. This will not always provide the basis for perception of the role that the other has to play in the work of his own discipline, but at least it poses the question to himself of whether there is a role beyond what his own discipline will be fitting him for.

We have in this a series of illustrative projects which are just at the beginning stage. For example, we are trying to examine the feasibility of developing what we might call social science annotations to legal phenomena. We feel that there are a number of areas in judicial decision making today in which social science data are either being cited by the Supreme Court or when not cited are being invited in the sense that they seem to be applicable. This view does not rest merely on the famous footnote in *Brown v. The Board of Education*,[2] but reflects positions taken by members of the court we would presume to be less social science oriented. So when one looks at the dissenting opinion by Justice Stewart in the *Colorado Apportionment*[3] case and we find Justice Stewart citing a range of political scientists headed by Bob Dahl[4] of Yale in support of his position, it looks as though there really is a growing recognition on the part of the Court as a unit of the role that disciplines other than law are playing in their own work. So at the moment we are taking all the decisions of the 1963 term as an initial point of departure, and we are doing a series of studies of criteria of decision making in the '63 term. And of those criteria we are going to try and determine which are based in the social sciences, and of those which are not based in the social sciences where would criteria from the social sciences have been relevant. And then we are seeking to take one or two of these instances in which data from the social sciences have been developed and find some way of incorporating them into publication, ultimately and ideally perhaps into amicus briefs or somewhere else where we can put them to some kind of test.

We have a couple of other studies which have been under way for some time on which we hope to have some findings very soon. Red Schwartz has been very much interested in the whole question of compliance and has been engaged in a study of the criteria for compliance with the tax laws. We hope that by the end of the academic year we will have some findings to report. He's had somewhat grudging cooperation from the Internal Revenue Service, but nonetheless we should describe it as cooperation, at least until they say that the material is confidential and can't be published. But there has been substantial progress there.

Jack Coons did a preliminary paper a year ago which he is now engaged in enlarging on the uses of compromise in dispute settlement within a judicial setting. We are raising the question whether winner take all is really the way in which the judicial system operates or whether it is not rather sometimes an end product. Is the institution itself not geared more toward finding ways out which are face saving ways, institution saving ways and which can involve a minimization of open conflict? These are some of the particular projects.

We have had a series of students performing we think somewhat unusually. I don't want to embarrass our senior fellow who is with us and participating at the conference today, Michael Barkun, but Michael, who is receiving his Ph.D. in political science this year has, as an example, completed four courses at the law school. In addition to his basic training in political science, he has also done extensive work with the sociologists. We feel that we have an environment in which this is now not only feasible but the accepted way of going about it. And having a course in survey research with Don Campbell in psychology as well as sitting in on Brad Jenkins work in philosophy and going down for Bronson McChesney's seminar in international law at the law school is now no longer a unique or unusual thing. We haven't yet reached the point where we have a speed boat waiting outside the Evanston campus to whisk us down to Chicago, but somehow the El seems to run on a fairly regular schedule, and you'll find a law student or two or a couple of political science or philosophy or sociology graduate students traveling between the two campuses like one would ordinarily travel between two buildings. That, by way of introduction, describes the kinds of things that are going on at Northwestern.

2.   The Denver Project

ROBERT G. YEGGE*

Our program has a legal name: a Program in Judicial Administration. The name may be misleading; the program is not concerned merely with judicial administration. Rather, we are interested in the administration of justice. But maybe there is some good reason why it has a legal name. Unlike the projects of some of my colleagues here, our program is completely based in the law school. It involves some of the other disciplines, nevertheless it is basically a law school program. Hence my discussion will deal with social science in the law rather than with law and the social sciences.

To understand this kind of program in a legal setting maybe we ought to suggest some prior conditions of the legal universe which really must be understood before the relationship between law and social science can truly be considered. In the legal world there isn't any particular systematic body of organizing theory or principle as there appears to be in the social sciences. One might suggest that the concepts of "justice" or "doing justice" come close to an organizing principle, but to go much beyond that I don't think we have any evidence. A further problem is that the law really hasn't defined or operationalized the concept of justice. It has been suggested, of course, that the term "justice" defies definition. I asked a law student, about a year ago, to search the American reporter system to find judicial definitions of justice. He came up with five, after working an entire academic quarter on the study. Each definition said something like "it's nothing more or less than application of legal principles to existing fact situations." Well, that's lawyerly. But does such a definition get to the concern for justice which I think the people here really want to explore. It has been suggested, and I think maybe rightfully, that the circumstantial problem of *when* is justice would be more worthy of examination, and maybe this is where social science can be of some value to us.

Without a body of systematic theory, the law is not really conditioned to consider the broader questions of social control which are the concern of the social sciences. Rather, the law frequently focuses on individual, concrete, what I like to call "brush fires" or individual cases. I don't mean to run down my own profession by calling cases "brush fires". However, lawyers are not generally considered in connection with the larger framework of social control. The lawyer doesn't consider the law as a system of

* Director, Program in Judicial Administration, University of Denver (law, sociology).

control in the sense that Wilbert Moore[5] suggested that the legal system and the system for its administration might be considered a tension management system. Moreover, the lawyer finds no significance in this kind of conceptualization, at least on the practitioner level.

It was suggested last night that another prior condition might be that law practice is involved in the norms and their application and their definition while social science is not really involved in the norms themselves but considers the norms merely as data. This alleged differential interest between the practitioner and the social scientist underlines again the different roles which lawyers and social scientists are playing. And it certainly suggests a misunderstanding of these differential roles. Possibly the misunderstanding creates and is at the heart of problems of true collaboration or better colleagueship between the practicing lawyer and the social scientist.

In connection with our program we have conducted two seminars for law students. The students are undergraduate law students. The seminars are called "Methods in Social Research." The two seminars are (1) for students who have not been exposed to the material before, and then (2) for a group that has done some work in the area, done some research with legal materials involving social science methodology. The law students have evidenced recognition of a strong sense of importance in the concepts of social science for legal education. The constant problem of usefulness of methodology in legal practice has not been solved by the students. Interest has been stimulated in many students to pursue the subject as an academic problem. Applicability of concepts in methodology to legislative and general policy decisions has been grasped. However, the problem of universality in legal practice remains unsolved for the law student.

I'd like to ask a question as it is frequently asked by law colleagues in connection with this program, "What's in it for the law?" "What's in it for the law man?" "What can the lawyer get out of a program that involves law and social science?" Asking such questions, in such lawyerly phrasing, emphasizes the lawyer's exclusive concern for usefulness. And, role difference between the lawyer and the social scientist, which may be our greatest barrier to collaboration, is underlined. Unfortunately, the law wants to use social science as a handyman, to insist on its usefulness, rather than allowing a meaningfulness or significance to develop in a larger theoretical context. Nevertheless, let us consider the question "What's in it for the law man?" Who are these law men? As we see them in our program—these law men on whom we are focusing—they are the legislators, the judges, the practicing lawyers and law students.

As to the legislators, I don't think there is dispute, or very little dispute, that studies which social scientists can make formulate reasonable bases for legislative decisions. In Denver, we studied the content of the docket in the Denver District Court extensively to determine what really was going on in that court. And from the research, legislators were able to form some reasonable bases for implementing a constitutional amendment which reorganized the courts in Colorado. They solved the problem, not by merely adding judges (which seems to be the standard way of moving the docket), but by re-allocating judge time in terms of real data that showed the condition of that docket, redefining the roles of the judge, stressing the sort of things the judges should and should not be doing. This kind of use of social science data is of an obvious nature. On a higher level, it seems to me that both legislators and researchers for the legislature could gain a great deal from social science insight by gaining a perspective of law as an institution of social control in our society, and that this perspective might add wisdom to legislation through the legislators themselves. Certainly if we can predict behavior on the background of research, such should be useful to legislative formulation.

In the court system, there hasn't been a great deal done on the lowest level. The lowest court is the first contact that the people have with the legal system. The focus of a current study at our school is to determine the psychological and sociological distance between city ordinances, or statutes, and the citizens violating those ordinances. If one can find something out about this problem, possibly wisdom can be imparted to the legislative body in further enactments of law.

Let us look to the "law man" called judge and see what the possibilities are. Of course a judge wears two hats. He wears the hat of administrator of the court, and he is a decision maker. As for his administrative function, it doesn't take a great deal of looking to see that a court is a bureaucratic, formal organization. And frequently in the courts around the country there has been the perpetuation of the "quill pen" approach of administering a court. The administrative judge of Denver District Court, who is involved in our program, likes to tell a story about when he took office. He took a look around the court and he found that—and this was just a few years ago —he found that all of the entries with regard to documents and judgments were being made in gigantic leather bound books with pens. And it was taking great amounts of time to perpetuate this system that probably began with the establishment of the court. His first reaction was, and I might say a logical one, why don't we find some typewriters for these people. Today, with only elementary knowledge of social science, the court is storing the data regarding cases in computer form. For settling cases we are now relying on the theory of probabilities and the actuarial basis rather than the individual basis (as the law frequently insists on doing). We are able to predict how long a case may take to try, how many cases will be settled, thereby allowing a more realistic trial date setting for the court.

The other role I suggested for the judge is the decisional role which he undertakes. Because law is involved in the norms and not just in their study, he has some serious problems with the use of social materials. Professor Rosenblum has indicated that he has been trying to annotate social science materials. Maybe this is the approach. But I might merely recall a question on this issue which was posed at a conference in connection with our program by Judge Sterry Waterman, Circuit Court Judge of the Second Circuit, in this manner: "Should judges—and I mean by judges those who decide—follow precedent awaiting legislative change on which they can fix their judicial stamp of approval or, alternatively, act in an affirmative manner in establishing patterns of social planning based on social research?" It is this sort of question that truly bothers the judge when he looks at social science research. I do hope that my colleagues, specifically Professor Rosenblum, can in their research assist us in answering or at least enlightening ourselves on Judge Waterman's question.

How about the practitioner, this last "law man." The adversary role of the practitioner is misunderstood by the practitioner himself. From an ethical point of view, the adversary role needs examination. As a part of our program we have been interested in teaching and studying professional responsibility—the role relationship of the lawyer. It is important to impart to a law student an understanding about the Canons of Ethics. The canons are devices to regulate inherent tensions in a strife-laden professional world. These canons are frequently aimed at each other. And when they are, it takes some understanding by a law student to see the inherent tensions and conflicts involved. We are presently involved in an empirical teaching project with law students. We are exposing students to the role conflicts which they will eventually observe in practice and letting the students discuss these conflicts so that they will have a basis to make some decisions about those conflicts when they run into them in the real world.

Besides an adversary, a practitioner is a counselor. Generally he is officially designated as such by the Supreme Court of his State. And as a counselor he is supposed to know something about counseling. But how much does he know about counseling? I suggest probably not very much. The cases don't tell him a great deal about that function. Hence we have a study presently being conducted, using current anthropological data, trying to examine the counseling relationships of the lawyer and his client.

The lawyer is also a fact gatherer. But how much does the lawyer know about gathering facts? He's good at the law, but is he very good at fact gathering? There have been some interesting things done in this area. Two of our law students, as independent study, are attempting projects involving social psychological data, one of which is titled: "Research Design in Sampling Techniques Used as Evidence in Trademark Violation Cases,"—an examination of kinds of design which were used in evidence in a variety of trademark violation cases. Here it seems to me that the methods of social science can be of particular value to the practitioner.

These are some of the things that are going in our program. In summary, the experience in our law school with law and social science that the greatest task of the law-social science area at the undergraduate level is to sensitize the pre-law person, or pre-social science person, in the role difference between the practitioner (the lawyer) and the social scientist.

3. Law and Sociology Project at Wisconsin

HARRY V. BALL*

The Sociology and Law program at Wisconsin is now five years old, by some standards it is two years old. The phases I will describe are basically two years old. So it's another relatively new undertaking. There have been a lot of abortive efforts in the past to develop relationships between law and social sciences. Most of these were motivated, in line with Professor Berle's talk this morning, on the idea of the lawyer as a social engineer. And I would say that his approach was relatively typical. The lawyer performs as *l'animal universel,* and the social scientist as a hired gun. Some people are far more outspoken along this line than Professor Berle.

The basic idea in the Wisconsin Sociology and Law program is that integration within the same person is more important than integration between disciplines at the outset if you are going to develop an interdisciplinary program. To be interdisciplinary a person must be highly competent in at least one area. And I mean highly competent. It is my view that the best interdisciplinary work is done between people who are exceedingly competent. A great deal of what is called interdisciplinary work is sort of the muddling work of people who are competent in relatively nothing. So I had biases when we started this thing and began with assuming that we would deal with people who were highly competent in at least one area and add something additional to their training.

So we began a training program. This was really a tooling up operation. We started with a group of five social scientists. These were quickly joined by other social scientists. Soon we numbered about ten; and they began a program of actual introduction to legal process. Now this was not a series of seminars devoted to sitting around talking about law and social science. These people were there to study the same introductory materials to legal process that the law students got. They were taught by a law professor. And they were students of this law professor. And the program for an entire semester, occupying roughly one-half time for these people, was devoted to their beginning to learn something about the legal process. At the end of that semester, each of these persons began his private tutorial. Now the premise in these peoples' training was that none of them would become legal specialists, that none of them would become necessarily sociologists of law, for example, or economists of law. But that rather they would now learn enough law that they could begin to add legal vari-

---

* Director, Program in Sociology and Law, University of Wisconsin (sociology).

ables and legal considerations into whatever research they were engaged in within their own specialties inside the social science profession. That was one of the very definite commitments. This was a deliberate decision, for the simple fact that there are very limited career lines for people who want to call themselves sociologists of law. It's probably the most general of occupations. There *are* career lines through various kinds of specialties. The goal therefore was not to take people out of their career lines but again to add something to the career lines which they were already establishing as young social scientists.

After they completed that introduction they were assigned to a senior member of the law school faculty for their tutorial which lasted for an additional five months. The tutorials consisted of meeting at lunch once a week. If a person was, for example, an industrial sociologist he met with the senior man in the field of labor law. If he was interested in community organizations, power structures, political cultures, he met with a person concerned essentially with state and local government. If he was interested in the professions, well, this person got a special treat, he got to meet weekly at lunch with Willard Hurst. So that the tutorials that these young men were receiving were from the top level people of the law school faculty, in the popular jargon the very men who would be least interested in having lunch every week with a social scientist. They were the old timers; they were the old men of the Law School faculty. Their average age was about 55. So we immediately put these young men in touch with these older men. This went on for the course of one semester out of which hopefully these people began a research project that would have significance both from the standpoint of social science theory and substance, and also from the standpoint of the law teaching profession. These studies were not intended to be major contributions to research areas; they were essentially intended as learning experiences, so that if a social scientist found out that he really was walking down a dead end street, he had no commitment to continue this study. His commitment was to abandon the study and to start on something that would be more productive from the standpoint of his own learning experiences.

Then we have some strange kinds of studies: The industrial sociologist finds himself for a change not doing factory studies, but studying the peculiar collective bargaining arrangements in union-employer relationships that exist in the area of the driver-owner. That is, the person like the ready-mix cement driver who happens to own his own truck and has say $30,000 capital investment. And the peculiar relationship: Is he a sub-contractor? Is he a union member? Is he a what? Now this doesn't fit any of the models that people have in mind when they talk about collective bargaining in the Wagner Act, where you think of huge factories and so forth. This is a very strange kind of relationship. Now our view is that this is a pioneering relationship, not because we expect all workers in the future to have $30,000 investments in ready-mix cement trucks, or in the typical business in the future. The workers will actually have, collectively speaking, a far greater financial investment in the actual equipment of the economic operation than does the employer (which is the case in all ready-mix cement businesses). If you view the amount of education that people have as capital investment in most cases the total amount invested by these people in their training and education exceeds the capital investment of stockholders in the corporation. So that we think that by looking at cement mixers we may be looking at an issue which can emerge and can radically affect the whole shape of employer-employee relationships in the future. Still this is a very small thing. The main object is for the social scientist to learn something in an area which is sufficiently unstructured that he can make all kinds of mistakes and nobody will know it, because not enough people have thought about it yet. It is sort of free floating situation. These people are now proceeding with their research and we've also added additional social scientists to the training dimensions of the program.

When we reached that point we started off on the lawyers' side of the thing with a few grants of released time for men who have been doing social science type research. And then we instituted a voluntary seminar for law faculty men who were interested in the law study of social science theory. This really constitutes the basis again for all social scientists in this program to now confront a host of lawyers. We now have roughly 50% of the full time faculty of the law school taking this seminar. The seminar basically talks about sociology. The lawyers are not yet ready to talk about law in sociology. This has been just two years; we haven't reached that point yet, though we are approaching it. But it has been a very careful kind of training program. The lawyers have now finally become convinced that there is no pay-off careerwise for young social scientists to annotate and evaluate all of the social science literature pertinent to a particular interest of one of the law faculty. The social scientists are simply not going to do this for the lawyers. The lawyers have now decided that they have to reach a point of self-confidence where they can read social science journals and evaluate the validity of the research methodology and statistics. The goal of this seminar is simply to bring the lawyers to the point where they can read professional articles in the social sciences. In other words, to have lawyers reach a point of social science competency to be added to their very high level of legal competency. This is the same goal that the social scientists are trying to achieve on their side: a certain minimal level of legal competency on the top of their high level of competency in the social sciences.

While this training process proceeds we are also introducing various dimensions at the student level. We give fellowships to Ph.D. students if they will complete a minor in law. Wisconsin has had a minor in law program in the social sciences for years. It has seldom been used. We are providing fellowships for social science students who will take a full-bloom minor in law. And now we are structuring and elaborating the kind of courses that these people should have to constitute this minor in law, courses that will insure them the level of competency that we think the social scientists are giving to their segment of the training program. We have graduate students in the social sciences whom we are supporting with fellowships while they do their dissertations, so long as they do their dissertations in a law-related area. So far this is usually a backdrop for sending the student on to law school when he completes his Ph.D.

We have fellowships for law students which start at the end of their second year of law school and provide summer seminar training for them and pay their way through their third year of law school. In this way, in addition to this third year in law school, they add the methodology sequence in the sociology department to their third year law school courses. They come back then for a second summer after they have graduated from law school. If they are bright enough and motivated enough and good enough they can complete an M.A. in sociology four months after they graduate from law school.

A lot more social scientists with Ph.D.'s will come out with minors in law but many more lawyers are graduating who will have added at least substantial segments of social science exposure to theory (such as methodology) in a very short time after they graduate from law school. In some cases they will likely have the supplemental degree. Whether or not they decide to go on to a Ph.D. will be entirely their business. We might encourage some more than others, but that will basically be their decision and it is not the essential goal of the program.

In addition to that, the Wisconsin program got very serious as to whether or not social scientists were generally interested in getting involved more in studies of legal operations, and of the manner in which the law was operating. We surveyed all the members of the American Sociological Association and on the basis of that started a Law and Society Association[6] which now numbers about 700 members. Mr. Selznick[7] is on the committee, Mr. Yegge[8] is on the committee, and we at this point don't know exactly in what direction this association is going. But we are planning to put out a Law and Society Bulletin beginning in September, 1965,[9] which hopefully will not compete essentially with existing journals. It will be some kind of an elevated newsletter; that is, it can include news of programs going on, research studies, the kind that the other speakers have described; it can also be a place where a person who is thinking about a research possibility can actually expose his proposal, can ask for criticism; and it will come out frequently enough, we hope, that there will actually be an honest possibility of others responding. We want to reach the various people who know about related research or who are engaged in a similar problem themselves so that they will actually be able to immediately get in touch with each other. Its main purpose is to be an actual vehicle that can provide a means of continuing communication between people who are in this area. The committee of the Section on the Legal Profession of the American Bar Association is setting up a committee on law and social sciences. We have approached them just to find out, for example, if they would be interested in an experiment in which their newsletter and our newsletter would be published from the same source, so that the members of both sections would automatically receive the newsletter of the other. We have hopes of making it possible for each to communicate within his own profession, but also for one profession to know what is going on in the other. Again, this very simple technical procedure would make this communication more possible than if every developing association starts having its own newsletter, which is one way to proliferate ignorance. You simply create boundaries around all kinds of things; people don't know what is going on anywhere else.

In a sense it is really unfair for me to be representing Wisconsin. I have been the director there for some years, if I say five that means that I was director of a one-man program there for three years. If I say two, that means since we have had a more expanded program. But in February I will go to the University of Hawaii where we hope to set up a Law and Society Institute which faces the ultimate challenge—not how you deal with law professors, but how you deal with practicing professionals. One of the real reasons why I am very eager to go there to try this is that there is no law school in Hawaii. So you have no alternative but to try to get whatever kind of assistance you need, or develop whatever kinds of collaboration possible solely with judges, administrators, and practicing attorneys. There are no law professors around. Who knows, we may have to bring one in. But, at least at the outset, this is the situation that prevails there, so it will raise a chance again to try some more experimentation along this line to see how problems of communication can be reduced and find out what the shared interests are and what kind of assistance can be rendered where the interests are shared, and at the same time try to maintain the proper professional identities on both sides. Because I think it is very naive to think, for example, that social scientists and lawyers necessarily share all their interests, even in areas of forward innovation (if one is a very applied social scientist).

In at least half the instances in which I have been involved concerning legislative innovation the major obstacle to the innovation was the legal profession, the organized bar, which does as a matter of fact have a vast number of vested interests. I have the feeling that Mr. Berle, when he speaks, is always talking about the lawyer who is now a successful senior partner in a Wall Street firm. Or the lawyer who has graduated from the Ivy League schools. Do those instances suggest the typical practicing lawyer in the United States today? In no way do they reflect the disorientations. For American lawyers are under tremendous tension because they are now being bombarded by their organized professionals all over the place to perform in this role in which Mr. Berle tells them to perform. This is another way of being told by the men at the top to cut their own throats economically. In a sense, it is a very difficult demand to make of a profession, although many of them do put themselves into economic extinction for noble purposes. Still, given the character of the organized bar in the United States today, can the legal profession ever become a major source for innovation along the lines that Mr. Berle was describing this morning? I myself am very, very dubious about it. But on the other hand I am more than eager to try to find out in what senses his aspirations can be fulfilled and what the major obstacles are; and what kind of things can be done to make it possible for lawyers who, in many communities, are part of the national leadership group, to establish an identity and orientation which is community wide, which reacts much more in terms of development of the great society, and much less in terms of the burden of their own immediate short term economic needs. I don't think anyone who wants to mess with lawyers ever dares deny that these people have some very important interests. Likewise, I don't think any lawyers who will want to mess with social scientists should forget that they, too, have some very special interests. One of these is, that they want to be able to study lawyers and judges. They don't want to be just colleagues and collaborators and co-conspirators. They also want to be able to use the lawyers, judges and administrators as objects for study. And very often you find that you get the greatest welcome from these people when you are prepared to enter their conspiracy. When I talk about conspiracy, I am simply talking about public agencies made up of lawyers and administrators who are more than happy to have you come and evaluate their work and keep your mouth shut about what you find wrong. But if you show that there are very general tensions, or evaluate their program and simply show that given the procedures they have adopted it is almost inconceivable on theoretical grounds that they could achieve the ends for which they were established, they don't welcome this kind of research. It is going to be outside their immediate problems.

4. Center for the Study of Law and Society at University of California, Berkeley

PHILIP SELZNICK*

I think by now everyone here must be somewhat overwhelmed by the portrait of initiative and energy and "Gung ho" commitment to the development of law and the social sciences that seem to have spread across the country. I think that we are dealing with an efflorescence of interest in a very old set of problems because speculative thought on law and society is probably as old as the self-conscious quest for justice, and I take the view that everything we are doing here ought to be seen within the larger context of the history of thought in these areas.

---

* Director, Center for the Study of Law and Society, University of California, Berkeley (sociology).

I myself don't have a very strong commitment to serving lawyers or the legal profession. I think that we are mainly concerned with the extension in society of ideals associated with justice, as well as with the effort to develop new approaches in scholarship that will cast, we hope, some additional light on some very ancient problems. For example, in philosophy for many years there has been discussion of problems such as determinism in human behavior. A social science approach can permit us to frame the question in a new way and perhaps help us to take a step forward.

At Berkeley, what we have done is set up an interdisciplinary institute which we call the Center for the Study of Law and Society. Just to very briefly indicate its administrative status, it is what we call at Berkeley an organized research unit. The hope is that this will be something continuing. It has some initial support from the Russell Sage Foundation and it also is in the business of raising money itself for specific projects. For example, some funds were received from the President's Committee on Juvenile Delinquency and Youth Crimes for some explorations of the ways the law impinges on juveniles. In addition to this quest for funds for specific projects, we have some possibility of gaining support from the University budget, at least in some very modest way as a basis for a continuing institution. Being an institute we are necessarily somewhat eclectic, that is to say, the effort is not so much to impose a program but rather to respond to opportunities and interests as they may be manifested by members of the staff of the University of California. To some extent this includes the statewide University and we have people who have received some support from us who have been at the University of California at Davis, and at the University of California at Riverside. That's basically the kind of institution we are trying to develop.

I am much too impressed with the importance of doctrine not to make some effort to suggest some of our lines of research and directions of thought. There are a few themes that have tended to emerge in our work and they are related to the problem of values we discussed earlier. The first theme that I would like to mention might be summarized as the study of the social foundations of legality. Here we operate from the following premises: that there is an ideal of legality and that this ideal is manifested in various ways in positive law, particularly in the law associated with due process and the attempt to achieve fair procedure; that this ideal and these legal principles and rules are only partially embodied in the institutions of our society that they ought to influence and direct; that we need closer studies of the dynamics of these institutions in order to help elaborate principles and rules for the guidance of these institutions in accordance with the ideal of legality.

Now these institutions include some of the conventional agencies of the law itself. For example, one of my colleagues, Jerome Skolnick, is now completing a book on the police.[10] And his interest in police practice is in the study of the variety of law enforcement patterns that are engaged in by the police: the interaction between police officials and various types of criminals, the significance of this for the way of life of the law enforcement officer, his perceptions of the world, and so on. All of this inquiry is guided by the basic question: To what extent is the ideal of legality in fact built into the law enforcement agencies themselves? As we know, of course, from the actions of the Supreme Court and other judicial bodies, there are many serious questions regarding the capabilities of these institutions to meet the moral demands that are made upon them. On the other hand we also realize that these institutions are different—they have different missions, different goals, different problems, and the way ideals will be built into these institutions is necessarily going to vary.

Another problem with which we have been concerned is on a more theoretical level—we have been conducting a seminar with a number of members of our law faculty that has been extremely stimulating. It has to do with the nature of the adversary principle. The conventional view, of course, is that the adversary principle has a very important role to play in the achievement of fair proceeding. If we look closely at this principle and try to pin it down, we find that is a rather slippery proposition and that it needs a great deal of analysis. There are differences of opinion that emerge within our group as to just what we are talking about. Should we have a strong view of the adversary principle that specifies some certain rather specific conditions or attributes? Or should we have a more general view that permits us to study variations in adversariness in various institutional settings?

One of our graduate students, Philippe Monet, is doing a very close study of the Industrial Accident Commission in California. The problems raised in the history of the Industrial Accident Commission pose serious questions regarding the role of adversariness in the adjudication of claims and we hope that by looking closely at special experiences and at the same time pressing always for the theoretical relevance of what we are doing, we will produce some modest contributions to scholarship.

There are, of course, many other institutions that need study, some not entirely within the law enforcement area. We have an interest in the problems of correctional institutions. But, again, we engage in critical analysis of the correctional institution from the standpoint of how the ideals of legality bear on these institutions. We are interested not only in the problem of rehabilitation and in the reconstruction of these institutions in the direction of the rehabilitation model, but also in what this model means for the administration of justice within these institutions.

We have also been much concerned with the so-called problem of private government. Here the same general issue emerges. If we take a university or a business corporation or what have you, what are the potentialities or the obstacles within these institutions for the extensions of the ideals of justice. Now this complex of the social foundations of legality is one basic theme.

Let me just mention a couple of other things. We're interested in the broad area of law and culture. I mean this not so much in the anthropological sense as in variations in the conceptions of a legal order. We suppose it makes a great deal of difference in society what it asks of a legal order;

what demands it makes upon it, how it proceeds, the contribution that the law can make to the society. It makes a difference for example whether you think of the law as educator. And also in that connection, is there a difference between the pedagogical stance of legal institutions in the Soviet Union as described by Harold Berman[11] and the educational posture of the law, or images of the law as it appeared in the classic Greek point of view? Both are formally similar, but I suspect substantially quite different. We think it might make a great deal of difference if you have a highly instrumental approach towards the law. If the law is concerned as basically instrumental, other values might be disparaged. For example, some law professors I know are perfectly willing to say they really aren't too much interested in the so-called principled bases of the Supreme Court's decisions, as in the reapportionment cases, so long as the proper political outcome is won. That is a somewhat radical instrumentalist view of the legal system. Some cultures have taken a view of law as fundamentally the embodiment of awesome authority, and this of course makes a difference. So this whole area of conceptions of the legal order is something that I hope we can do something with, but, of course, it takes a high order of sensitivity to pursue the matter.

We are interested in the emergence of potentially new branches of the law. Is there something emerging such as a law of welfare? Do we see out of the whole development of modern welfare institutions and welfare legislation some principles that provide bases from which to reason as new cases arise in the course of adjudication? Is there something new in the whole field of consumer law? Are we seeing the development of the legal perspectives that draw upon social change, that represent, as it were, incipient law, that may make a considerable difference so far as the evolution of our own legal order is concerned? These I think are some of the themes that emerged from our discussion before.

I have a modest optimism in all of this. I think that we start from the proposition that this generation is going to do something about law and social science. The payoff will be in the kind of jurisprudential writing that comes out of it. I think this will require work on all levels including all of the things that have been mentioned today, but ultimately it seems to me we are either going to make some contribution to jurisprudence by way of the energies and concerns now stemming from social scientists or we will probably not have advanced very far.

5. The Research and Graduate Study Area—Dialog

The Conference Chairman led off the discussion which followed among the authors of these papers and other conference participants.

MASSEL—Looking at the various programs that have been described, it seems to me that many of them are focused upon law students and what takes place in the law schools, what might be done in the law schools. How much of the work that is going on, as you see it, results in developing lawyers who can do the job of acting as lawyers in the representation of private clients, or the representation of the government, more effectively than they are today? May I suggest the basis for my question is that the function of the lawyer is not merely one of making a contribution to society as a citizen, but also the representation of clients. Now how much of this work, and what phases of this work, will end up with the development and preparation of lawyers who will have better skills in carrying out what we conventionally regard as the function of a lawyer?

ROSENBLUM—Skill is a matter of technique, and I think that what the four of us were talking about this morning was not so much the technique itself but the uses to which the technique could be put. Phil [Selznick] mentioned earlier the question about the extent to which new areas of law are emerging—the law of welfare, the law of the consumer. And I think that in this area we are not simply training the traditional lawyering skills that Bob [Yegge] was talking about earlier, but we are concerned with the areas to which those skills can be applied, and when we are dealing with those areas, we are reformers in a sense. I say that without blushing. I think that we are seeking to do something in the way of innovation through this union of law with the social sciences. The union is designed perhaps to make law look at itself, and to ask to what extent certain aspects of lawyering have been concerned with the reinforcement of levels of stratification within the society, by keeping the law unavailable to some elements of the community, by priding ourselves on the role that law plays procedurally, but not looking at all on the substantive functions that are performed by the law with regard to major segments of the community. Insofar as law practice was based purely on the law of supply and demand, where the ability to pay is a prime factor of getting access to the legal mechanism, then what is being performed through this access is a reinforcement of existing structures. To the extent that we are making law available now meaningfully to the consumer, to the extent that we are concerned with the relationship between the law and the poor, which is really the subject of a forthcoming panel, I think that the social sciences in performing their function as social sciences are requiring that law take a look at itself. The kinds of decisions that the Supreme Court makes today in the area of apportionment, in the area of civil rights, in the area of providing counsel, are the consequences of the newer social concerns and the newer awarenesses on the part of lawyers of what the social scientists have been doing and of the awarenesses of the social scientists about the importance not merely of the application of legal techniques in the resolution of disputes, but of the equal application of legal techniques to every strata of the society.

MASSEL—Now this involves an examination of the legal system, and how the legal system is operating from the policy standpoint. The question I raised did not move along those lines, but rather along the lines of whether anything that was being done would either directly or indirectly improve the skills of the lawyer. And in that connection may I point out that the development of the skills of the lawyer in the areas we are discussing does not require that the lawyer have the skills of the mathematician or the statistical mathematician in being able to carry through sampling techniques, or the skills of the accountant, or the skills of the economist in carrying out a study which gets into such questions as the definition of the market. The skills of the lawyer call for the use of the materials which will be produced by the people in the social sciences. The skill of the lawyer in handling the information gathered on a statistical basis or a sampling basis is a skill which relates to what we call the conventional skills of the lawyer. The question I was raising was whether, in the work that is being done, either directly or indirectly, this work is contributing to the skills of the lawyers who go to law school in order to develop educationally and through training the skills of a lawyer. This is not to deny the usefulness of all of the work being done in the examination of how the legal system works, and it is not to deny that this would be useful in and of itself, but it is to raise the question of whether the work which has been described here produces lawyers with better skills, as part of the whole question of whether our legal system is working effectively.

SELZNICK—If scholarship can add something to our understanding of what lawyers can do, and particularly in new settings, and if this is then communicated, then presumably it will add something to the skills of the lawyer. But I think there is perhaps relatively little interest in enhancing the existing body of skills. I think this notion of reconceiving the role of the lawyer is likely to be more stimulating to a social scientist than this job of simply adding to existing skills. For example, Dean Newman at our law school is interested in the role of the government lawyer, and the extent to which the Office of Solicitor General, for example, has been active, not only in defending the government when it is challenged, but also in the more positive role of devising procedural rules of fairness, etc., for government agencies. Well again, if that role is recast and reconceived, it will change the work that is done and in that sense affect the skills of the lawyer.

YEGGE—One of the judges of the Juvenile Court in Denver said this: "When will the lawyers ever learn to keep their nose out of the court. When we pick up a juvenile offender in our court, who has no prior record, but has done some mischief, we put him in juvenile hall for the night, and probably give him a lecture, for whatever good that is, and let him go without filing any charges. If a lawyer appears, the lawyer immediately insists on information, and hence a full blown trial follows, and probably conviction follows as well." Now here's a case where, if the judge understood the operation of the behavior of that court, the lawyer would be well advised to decline the case for the good of his client rather than pursue all of the legal remedies.

ARENS—It has been my experience in the District of Columbia that most lawyers conversant with local court practices have attempted to avoid adversarial proceedings by stepping in at the earliest possible moment with a view to securing informal conferences with prosecuting officials in order to do precisely what Professor Yegge has suggested is most desirable: The avoidance of the creation of a damaging record, particularly in the case of youngsters involved with the law. It is only the incompetent lawyer who will always insist upon the full blown adversarial proceeding. It is precisely the person without legal counsel who will stumble about and make demands for a formal hearing when informal conferences can easily secure the result which would appear to be the most desirable. I believe lawyers have shown considerable sophistication in securing exactly those results.

DOWD*—Maybe this is an area where the social scientist who has to deal with things that do involve legal problems, is somewhat unsophisticated in the law. I am not talking about specialists. I mean the concept of a legal right as opposed to a social right; the concept of what defense means, what is the significance of guilt, what is the significance of a legal determination as opposed to a non-legal determination. I think that anybody who is going to constantly be concerned with these problems—in other words, the social worker, the person who is working for a public aid agency, maybe from the undergraduate curriculum as well as in graduate study, should have an idea, for instance, of what "constitutional" means, an idea of what "legal procedures" mean. There is a role for legal education at that level, I think. There the problem is just as severe as the need of social education for lawyers. Policemen need it. I think all sorts of other public servants need it.

SELZNICK—I think to some extent we have to recognize there are some areas of ignorance here. We don't know, for example, how much and under what conditions a concern for legal rights actually has a psychological benefit for the individual—I'm not talking about other benefits, the kinds of things that the law is classically developed to take care of, but the payoff for the protection of legal rights in the simple fact of dignity, being treated as a person, and so on. I think this has a very important role to play and it has not been fully recognized. On the other hand, we don't

---

* Professor Donald W. Dowd, Villanova University (law).

know for sure, just taking these matters as psychic benefits, whether they are outweighed by some other considerations in some special circumstances such as in juvenile court hearings.

POWELL*—Professor Selznick, I wonder whether the definition of the policeman as an "enemy" by adolescent delinquents isn't a reflection of something more general and more serious, namely, whether the 25 percent—or 15 percent—of the American people who don't participate in the American way of life don't define the policeman as an enemy. And then this passes on to the adolescent and appears in the form of adolescent delinquency.

SELZNICK—There has certainly been a considerable amount of concern for just that—that is, the extent to which, the possibility at least, that we are dealing with a very important matter of perception, perception that affects the viability of social control. There certainly is a considerable amount of law enforcement that is experienced as unjust and discriminating. Whether it is in fact unjust and discriminating isn't necessarily the point. But it certainly is experienced as unjust and discriminating. Some of that derives from the social backgrounds of the individuals. Some, however, from the rather immediate situations in which they are placed. The police come along, and on a good actuarial basis will throw more resources into a certain area of the community, will be more alert to offenses in a certain area of the community and so on. And they are perfectly right if you are going to ask, now what is the probability distribution of these offenses? On the other hand, if you live in an area to which this special attention is given, this is going to affect your response to law enforcement, and this is certainly one of the basic problems in this area. Again, however, we know that this goes on, but we don't know how much it goes on, and really not too much about the conditions under which it varies.

MASSEL—What, as you see it, is the influence of your programs on the people in the social sciences from the educational standpoint, the graduate students, as well as the undergraduate students?

ROSENBLUM—I think we have all done our part in the past to create structures of mutual misunderstanding, but I think that we are in a period in which we are really engaged in fairly substantial undertakings to rip those barriers down. The old dialog used to be in terms of what can the social scientist do for the lawyer? What can the lawyer do for the social scientist? I think that is really outmoded at this point. The question, or the series of questions, is the extent to which social science provides components in the law, and the extent to which law is a component of the social sciences. And we are recognizing more and more through the kinds of things that Professor Wasserstrom has done,[12] through the kinds of things that are going on in the various programs, through the kinds of things embodied in Mark Massel's research in economics and law,[13] so that these are

---

* Rev. Ralph Powell, O.P., Aquinas Institute of Philosophy and Theology, River Forest, Ill. (philosophy and sociology).

the natural affinities which should be probed in the natural course of a student's training regardless of which disciplinary route he is following.

MASSEL—Do you see very much of an influence of your work on education in the social science areas and in philosophy and history? What's happening at Berkeley?

SELZNICK—I think it's much too soon to expect this kind of influence although I personally believe it is inevitable. I think it is a question of whether things are produced that people can read, that make sense, and so far we don't have a great deal of that. That works both ways. I think that there is a great need for a literature on the law that is available to the educated non-lawyer. We don't have very much of that. And this is one of the barriers to communication. On the other hand, there is a great need for a literature on the law from the social scientist that makes sense to the lawyer, not in the sense that now he can't read it, but in the sense that it says something that seems worth saying. Now this might vary all the way from a straightforward, very useful piece of analysis of Professor Carlin's[14] on the nature of law practice at the lower socio-economic levels and what image of the law this brings forth—I think many lawyers have found this a very useful social science study—all the way to what I think may become useful pieces of socially oriented legal history that cast some light on the evolution of law in various fields, on the growing points and direction of the law, and that may influence the thinking of lawyers. I don't think we can expect in the world of the mind quick influences of this kind. You build up a literature and then it takes some years before this literature even becomes known. These days it is not so difficult as it was earlier.

Part Three
THE UNDERGRADUATE CURRICULUM

CHAPTER III
THE BASIC COURSE

1. Preliminary Dialog

Some of the restlessness to discuss the question of introducing "basic courses" in law into the undergraduate curriculum is evidenced by the following interchange that took place even before the subject was reached on the conference agenda. It serves as an introduction to this chapter. In addition to Professors Selznick and Rosenblum and the Chairman, the participants are Professor John Duff (history), Seton Hall University, and Dr. Michael Barkun (political science) of the Program in Law and the Social Sciences at Northwestern.[1]

DUFF—As a teacher primarily of undergraduates, I am glad to see the conversation get turned around a little bit. Frankly, this morning when Professor Berle spoke, he apparently assumed that everyone here was a lawyer, and most of the discussions assumed that as well. I am not a lawyer. I must admit I know nothing about the law whatsoever, but I am interested in learning. I came here at the direction of my school primarily to find out about forming undergraduate courses so that we could perhaps restore the law back to the undergraduates. In the 19th Century law was a consideration for undergraduates. It was primarily the lawyers who set it off in law schools in the urban centers away from the rural campus, which is the situation now at Seton Hall. We would like to get the law back in the undergraduate field simply because our students are asking us questions about how the Supreme Court arrives at its decisions on segregation, on obscenity, on prayers in the school. This entails a special knowledge that an historian often lacks. We are interested in finding out more, but frankly, it has been my experience that the people in law are not much interested in teaching undergraduates anything about the law. They are interested in keeping law on the higher level. Moreover, most of the proposals that have been discussed here seem to be aimed at the graduate student and not at the undergraduate. I wonder if there are any comments on that.

SELZNICK—In their beginnings these programs, which happened to be training programs for graduate students and research programs, certainly are aimed at the graduate student. I think that within a very few years these programs will produce precisely the kinds of material that will be of great value for the undergraduate curriculum. I think you've got to develop these materials and it's not the undergraduates who are going to do that. But it's the undergraduates who will be able to read this stuff when it comes out, and this material will provide a good part at least of the text reading and supplementary reading that can help to build up an undergraduate course. I think one of the difficulties with teaching law and social science right now at the undergraduate level is the lack of a really apposite body of materials. I am not saying that it doesn't exist; I think it can be produced, but so far it lacks the concreteness, it lacks the presentation and the form that would be really useful for the undergraduate. That is much less true of constitutional law than it is in other areas, and of course there are many places where a course in constitutional law is being taught.

DUFF—There are admittedly constitutional law courses and I think any adequately prepared historian knows the great constitutional cases and the issues behind them, but what I am getting into is the idea of the course where undergraduates—I am talking of all undergraduates—could become acquainted with the law, its ideas of torts and contracts, etc., to find out perhaps if that is their vocation, or even to just have a layman's knowledge of it. It is apparent that in Europe the average citizen seems to know a great deal more about ordinary law than an American does. Why are Americans so puzzled about the decision on prayer in the schools? They simply don't know the law behind it; they don't know the law behind the segregation decisions; they don't know the law behind the obscenity decisions—this is a deficiency I think it is vital to correct. How much real value today is there in knowing the legal basis of *Gibbons* v. *Ogden*[2] on the commerce clause. Is that as much related to the individual as the other cases? This is the point I want to make. It is difficult to get people to come from the law schools to offer these courses. You are almost faced with the alternative, as Professor Summers of Oregon suggests, of persuading the historians and political scientists to get a little knowledge of the law so they can do it themselves.[3] But this seems to be practically hopeless to me.

BARKUN—I wonder if one of the obstacles here isn't the feeling on the part of the legal profession that the presentation of the law in some form to undergraduates and hence to laymen represents a threat to the profession, and I wonder also if an underlying assumption in much of legal compliance isn't the notion that in some way legal compliance is dependent upon the law being surrounded with some aura of mystery?

MASSEL—Is your program at Northwestern serving to break this down?

ROSENBLUM—Yes, Mike [Barkun] is serving to break it down himself. He taught a course, one of our new courses, with a very pretentious title and it's just as pretentious as the title is, called "The Political Life of Mankind," that has a legal dimension to it. But in response to the question, I think it is very important to have a legal dimension to the courses in history, philosophy, political science, sociology and so on, but not for the purpose of enabling the student to find out whether law is going to be his vocation or not. On the contrary, we should not be engaged in turning our undergraduate curriculum into a prep school environment, into preparing students for law school aptitude tests, in trying to give them a preview of what their professional life might be like. The objective here is to give them, as emerging members of the community of liberal arts people, some notion of the part that law plays as a liberal art in this sense, some notion in looking at torts not to be able to say to a friend who trips on the staircase, this may be worth $10,000 to you, but rather to be able to see how tort law itself has been a product of community attitudes and how it is molded by and in turn molds these attitudes. I would want to disassociate (we've made every effort to in our undergraduate program) fully from our courses any notion that this is to give you a bird's eye view of what awaits you. Students are urged if they have any notion that this is going to prepare them for law school, to get out immediately and save themselves from getting into trouble, because what we want at this stage is a stimulus to imagination and the ability to see connections between seemingly remote disciplines. The student who is able to say by the time he gets through with the law-politics course, that he sees some connection between legal reasoning and the dispute among schools of architecture, or schools of poetry, or schools of historical interpretation, is to the minds of those of us connected with our program accomplishing far more than the student who comes up afterwards and says, "Gee, now I really know that I want to make law my career."

DUFF—I think that is an entirely sensible attitude. I think you misunderstood me if you thought I wanted such a course—this is exactly what I wouldn't want, an LSAT[4] preparation course. This would be ridiculous. I just want a course that would help add to the well-rounded student some knowledge of the law for his everyday life so that he could appreciate law a little better. You can see evidence today, when the *New York Times* every Sunday runs a section just on the law—obviously aimed at the layman —that there is much interest in it.

MASSEL—Incidentally, in case you feel, Vic, that you have a course title which is quite imposing, I heard the other day of a fourth grade student who handed in a composition which was headed, "The Universe and Other Things."

ROSENBLUM—Let me try and get my point here across at the risk of digging a real deep hole. I don't think that we are engaged, or should be engaged, at the undergraduate level in teaching law, substantive law, torts law, contract law, property law, constitutional law, administrative law. I think what we are engaged in teaching about is approaches to law, the methodologies of the law, the relationship of the law to other forms of knowledge, the reliances, if you will, of the law on other forms of knowledge, because what is it that we are dealing with? Are we mesmerizing ourselves into believing that there is something in the way of court declared law apart from those elements that create what Phil [Selznick] has called the social foundations of legality? If we go back and use little more than Cardozo, we find that there are the avenues of history toward law, the avenues of philosophy toward law, the avenues of politics, the avenues of sociology—all of these are part of it, and what we want our students to become aware of at the undergraduate level are the things that contribute, and the ways in which they contribute, to the molding of the law. Whether we want our undergraduates to know how the last clear chance doctrine would apply in an injury case, would seem to me to be entirely beyond the scope of what we want to achieve in undergraduate education.

DUFF—I know, but I still can't help feeling that you're arguing almost as if you put it in an analogy, why teach an undergraduate physics course if you're not going to be a physicist? All I am trying to point out is that, as Dr. Barkun from Northwestern mentioned, there is, it seems to me, a tendency to try to veil the law in mystery, to make it something people don't understand, so that when one enters a lawyer's office to sit down and have a discussion on the particular legal problem with you, he has to be in the position of a complete supplicant to the lawyer. Now I am not saying I advocate barracks-room lawyers, because I am not trying to do that, but I just want to have a course that would give a person a liberal knowledge of the law.

ROSENBLUM—I would say you were exaggerating the significance of one dimension of the law, because after all if you're going to have someone coming in talking about the last clear chance doctrine, or talking about consideration—this is one small dimension which perhaps may be nothing more than the oughtness of a society. This may be a declaration by a court about how people ought to behave. And should a student at the level of the liberal arts not know much more than that? Should he not know that there are areas of the law which have not been available to some parts of the society? Should he not be able to see the contrast between the things that the law declared as it ought, and the things that the law hasn't looked at? And within the domain of what we are trying to do in our undergraduate teaching, I think we're trying to open gates to the bridges among the various disciplines, and not to communicate a batch of substantive knowledge which is more the domain of the professional school.

DUFF—I don't think we are really arguing at cross purposes here. I think we are moving in the same direction, but what you would suggest then is the role of law as such, or even the history of philosophy of law, on the undergraduate level?

ROSENBLUM—To give the student an appreciation of the method of law's evolution and declaration, to give him some notion about the efficacy or the adequacy of its functions, the notions of its method, the ways in which change is achieved in the law. Because if a student sees law as something which is static and irrevocable, then he becomes addicted perhaps to the notion that this is something which can be learned for now and for all time, and to form a highly warped notion of at least American legal institutions.

DUFF—This is perfectly reasonable. Now, how do we go about imparting that?

2. Teaching the Basic Course—Materials

Two specific approaches to a basic course were presented to the conference. The first, for general undergraduate consumption, was outlined by Dean Richard Wasserstrom of the College of Arts and Sciences at Tuskegee Institute, a former law professor at Stanford. A seminar-type basic law course was suggested by Dr. William H. Roberts, Head, Department of Politics, The Catholic University of America.

(1) MATERIALS FOR A BASIC LAW COURSE FOR GENERAL UNDERGRADUATE CONSUMPTION

RICHARD WASSERSTROM*

There are at least three different functions that a course on the legal system for undergraduates in a liberal arts college might fulfill. The first justification for having such a course would be that of acquainting students who are not prospective lawyers with the legal system and its roles, past, present and future, as an institution, a very important institution in society. There are few institutions in society that are as highly developed, as complicated, as rigorous, and have as pervasive an influence as the legal system. And there is a fairly persuasive justification, therefore, for having a course which would concentrate primarily on a study of that institution and its place in society.

The second function of such a course would be as a vehicle by which to interest and to thereby recruit able undergraduates for the legal profession.

And the third different function such a course might have is to serve as a vehicle by which prospective law students could evaluate their aptitude for the study of the law.

Now, while these three functions are not necessarily mutually exclusive, I do think that each would require a somewhat different focus for a course to undergraduates. Thus, if we are concerned primarily with the development of a vehicle by which prospective law students could evaluate their interest in and aptitude for the study of law, then I would think that we would want a course that would simulate to the greatest extent possible the character and characteristics of present-day law study.

On the other hand, there is no necessary reason why a course designed to teach about the legal system to non-prospective law students—*about the legal system and how it works*—need have any such focus. I suppose

---

* Dean, College of Arts and Sciences, Tuskegee Institute (administration, law).

that a course that was designed to interest and recruit undergraduates to the legal profession ought to give them some taste of what law study would be like, although perhaps it could have broader focus.

Now, for myself, I don't have any difficulty in assigning priority to these three different functions and in deciding which of these is the most important role that an undergraduate course might fulfill. To begin with, I think there is no lack of qualified and interested applicants for law study. Therefore, I doubt very much that the primary purpose of such a course ought to be to interest and recruit able undergraduates for the profession. Although we never have enough *highly* qualified applicants, we always have plenty of applicants for law school. Furthermore, I think that relatively few students who attend law school discover *after* they get there that they were not interested in the law—although some of them do—that they made a mistake. I don't think that this is a serious or momentous problem in legal education. Furthermore, I think that the law schools have, by and large, devised reasonably good measures by which to assess aptitude for law study. For example, the law school admitting exam, among others. Therefore, I doubt that the development of a vehicle by which prospective law students can evaluate their interest in and aptitude for the study of law, is a vehicle that we desperately need to develop.

On the other hand, there are, I submit, at present, in the undergraduate curriculum, relatively few opportunities for an undergraduate to learn, simply as a part of his liberal education, in a relatively systematic fashion, about the law as an institution. I think the typical experience is that one or a few political science courses in constitutional law, and possibly a philosophy course or two in the philosophy of law, constitute the maximum number of opportunities whereby an undergraduate could study the law in anything but a peripheral fashion. And because the legal system has played, and does play, such a role and set of roles in our society, I think that there is a real justification for making its study a part, or a possible part, of the liberal arts education of undergraduates. Now this is not by any means a novel suggestion on my part; and certainly for the past ten years, at least, people in legal education have been wrestling with this problem of whether such a course should be offered and if so, what kind of course it should be.[5]

For three of the school years that I was on the faculty at the Stanford Law School, I taught a course under the sponsorship of the Law School in the undergraduate liberal arts college on the legal system; and I had an opportunity to use at least two of the sets of materials that have been developed commercially for such a course. It is my own view—it is my thesis that I will try to propound this morning—that none of the materials that have so far been developed for such a course are at all adequate for a course of this type. They all suffer, I think, from extremely serious defects. Let me say something on the materials I am thinking about: Probably the first set of materials was developed by Harold Berman of Harvard.[6] This is largely a collection of cases dealing with approximately one-half dozen different substantive areas of the law. Another set of materials was developed by two of my colleagues at Stanford, Harold Shepherd and Byron Sher.[7] These are materials devoted exclusively to one theme, the theme of contracts, and again, are largely case materials somewhat different, though, from what you find in the typical contracts course.

The third set of materials with which I am most familiar is a set of materials developed most recently by, or at least put into final form recently by Hurst, Mermin, Garrison and Auerbach at the University of Wisconsin.[8] These materials try to deal with the judiciary, the court system; a separate section on legislation; at least a third section on administrative law. While containing a fairly large amount of case material, there is substantial non-case material: excerpts from legislative debates, a number of excerpts from articles on various subjects. These materials are all organized around the theme of the development of the law of Workmen's Compensation, the earlier common law aspects of the same problem, the fellow servant rule, and the like.[9]

Now, it is my thesis that almost all of this material rests at least in part on the assumption that the method which is used more than any other method to teach law to law students, is also *the* method of teaching about the law to anyone, including undergraduates. But this involves, I think, a dreadfully serious mistake. The materials used in law schools—I am talking now of this case method broadly conceived—the materials used in law schools are designed, I think, as much as anything else to develop certain habits of analysis and inquiry—habits of analysis and inquiry that legal educators feel it very important to develop in students. For myself, anyway, the justification for the case method is that this is a remarkably effective way by which to develop these habits of lawyer-like analysis and inquiry.

I think in part—in very substantial part—these materials when used in law schools are effective because they are permitted to operate throughout a hopefully coherent three-year program. They fit into a fairly sustained exposure to legal materials; they can afford, if you will, to concentrate on relatively narrow aspects of the legal system just because in the course of the three-year curriculum the students will thereby see a great deal of the legal system.

Now, I must say, some of the things I am going to say I think are also relevant to theories about the legal system, but they are more relevant to such an undergraduate course.

I think the case method, as I said, is ideally suited to teach people how to think and reason in the way in which at least law professors think lawyers ought to think and reason. I don't think that there is any very good reason to suppose that this is necessarily a desirable device by which to teach people about the law—to give them what might be called "the big picture." And it seems to me that a one-shot proposition in the undergraduate curriculum ought to give them a bigger picture than the case method permits. I think this reflects a kind of parochialism on the part of law school teachers —"If it's good enough to teach lawyers, it must be good enough to teach anybody else about the legal system."

Another necessarily related feature of the case method, and hence of the materials such as Shepherd and Sher and Berman developed and, even to a considerable extent, the materials developed by Hurst, et al., is that they concentrate largely upon appellate court decisions. These are the bread and butter of the case method. And after all, appellate court decisions are really only one very small slice of the legal system, although they are the slice that law professors find intellectually most appealing. Typically, too, the materials that have been developed for undergraduate courses focus upon given or selected areas of the law—I have indicated Shepherd and Sher on contracts, Hurst, et al., on workmen's compensation, Berman on four or five areas. Thus, not only do we have a slice of the law in the sense that we are presented primarily with appellate court decisions, but we have a slice of a slice—if you will—because appellate court decisions are on one or a selected number of substantive legal areas.

No, I just don't think that these materials do a very good job. I don't think they realize any number of objectives that such a course can and should realize. I would propose that new materials, better materials, are needed; materials that would break away from some of the parochialism of legal pedagogy; materials that, too, would break away from what I think is a curious habit of mind of law school professors—and that is if something is interesting, something is dramatic, exciting, poignant, it is inherently suspect and to be avoided. And I think this is unfortunate, both because it is silly and because necessarily it prevents one from exposing the students to the richness of legal experience; to the varieties of activities, enterprises and problems with which the law is concerned and which concern the law. And many of these problems, many of the reasons why the law is an important institution is because these problems are the very real problems of very real people.

The materials that I would propose that someone ought to develop would frankly seek to be a survey. They would seek to give a macro-cosmic rather than a micro-cosmic view of the legal system. Now, such a course might cover all or some of the following topics: In some cases where I have been able to think of particularly appropriate reading selections and where I have known about them—and I must say that there are a few, or a great many that I don't know about—I'll indicate them.

I think that one topic that should, or at least might be, covered in such a course is, broadly, the development of legal systems. And if one had a penchant for the chronological, one might begin with the primitive law. But what does it look like just before, or just when you're developing in a society a legal system? And I would suggest that you might do this before you try to ask the question of exactly what a legal system is—which is, after all, one of the most perplexing problems of all.

And then, certainly, I think that there ought to be some attention to the development of the common law system over the past six or seven hundred years.

Now, I don't think that it's cheating to use discursive material. If somebody has written a pretty good article on the development of the common law, it isn't cheating to tell the students to read it—although again, I think the pedagogy of legal education would suggest that at least in the classroom it would be cheating just to ask them to read it because then you can't ask all the clever questions you might ask about slaves' tests.

Apart from this—and this is an area which I know the least about and so I am weakest in, and I am sure there are other aspects of the development of legal systems—you might turn to a much more concentrated look at the Anglo-American legal system. And I would think that one of the things, but only one of the things, that one would certainly want the students to see, is the nature of legal analysis: What is it? How is it that a lawyer would look at a tangle of cases and analyze them? And here I think that the appropriate vehicle might be selected cases in the appropriate areas that you wanted to have them actually read into. And if you wanted to be able to pose some of the nice questions that we pose in law school classes, you could take any one of the stock set of cases that adapt themselves so nicely to this purpose: the development of torts of product liability and the kind of things that I think Levi does quite nicely in his little book on *An Introduction to Legal Reasoning.*[10] If you don't want to use that, you could just use the cases and give them your own analysis. But I don't think this ought to loom as an overly significant portion of the course.

And again, to repeat what I said, *most* of the materials that I've seen treat this as the central focus of any such course, if not the exclusive preoccupation. I think this is instructive, as I think almost all things we try to do in liberal education are instructive; not because you want to teach the students about substantive law, or anything else, but to give them a sample, an illustration of what this kind of thing is like, so that if they are bright and attentive and are being taught well, they can make certain kinds of intellectual inferences to the effect that if this is what they do in this area, then they do probably the same thing in lots of others. So—something on the nature of legal analysis—a good exposure to a half dozen or a dozen cases and all the questions they do and do not answer.

And then, I suppose that maybe this ought to come first, some kind of brief discursive treatment of the nature of the system itself. Now, hopefully, this wouldn't be necessary, but I imagine for lots of undergraduates, a brief discussion of the role and structure of the court system, the legislature, and the executive might be necessary. (The number of students who know absolutely nothing about the organization of the federal courts and the state court systems is absolutely appalling.)

And then I would like to really turn to some of the things that law schools somehow never really get around to talking about that are essential or significant aspects of the legal system: What about the men who made this system and who make it? What about some of the titans of legal systems, the great judges, and the great lawyers; and why were they great? Now, we obviously can't ask them all to read Beveridge's *Life of Marshall,*[11]

but I don't see anything wrong with asking them to read a couple of shorter
biographies of judges, of lawyers—maybe Catherine Drinker Bowen's
biography of Holmes;[12] maybe a biography of a lawyer or two. Even if
they are bad biographies, one can learn a good deal about the kind of man
it was who wrote this. I think of Nizer's book,[13] or a book on Darrow. I
think they ought to see that the legal system is manned by people and some
of them are very exciting people; some of them are very curious people,
and some are remarkably dedicated and intelligent people.

   Then another thing that we certainly ought to do in such a course, and
I think we really ought to do more of in law school, is to let the students
really see the anatomy of a legal case. I think there are comparatively few
law students who ever get to see this directly. Start with the incidents involved—and I don't see anything wrong with making it an interesting in-
cident; maybe a murder—you know! And then: What do all the legal
papers look like? I would reproduce, at a *minimum,* all of the legal papers
that might become a part of the trial file in the case, with the complaint
and the subpoena. And let them see all the fancy language that means
absolutely nothing that's on these documents. Let them see what a lawyer's
brief looks like; let them see that sometimes they are fairly down-to-earth,
that one can read and really understand what the lawyer is talking about,
that he is not using a lot of magical names and Latin phrases; let them see
—say, a sample office memo that might have been prepared—all of the
court materials and briefs. And, I suggest, a copy of the attorney's bill.
Now that's something I never saw at law school; and I'd *still* like to know
what a bill would look like. My only work has been—you can see, I've
done nothing but indigent defense work.

   Then—and I *do* think they ought to see what these documents look
like—I think maybe (because we want to break away from just the judicial
aspect of this) do the same kind of thing with a piece of legislation. Maybe
the best thing to do is make it up rather than using an actual one. But the
nice thing about the law is that there are enough materials so that you
can always find something that has been done that is much better than you
can imagine. The Hurst collection[14] does try to do some of this in connection with legislation. But—again—I suppose something more could be done.
They ought to see what the committees went through; maybe a sample of
the transcript, and everything.

   And then (to pick up something that was mentioned yesterday), I
think in such a course it's quite useful to have the students make some
visits to the courts. I tried to do this every year with my students at
Stanford. I don't suppose their experiences are atypical. Most of them
had never set foot in a court before. I think many of them were frankly
surprised to discover that the courts were open to the public. And—I'll be
frank—I used to take them to the criminal court. After all, this is what is
interesting. And I told them that this is the greatest piece of free entertain-
ment available in the United States today—that you can walk into a
criminal court in San Francisco almost any time during the day and find
almost any kind of gory crime. You can *see* what a defendant looks like!

He's really a person. And the jurors aren't always very attentive; and it's amazing to see how inattentive the judge can be. And this is part of what the legal system looks like. I was usually able to arrange to have them go into the chambers sometime during the course of the trial and have them talk with the judge; see when he takes off his robe that he wears a suit, you know. And if the judge is cooperative this can be an interesting experience.

And we would talk about what we had seen when we came back. I did try to find out ahead of time what cases were up, and we would talk a little bit about the particular offense involved before we went. And I found this a quite successful part of this course.

And then finally—this is another thing that I think is really quite important—I can't understand why legal education shies away from it: And that is that there is great rhetoric in the law. I mean, we have had some of the great stylists of the English language, among others, saying things that are important; sometimes very beautifully; and I think somehow in such a course, students ought to have a chance to see some of the magnificent rhetoric; some of the ways in which men have been able to use language to express so well and so movingly some of the important things they wanted to say. I think, for example, of Justice Frankfurter's concurring opinion in the case of *Wieman* v. *Updegraf*,[15] involving the loyalty oath. There are some opinions by Justice Jackson, I think in the *West Virginia*[16] case—a number of them— anybody could find them. Somehow, we seem to edit these out of the case books. You know—"If they read that well, they're probably bad law." I think that this is nonsense! And, of course, some of the fine British judges used magnificent rhetoric.

Well, when you get through with this, then I think you ought to raise some of the questions about what are the alternatives to the Anglo-American legal system. Let's not be provincial and parochial. There are a lot of things about it that are best curious and at worst barbaric. What about precedents in case law in the perennial problem that we all talk about? They at least ought to try to engage in some thought experiments about alternatives to this. Ask them to try to formulate a legal system that wouldn't in some sense treat like cases alike—if that's what precedent comes to. Or—how to be different? And then I would focus on the Anglo-American criminal law, which is where I think we look the sorriest. And I think there are some nice things that have already been written on the comparison of the Anglo-American criminal law and that of other countries, which we somehow don't think of as any more civilized than ourselves but somehow run a much more civilized system of criminal justice. I think one of the nicest books that explores this is a recent book by Sybille Bedford called *The Faces of Justice*.[17] She has a fairly lengthy discussion of a very interesting case that occurred in West Germany after the war. I think it's a particularly nice case because it's hard to think of the Germans—it's hard for *me* to think of them—as terribly civilized. And yet, compared to the typical Anglo-American criminal justice, it's a model of what a humane or sensible system would do.

And again, I think another institution that's worth talking about, where we *have* developed a fair amount of materials, would be the whole institution of the jury. Does it make sense? What are its limitations? And certainly here, as well as any other place where they have been developed, I would draw on the materials that social scientists have developed and that give us more information about these institutions. Some of the studies on the juries have been printed—or at least *hints* have been printed about what they are going to tell us whenever they get around to printing it—and these raise some very interesting questions.

Then from this, I would want to look a little bit at the influences of society on the law. It is a two-way street. I think excerpts from Jerome Hall's book, *Theft, Law and Society*[18] are quite appropriate here, and I am sure there are others.

Then, I'd want to ask some questions about the presuppositions of a legal system. Are there different conceptions of the nature of human beings? Does our legal system reflect a particular conception? Are there other systems that reflect others? And here, Berman in his book on Soviet justice,[19] at least I think, makes a fairly provocative, if not wholly persuasive case that the Soviet system has a quite different view of the nature of man and correspondingly the role that the legal system ought to play in respect to man. It is obvious to me that our legal system makes a number of assumptions and therefore acts in certain ways, and I think these are reflected in the adversary system, and in a whole lot of other things that are connected.

Similarly, or related to this, are there different conceptions of the way in which disputes might be resolved? Can there be legal systems that would approach these things quite differently? Again, here you might talk about the adversary system versus alternatives to it. Unfortunately, there has been comparatively little in the way of discursive materials that are, I think, much good on the question of the adversary system. I think, as Phil Selznick pointed out, it is one of the areas that somebody ought to do a lot of work on.

What about the economic assumptions of a legal system? Again, I suppose some of the things that Cahn,[20] among others, was saying yesterday would certainly be relevant here. How accessible is justice? To what extent does Anglo-American law incorporate or depend upon the acceptance of the capitalist?

And then, the conceptions of justice and the conceptions of freedom. To what extent are these built in? How might they differ without changing the system? And after this, I would want to have a bit on the legal profession itself—it's terribly important, this part of the law. What are the economics of the profession? What are the ways in which we select people for the profession? Are these sensible? Could they be improved? And what about the ideology of the legal profession? Riesman has one quite interesting piece in the *Stanford Law Review*[21] which tends to deal with some of these questions, and others.

And then I suppose, finally, if I had time and could think of anything interesting to say, I might try to talk about alternatives to legal systems themselves—figure out what would happen if we didn't have a legal system; what kinds of things could you and could you not do?

This is roughly what I would do—a kind of "panorama." And I think it wouldn't be too hard to organize such a course; and to get such materials. Hopefully, they would be constantly revised as our social sciences that study the legal systems so eagerly developed new and more interesting theories and collected more interesting and relevant information about the "beast" and how it works.

And I think that such a course—if one developed it and taught it— would serve a number of the purposes of liberal education; it would acquaint the students with some of the *richness* of the system, and would do a much better job than the existing materials permit.

(2) A SEMINAR APPROACH TO TEACHING LAW IN THE UNDERGRADUATE CURRICULUM

WILLIAM H. ROBERTS*

I would say that liberal arts education, like any other type of education, is primarily and basically concerned with disciplining the human mind; with enforcing a discipline on the human mind. In liberal education we try to discipline the human mind as far as the basic questions, the basic problems of life, are concerned.

How do we face reality, on whatever level—metaphysical reality; the reality of human and social relationship? We cannot go any farther on the liberal arts level. And then comes the professional level. On the professional level we try to do something entirely different. We try to discipline the mind to deal with certain human problems applied in a concrete situation. Professional training is not scientific training, and it ought not to be scientific training. The lawyer, the doctor, are trained to apply certain scientific findings to concrete human problems, whether they be legal problems or whether they are problems of sickness and health. Quite different, again, is graduate training. In graduate training we try to impose upon the human mind the discipline which is necessary to discover new knowledge; or to apply knowledge to a broad area of problems—pure science and applied science. But on each of these levels we have to try to discipline the mind in entirely different ways.

In the liberal arts curriculum, it is *not* our task to give professional training or research training. We vitiate the liberal arts approach if we try to be semi-professional—we can never be professional; we can only be

* Head, Department of Politics, Catholic University.

semi-professional. And that, in my opinion, is worse than not doing anything. The professional education and graduate education today, in our complex world, need more and sounder liberal arts education than ever before.

Now, law, in my book, has always been one of the most important vehicles for *really* imparting good liberal arts education. In Greece—in ancient Greece—that was a foregone conclusion. Plato accepted it as a fact that what we call liberal arts education is based on a survey of the nature and function of law—not legal details, but the nature and function of law. And then in the Middle Ages we have, naturally, as you know, the *trivium* and the *quadrivium;* and in the *trivium* we have rhetoric, grammar and logic; and in all three—and that escapes most people—law was used as an essential vehicle for instruction, not *qua*-law, but *qua*-vehicle of instruction. And then we come to that excellent statement by Woodrow Wilson that the college student has to know "what law is, how it came into existence, what relation its forms bear to its substance, and how it gives to society its fiber and poise of frame."[22] Now, I believe that is very well expressed. We still can say exactly the same thing today.

And I believe Mr. Berle was quite right in saying that the lawyer is used as an intellectual translator.[23] But he failed to say one thing: the *liberally* educated lawyer, the lawyer who had a good liberal education before he went to professional school, before he became acquainted with the techniques of the trade.

Now, who can give such a course? Mr. Berle said yesterday that it can best be handled by an educated lawyer (and he meant, obviously, a liberally educated lawyer). I completely agree with him. I do not believe that such a course can be offered by anybody except by a man who had legal training. A man who had no legal training will always "nibble" at the edges of the law. Whatever he may know about the nature and function of the law, he has to know the professional mind; he has to know the techniques of the law. I would even go further than Mr. Berle did. I would say that such a course has to be taught by a man who had a good liberal arts education, legal education, *and* experience in the law. Why? Because only experience teaches us where the limits of professional knowledge are. Paper is very patient; you can put everything down on paper. But *where* are the actual limits of the professional knowledge and the application of our professional knowledge? That, only experience teaches us.

We don't go to a young lawyer just out of law school because he may know all the books; he may have been first in his class at Harvard, but he still does not know where the limits are. And heaven protect us against the young man coming out of medical school! He learns the limits only in experience. That is exactly the same with the waistcoats in the Pentagon. There are a few armchair strategists, but it is only the soldier, only the professional soldier, who actually knows the limits. Therefore, ideally, the man who teaches such a course should have a good liberal arts education; he should be legally trained; and he should have practical experience in the law.

Where is the place for teaching such a course? We have here at this university in each department what we call a senior coordinating seminar. I have taught a law course for, I believe, nearly 20 years in the senior coordinating seminar of the political science department of this University; and looking at it with an experience of about 20 years, I would say I cannot conceive of any department that could offer the same possibilities for introducing law into the liberal arts curriculum. After all, as Aristotle said—and I believe it still holds—politics, like philosophy and theology, is a discipline which ties practically all the threads of society together. We may teach law in other disciplines, too; but we will always get it from one particular angle. As Professor Carl Friedrich of Harvard said in his recent book,[24] after all, legal thought is only part of political thought. It belongs, in my opinion, in the political science department, nowhere else.

And now I should like to speak about the materials which can be used to introduce the students—and I mean the liberal arts students—to law. I should like to say that my seminar has never been a lecture course. I consider myself, as I say in the first session of the seminar, as the director of the seminar, and I let the boys and girls work out their assignments by presenting them to a group, subject to continuous cross-examination by the group and myself. What are the sources? Well, here I am rather pragmatic and adaptable. Ideally, I have a look at the group. The students come in for a personal conference at the end of their junior year and I can size them up and give the assignment before the end of the junior year so they have all summer to really prepare themselves.

There are, needless to say, two great legal systems in the West, the Roman legal system, or the civil legal system, and our common law system. And first, I want to get them acquainted with the principles of these two legal systems. And here we have one older book which is not any more in stock, the book of Sait (of California), *Political Institutions*,[25] has four excellent chapters on the Roman system and on the common law legal system. Then, I use Lord Bryce's *Studies in Jurisprudence*[26]—and some of these studies comparing the two legal systems are marvelous; excellent for an introduction to the nature and function of these two legal systems. As far as common law system is concerned I use *The Common Law*[27] by Holmes, and also Pound's book, *The Spirit of the Common Law*.[28]

But the important point in liberal arts education is really to make our people familiar with the *working* in the mind. Now that can be done in chemistry, it can be done in physics, and it can be done in the law.

And here I agree with Dean Wasserstrom that biographies, well-selected biographies (taking those chapters which deal with the making of the legal mind), are understandable by everybody. There are any number of them. We have good biographies of Roman lawyers, ancient and modern; we have excellent biographies of British and American common lawyers. I read the other day a recent biography of Henry Stimson and his legal practice, and I must say that it is wonderful. It shows here exactly how the American legal mind works.

There are some statements (you know he practiced with Elihu Root) made by Elihu Root which, just for a young man or a young woman, are brilliantly illuminating as to the working of the legal mind. Then I use frequently selections from the Holmes-Pollock correspondence.[29] Here we have an American and a British contemporary going over practically the entire range of legal thought and legal problems in a fascinating way.

So, I deal first with the principles of the Roman legal system and the common law legal system, and with the working of the legal mind. And then I try to take up modern philosophies and theories of law. I take first the Catholic modern philosophies of law and this year I used Dabin; and the modern American theories of law—and I use Cardozo: his two series of lectures, *The Nature of the Judicial Process*[30] *and The Growth of the Law*,[31] and Hegel, *Judicial Legislation*. And they have worked out very well. And then, if I have time, I try to introduce them to certain selected aspects of the American legal system—on a non-technical basis.

I do not use cases because I believe the use of the case method is a very specific professional method, and I wouldn't try to use that method on the liberal arts level. When teaching in law school, I discover again and again that the people who use the case method in the liberal arts curriculum are worse off than those who have never heard of it, or have never taken the particular professional tests. It is exactly like the difference between pre-med courses in biology and the schools of medicine biology courses. There is no use introducing into biology courses actual medical professional training. I steer clear of that in my senior seminar.

Now, I conceived it to be my purpose to really speak about the liberal arts curriculum, not about the social sciences in law; that is an entirely different problem. The social sciences are one part of the liberal arts, but only one part. And if we put it in these terms, as we have done, then we come out with what we did: We speak about the problems of graduate education, but not about the liberal arts program; and I personally do not believe that the interdisciplinary approach, as we conceive of it today, has many advantages. If we try to introduce the interdisciplinary approach to teaching in general, we shall develop schizophrenics, amateurs.

I might well have given a title to my paper by saying, "The *Limits* of the Teaching of Law in the Liberal Arts Curriculum". There are limits; and if we over-step them—like everything in human life—we vitiate and do harm rather than promote what we are doing.

3. Law Approaches the Liberal Arts—Four Views

Motivations and methods of approach for teaching law to undergraduates were treated by a panel that included three law teachers, Professors Francis E. Barkman of the University of Toledo, Richard Abbott of Carleton University, Ottawa, Canada, and Robert Goosetree of American University, and a sociologist, Professor Harry V. Ball of Wisconsin.

(1) UNDERSTANDING LAW AND OUR SOCIETY

FRANCIS ELWOOD BARKMAN*

I think we ought to stop for a moment and discuss briefly the nature and function of the lawyer in our society. I would guess that most of you regard him as a rather glamorous figure, starring on television. This is far removed from the popular image of him, as reflected in the line of jokes about shysters, a man who is slippery, not quite clean-cut, not quite decent, but nevertheless very handy to have on occasion when one is in trouble.

It is unfortunate that this popular image is in part sustained by the way the lawyer conducts himself. A survey was recently made as to the attitude of the public toward lawyers in Missouri.[32] On the whole, the lawyer had a lower status than many other professions.[33] Laymen who had used the services of lawyers had, on the average, a higher opinion of lawyers than laymen who had never used a lawyer.[34] The users of legal services had a favorable opinion of their personal lawyers and an offsetting lower opinion of all other lawyers.[35] This study makes it clear to me that, on the whole, lawyers have not explained to their clients the nature and operation of the adversary system, and suggests that they might have been less than completely candid in explaining to their clients how they achieved, or failed to achieve, results as compared with the client's expectations.

We lawyers have become much concerned with our public relations and public image; nevertheless, there is a widespread reluctance of the individual practitioner to regard this problem as being as important as it is. His daily life is too intense and competitive, and dominated by the need to make money in order to survive. He, like the physician, derives his living from his practice; economic necessity limits what he can or cannot do.

This economic necessity can be seen in the nature of the material he selects for his continuing self education. Although I teach at the University of Toledo, I am also the Chairman of the Toledo Bar Association's Law Institute Committee, which conducts a continuing legal education program of 24 sessions a year, in each of which we lunch and then spend about 45 minutes on recent legal developments. Those who attend always stress the

---

* Professor of Law, University of Toledo.

primacy of *"bread* and *butter"*. Sometimes I think they literally expect to hear the cash register clank as they walk out the door after hearing of recent developments. I am sorry to report that they are *not* interested in law reform; indeed my most poorly attended meetings in two years were those where a Negro lawyer discussed the responsibility of the bar in civil rights cases, and where a woman lawyer undertook to discuss the obligations of corporate officers as fiduciaries. This suggests that the law as a profession, reflecting the prevailing attitudes of our society, or its governing elite, does not want to face the issues of discrimination against Negroes and against women, topics which are outside our ability to solve here today.

There is another problem which the attorney faces and from which other professions are comparatively free: guilt by association. A clergyman can minister to the spiritual needs of a prostitute, or a doctor can heal her venereal disease, and society will, quite properly, applaud their socially useful efforts; but let the lawyer undertake to protect her legal rights on any criminal charge whatsoever and society will regard him as being her new pimp. Our society has simply not learned that the real security of each citizen in our legal system is most fully guaranteed by seeing to it that the legal rights of *all* citizens, not just the wealthy and the politically powerful, are represented by competent counsel. The greater the unpopularity of the cause, the greater is the abuse to which the community subjects the lawyer. It is tragic that the difficulties in getting lawyers to defend unpopular causes extend throughout our nation. And law-society projects in undergraduate college education should drive home the importance of protecting the legal rights of each and every citizen, no matter how humble or reprehensible.

Now, I would like you to consider the nature of law in our society and how law has necessarily become more complex, just as our society has become more complex. When the average citizen thinks about law, he has some very simple-minded superficial notions about something which has been complicated by our tremendous growth.

Law is still regarded as something that Abe Lincoln learned in front of the fireplace, and the assumption is still widespread that is how to become a lawyer. The myths of Abe Lincoln, and a few other outstanding lawyers like Chief Justice Marshall, have done great disservice to popular understanding of the nature of our law and the role of the lawyer. Too many think it is only necessary to read the Almanac to win a court case. Very few know or could believe that lawyer Abraham Lincoln was paid five thousand dollars for an opinion on a complicated railroad reorganization.

This simple-minded approach to the law controls popular thinking in our society, so an objective of any liberal arts course in law-society had better be to rip this myth out and replace it with a more sophisticated and realistic notion of our legal institutions and the kinds of people who operate them. For now my point is simply that the image of law in a law-society project must have some reasonable relation to reality. Civics in the grade schools teaches the pupils that the legislature makes the law, the executive enforces the law and the courts interpret the law. Frequently lawyers unthinkingly mouth this old cliche. But it is not literally true, is entirely too simple-minded and has as much relevancy to law today as if we were to characterize the entire relationship between water and our society by saying it was for drinking by the thirsty person, washing by a dirty person, and fishing in by a sportsman.

The lawyer, in his education under the case method and in the performance of his role as an advocate in an adversary system, essentially performs along the lines of the Socratic technique in the best sense of the liberal arts tradition. There are many other kinds of skills he also uses, including negotiation on behalf of his client, which his legal education aims to develop. But where does he get his values? By and large, he takes his values from the needs of his client; all too often these values are translated in terms of something as tangible and fungible as money, and have little relationship to truth, beauty, or justice.

Legal education pays little attention to the lawyer's thinking about values. It seems appropriate to me that this conference is held at a religious educational institution, because my guess is that clients and lawyers tend to take many of their values from religion and education. I would hope that attention could be directed to this problem in the course of evolving any law-society project.

Going back to the lawyer's skills, he ought to be an educated man; yet, all too often, I can tell you from first-hand experience, I see them every year, a fresh crop of pre-law students with the bachelor's degree—they are ignorant, they don't know how to use the language, or they deliberately misuse it in the current fads which seem geared to destroy our ability to understand each other. So a third objective of a law-society project must be to improve communication.

I trust that it is abundantly clear that I whole-heartedly endorse a sound liberal arts program as the best possible way to prepare for law as a career, or indeed for *any* career. We need however to develop our knowledge of values in the liberal arts program and to do much more research and scholarship in the science of values. The same point was made at an Institute on Medical Malpractice[36] by the Chief of Surgery at the University of Michigan[37] last year. He indicated the most critical problem in medical education now is not technique, but judgment; that medical schools can take a butcher and make him into a technically and mechanically excellent surgeon, but the medical schools are not at all satisfied with their training of the medical student to deal with the important question— to cut or not to cut—and to realize that this question has to be decided in terms of what is good for the particular patient. Thus the medical schools, like the law schools, come back to the basic approach in the liberal arts, which, as I see it, emphasizes the question *why*?

As I go around and informally meet students on my own campus in the various undergraduate colleges, I am appalled at the lack of interest in this question, "Why?", both on the part of the student and on the part of the faculty. I was amazed to discover that this question is raised and discussed most frequently by engineering students, whose curriculum gives them the least amount of time to devote to the question. Perhaps this can be explained by their awareness of the complexity of our technology and the tremendous power and capacity available with growth. Perhaps awareness of the potential for destruction has aroused their sense of responsibility for avoiding destruction.

Let us assume that we are all agreed on the merits of a liberal arts law-society project. I want to direct your attention to some notions which should be rejected as the objectives of such a project. I agree completely that the justification for law-society is *not* in terms of giving a particular student an advantage which he would capitalize on only if he were admitted to law school, or which assumes that the project would be without benefit to him elsewhere. I fear that such thinking motivates many students to take courses in engineering law, business law, school law, or architectural law, and—I am sorry to have to differ with some of my colleagues on this—all too often the "liberal arts" courses in constitutional law, international law and administrative law. For the law student such courses have been presented as a maze of oversimplified generalizations which actually impede the development of his capacity in these areas in law school. The subject matter of such traditional courses emphasizes law as static, rather than as an on-going process. All too often the instructor has not been properly qualified for the task. Even worse than all of these is the usually implicit, but sometimes express, idea that the student will become capable of solving his own legal problems, a disservice of which I shall say more shortly.

As for the kinds of books for a law-society project that have been put out, I am inclined to agree very much with Dean Wasserstrom's evaluation. There is a paperback book to which I invite your attention, *The Citizen in Court*.[38] It presents the various possible impacts of the law upon the average citizen and does not perpetuate the old myth.

The subject matter of the law-society project must not be too simplified. Laymen generally feel that law is entirely black or white. They regard the legal system as a slot-machine, if you will. All you have to do is put in factors x, y, z, and any lawyer would know the result; if he doesn't give the result to you, he's incompetent or trying to jack up his bill, when really he ought to be giving the stuff away free. A client comes in to a lawyer and says he wants a will. The client has made up his mind already that he will pay no more than $10, or some other trivial sum, and that if the lawyer doesn't do it for that, the client will go instead to his accountant, real estate broker, preacher, or banker, or perhaps to the public library where he will borrow a form book to use to draw his own will. He will save money and he won't have to face the lawyer's prying questions. Occasionally a lawyer will do that same thing, and, when he does, we say that he has a fool for a client. As notable a lawyer as Samuel J. Tilden, who was almost elected President of the United States, drew his own will and precipitated most expensive litigation as a result. From the lawyer's point of view he has to know a great deal about the client, the extent and nature of his property holdings in various forms, the life he has led, the details of his sexual dalliances, if any, in order to draft a will which will achieve what the client wants. Don't misunderstand me. This kind of layman breeds expensive litigation from which lawyers earn substantial fees; but litigation of limited social value which should be substantially reduced or entirely avoided. In the law-society liberal arts project no student should be conditioned to solve his own legal problems; rather he should be trained to recognize the complexity of the problems and his own inadequacy to solve them without the proper professional guidance.

Instead, the emphasis in the law-society liberal arts project ought to be upon the relationship between the citizen and the legal system. In a democratic society that citizen is the basic unit of the society, or ought to be, if we adopt an intelligent approach which enables us to enfranchise the disadvantaged segments of our society. The objective of his education ought to be to make him a good citizen of that society. The constitution of the Soviet Union flatly states that among its objectives is to encourage citizens not only to obey the law, but to assume responsibility for the development of socialist society.[39] Now I am not suggesting that we adopt the Marxist lingo, nor that we try to solve, here, today, whether one is obligated to be a Good Samaritan.[40]

To be successful the teacher conducting the law-society liberal arts project must be qualified beyond present levels. I don't mean to imply that only a fully-trained lawyer can do the teaching, but I clearly do mean that a smattering of undergraduate political science courses is not enough. Here I would insist that the teacher have had substantial exposure to the operation of the legal system and the terminology of lawyers.

I recommend a course in Legal Process by two Harvard law professors which is still on an experimental basis.[41] These materials emphasize law as a process and show the interaction of our legal institutions through a set of problems presented for solution. Some mastery of technical language and judicial procedure is essential for understanding the materials and solving the problems.

Jargon brings us back to the problems of communication. Words are of special concern to the lawyer because they are his only tools. The liberal arts law-society project should consider the special way in which the lawyer employs words. Words are used in statutes or contracts to guide conduct. The recipient of the direction must interpret that guidance in the light of his situation. Others concerned may question the propriety of that interpretation. The social purposes of the statute, or contract, or rule of law, must be brought to bear in deciding this difference of interpretation. The lawyer's use of words is geared to solving his client's problems, to persuade the court toward that solution; he builds upon the post of the social structure by using words as bottles from which to pour old solutions and to replace them with new content. Lawyering then is the art of using words for social engineering. The law-society project must recognize this essence of the lawyer's craft.

One other suggestion for materials is the two-volume set edited by Ephraim London on *Law in Literature* and *Law as Literature*.[42] A teacher of the language arts could use these volumes and their ideas and themes in give-and-take which would be beneficial and fun for both teacher and the students in wrestling with the role of law in the "eternal" problems with which we have really not made much progress in two thousand years.

(2) A FRESH START IN CANADA

RICHARD D. ABBOTT*

It is made quite apparent to you that I am a rather youthful member of a youthful university in a rather youthful country, namely Canada. And Canada has been pointed out so often as the inheritor from both the United States and the British systems. Our legal education had the misfortune of inheriting the *worst* characteristics of both systems; that is, the worst for the *law student.* I want to say something about the framework of legal education as such because this will put the sort of courses that we are talking about now in their perspective in Canada.

The history of legal education in Canada until very recently was a professional—a very, very professional—history. We had followed the British system of taking a person in immediately after the level of high school and putting him in as an articled student to a barrister, and eventually, after six years of work, he would become a barrister and solicitor.

Recently—and I would say that by recently I mean within the last 20 years—we finally adopted something from the Americans in the sense that we expected people to attend a law school and take a law school degree before entering the articling period. And this, of course, was supplemented by a previous period—between two and three years—in some other college work, usually liberal arts.

Now, what occurred was that it was felt that this previous time in a liberal arts course was all that was needed by way of a brush with the social sciences for the lawyer. Once he entered law school, he settled in for a very rigid technical training—and I emphasize *training,* not education. When he came out he was ready for his one or two years of articling and then he was a lawyer. And so far our law schools regrettably continue this tradition of being technical schools without any real regard for the greatness, the great subjects of the law. In fact, it is only within the last ten years that jurisprudence itself has been allowed into the law school curriculum. International law, for example, is only now beginning to get in by the back door methods.

This means that as legal education stands in Canada at present, there is no great thinking being done about the legal system. I would hope that the

* Professor of Public Law, Carleton University, Ottawa, Canada.

undergraduate course in law in the social sciences, as part of a social science program, might meet some of this deficiency. It is the product of the deficiency of our present legal education system.

Before I leave this problem of the role of social science education in the training of lawyers in Canada, I would like to justify it to some extent. It is well to realize that in your system the judges, in their decision-making, rely on a much wider range of data than anything that our judges rely on. Remember that we follow the British custom of not looking to legislative history. Remember that we do not allow in a wide range of material on the social framework within which a particular law must be applied. We don't have an effective Bill of Rights. This great wedge allowing in a wide range of material is denied us. Our lawyers and our judges are expected to apply a strict legalism. Therefore, the role of social science materials in our system is very limited, and I would like to defend our legal education system on that basis. It is not much of a defense, I admit. I might say that the whole thing may be summarized that there cannot be Brandeis briefs in our courts; the vain attempts that have ever been made to put these in have failed miserably.

Having seen the role of social science in legal training, I turn to the other side: What about law outside the law schools? Here the history in Canada is almost nil. There was an attempt by the University of Toronto, which is the largest and, I think, the best of our universities, to have law taught as part of the arts curriculum. This was by necessity, because it could not teach a regular LL.B. program which would be recognized by the Law Society of the Province. In other words, it was using this as a back door method of getting around the strict professionalism of our legal education system. And their B.A. in jurisprudence continued until the mid 30's or so, when it was transformed into a regular LL.B. program. Since that time I don't think that there has been any teaching of law to speak of outside the law schools.

Then Carleton came along—and I emphasize that what I say about my own University, Carleton's experience, is unique to Carleton. We are trying something which is not being done elsewhere. I have since learned that Sir George Williams University (Montreal) is now offering in its Faculty of Arts a course in the Elements of Law. Furthermore, Victoria University (Victoria, B. C.) will soon be offering public law courses in connection with its School of Public Administration. Do not take what I say as being typical of Canadian schools. This is not so. It is unique. Now, Carleton was established very recently—1942—in response to the needs of returning veterans. It is oriented toward adult education; it is oriented secondly toward the training—I beg your pardon; now I want to use "education"—toward the *education* of civil servants. We are located in the capital city, Ottawa, and we felt it was one of our major roles to educate civil servants. A large part of our work is done at night; done for the convenience of civil servants and for the adult population of our city. From the very start it was felt that law, or some rudimentary brush with the law (in an educative process; not taking part in it as a defendant) was a necessary part of adult education.

And this was accepted. I am amazed to find that although it may not be an accepted part of a liberal arts education, it was accepted from the start at Carleton. Fortunately, we had practicing lawyers in the city, in the government service and in private practice who were more than willing to take on the task of teaching an undergraduate course in law, and they took on this job and did it well.

Well, then the lawyer, the incumbent of the faculty position, was elevated to the bench; and I happened to come along at the right time and fitted in with the plans of the University. And I took on the task of teaching the undergraduate course both as an evening course and as a day course, so that its role has passed beyond simply adult education to becoming a regular part of the course of the young regular full-time student in the university.

I also took over the teaching of an administrative law course which had been taught to civil servants as a necessary part of their course in public administration. I found, furthermore, that my role in the university has included the supervision of various undergraduate and graduate theses. Here I work as an appendage of the political science department and of the economics department. Whenever a student proposes an area for his thesis which is distinctly interlaced with legal considerations, then I am called in as the thesis supervisor, and I have found this a most interesting part of my role at Carleton.

Let me say something about the present organization of my department. It is called the Department of Public Law. It is at an equivalent level with such departments as English, history, philosophy, political science. It has its own departmental autonomy. It consists of one non-teaching chairman and has two full-time teachers. Both of us who are full-time teachers are lawyers; we have been trained in the law; and we have, oddly enough, both of us, economics background. We teach a range of four courses, one of them being an undergraduate course which I will discuss further now, and three others which I think you can pretty well pass off without too much comment: a course in constitutional law, a course in administrative law, and a course in international law. Add to these our role as theses supervisors. I think that this is a significant role, and its significance becomes greater the more I see of this particular conference.

The basic undergraduate course in law at Carleton seems to meet many of the requirements as to content suggested by Dean Wasserstrom. I am amazed to find how closely his content follows the course that I have been trying to teach. And we have accepted in our department your primary objective. Perhaps it is a more limited objective than the one that you have suggested. Our objective seems to be to supplement, to be an appendage to the normal range of political science courses. We seem to detect a limited view of the political science courses; a view which will take the organization and functioning of the political system down to the point of application and no farther. And we feel, in my department, that it is a necessity to tell the student something about the next step when you have the piece of legislation, when you have the orders in council, when you have the regulation. What is the next step? How is it applied? This seems to be our role. With this in mind, I want to expose my students to the full range of implementing tools that are available in the legal system. I want to remind them that there are places other than courts that apply the law, that interpret the law. I want to tell them something about administrative tribunals; I want to tell them something about how the law is made by private decision; about how contracts make private law; about compromise and settlement. I want to tell them about arbitration; I want to show them about the role of judge-made laws in courts; and I want to tell them perhaps there are alternatives. We have alternatives in Canada such as the Motor Vehicle Accident Claims Fund in Ontario, which is largely replacing the adversary fighting out of claims arising out of traffic accidents. We have the Saskatchewan Plan, which you may or may not have heard of, which is a workmen's compensation plan applied to traffic accidents. I want to tell them about these alternatives so that they can see that when political process comes to the point of application there are wide varieties of ways of application.

The way in which this is done is strictly the lecture method. I have, of course, assigned large bodies of reading. Occasionally I bring in cases, but the feeling that I have is, of course, that the case method is not quite suited to teaching at the undergraduate level. I quite concur in what Dean Wasser-strom said—that the law school method cannot be picked up in a single piece and put into the undergraduate system. I have tried the case method, however, with amazingly good success; and I am quite pleased with the reaction of my students to it.

Other than teaching about the institutions of the legal system and their characteristics and their roles and their functions, and showing that there are alternative tools of implementation, I try to deal with one or two problem areas each year. My problem area last year was the problem of licensing tribunals, showing the role of administrative tribunals. Last year, I also dealt with the problems of sentencing in criminal law, particularly with the law of habitual criminals and habitual sexual psychopaths. I thought that this was something worth introducing them to. Furthermore, it gave me a wedge to tell them about criminal procedure, and, of course, I did so.

This year I want to deal with restrictive covenants on the alienation of land. This is an area in which I can show the system of interests in land. I can show how one particular interest, namely the restriction on the use and alienation of land, can be misused, depending on your frame of reference, and how at least in Ontario, we have, first of all, methods of controlling that interest by judicial decision, which attack restrictive covenants on the basis of vagueness. If I find a restrictive covenant which says, "The land shall not at any time in the future be sold to a person of the Jewish race," I can point to the various cases which have shown this is too vague, or it does not run with the land, so that the courts have struck this down. Or, I can also point to the succeeding pieces of legislation which have made it an across-the-board rule that you cannot impose this sort of limitation.

And, of course, this is a vehicle to introduce them to the system of land law. I will tell them something about our land registration systems, etc. I must do so to make the example worthwhile.

The other examples, I think, are ones which have been introduced to us at this conference, for instance, the example of family law. I am sure this is capable of developing into a full example area to show them the range of tools available. Workmen's compensation has been, of course, fully developed as an example in Auerbach's book.[43] I would like to do the same thing for Canadian law.

All of this implies that I am only driving at the first of Dean Wasserstrom's objectives; but I do feel that my course is an introduction to the law for those who go on to law school, and I have noted so far that a fair proportion of my students do go on to law school, and the "back talk" that I receive through third parties indicates that it has been of some assistance to them. They indicate that legal training is excessively technical in the law schools; that at no time does one sit back and look at the legal system as a whole; there is no time; the course is too tied up with the technicalities. And they do look back on my course as the time when they did sit back and look at the complete legal system. I am now looking forward to the time when a course similar to mine will be imported back into the law schools.

Nothing of what I have said implies any dealing with the substance of the law as such. I am sure this is quite apparent. I have said something of the materials that I use, and that I use mainly a lecture system. I find that I am able to stir up sufficient class discussion to draw out the difficulties of my students. I have wide assignments of reading. I am indebted to American legal materials since you have done so much in this problem of sitting back and looking at a complete area of the law, trying to see its generalities rather than its technicalities. We have no textbooks in Canada equivalent to Auerbach or to Shepherd[44] or to Berman.[45] There are no books of this sort, and someday I hope they will be developed.

(3) SOME MOTIVATIONS FOR THE BASIC COURSE

ROBERT GOOSETREE*

I am sure all of us have had the same feeling of frustration after a faculty meeting in which weighty academic problems were discussed. In the past when I happened to have been a member of the Undergraduate Council at American University, and at another time when I was a member of the Graduate Council, I used to try to relieve this frustration by going

* Professor of Law, American University.

home that night and reading Veblen's *Higher Education in America*,[46] and I suggest that this may be perhaps a little cynical salt to be added to our fare for the past few days, which has been, as the Chairman said this morning, extremely rich.

I refer to Veblen because the whole question involved in this afternoon's panel revolves around the fundamental one of the purposes of undergraduate and graduate education, and ranges all the way from Veblen's view of undergraduate education, that the only purpose of a liberal arts college is to support the graduate school, to that set forth I suppose by some of the more extreme Deweyites, that would bring the undergraduate program into the realm of professional and vocational training.

Not wanting to commit myself to any of these extreme views, I would like to suggest that what we are concerned with here in terms of graduate and undergraduate education in non-law schools, and what we are concerned with in law teaching, are not two sides of the same coin or even sides of a die, but they are the same problem: the problem of attempting to get a degree of feedback; a problem of attempting to overcome several decades of cultural lag, not only in law, but in the development of the social sciences, which has permitted the legal profession to gather unto itself in the law schools a monopoly of teaching about law; for the very real reason that was suggested in the earlier discussions: that they are training professionals. However, it occurs to me that the law school should not be training professionals only, any more than the economics department should be only training economists to go into government service or to function as predictors of price fluctuations for General Motors. In other words, what I am suggesting is that the law school has the same problem of attempting to get some feedback from the social sciences as well as from the physical sciences that the social scientists have in attempting to get some feedback from the law school and from the lawyers.

I am not clear as to the reference to the social sciences, as to what some of them are: I don't know whether we're talking about history, psychology, geography, as well as the more traditional social sciences, to the exclusion of law. I suggest that each of the disciplines which comprise the social sciences, including history, psychology, geography, *and* law have the mutual interrelationships about which Professor Ball has spoken; and I suggest we are creating a false dichotomy in viewing law as other than a social science. It is a social science with certain professional applications, just as economics is. For this reason, I don't fully agree with Professor Roberts' division, his formulation this morning, in which I think he as a political scientist too modestly gives up much of the rich materials of law study to people who, unfortunately, may just become fixers or ambulance chasers; and gives up also to the law professor a monopoly under the rubric of professionalization. I don't think, on the other hand, that we can say that all the separate disciplines that we refer to generically as social sciences, including law, should be thrown into the same melting pot in a single discipline. I don't think that our educational institutions are capable of making an omelet. We are divided into disciplines; we're going to remain divided into disciplines, and for this reason I prefer to think of multi-disciplinary approaches rather than interdisciplinary approaches, particularly so since having had my initial teaching experience in a course for freshmen in integrated social science (under the old Harvard *Redbook* pattern) out at the University of Iowa. I learned a lot from it, but I am not so sure that the freshmen did. And I would suggest that perhaps the interdisciplinary approach is more suitable for the mature scholars than for the undergraduate, but that what we are trying to get a handle on in our discussions is a multi-disciplinary approach.

I share the feeling that has been expressed widely: it's too bad that law has been pulled out of undergraduate curricula as much as it has, and in a sense it's too bad that as much has been left in as has been left in, particularly specialized business law, which, I think, falls under the condemnation that many schools of business are trying to teach businessmen how to be their own lawyers rather than know when they need to see one.[47]

It is possible, and I am afraid in a number of instances it does happen, that international law, constitutional law, administrative law—all of the other public law areas which have remained in the undergraduate and graduate curricula apart from the law school, are conducted in such a way as to make the political scientist his own Supreme Court Justice. This is to be avoided, I believe, in the liberal arts curriculum. I think that this type of course appropriately calls for a different approach—not necessarily a different method, but a different approach, for the undergraduate social scientist, for the graduate social scientist, than the law school does. Our Chairman spoke of administrative law, and it is perhaps in this area the difference in approach, in my estimation, could be least because it is here that the law student most needs the materials of political science, economics, sociology, etc., and it is here, too, that the government student most needs some "hard" law rather than the "softer" law of the constitutional variety. He needs to know more about procedure in the administrative law field, perhaps, than he does in the general administration of justice. This is a personal opinion, nothing more.

Apart from this, though, how can the other social sciences, other than political science (for which Professor Roberts has spoken so eloquently), participate in this sharing out? And, if I may pray the indulgence of the social scientists, how can law participate in this sharing out of resources as well? I suggest we are not getting very far in considering various segments of the educational process as apart from other segments—of considering undergraduate as apart from graduate as apart from legal education—because the same problem is, really, involved at whatever level. The excellent discussion this morning of the introductory course for the liberal arts curriculum, designed to put a gentleman's knowledge (in the terms of the earlier view of the role of law in the liberal arts) back into the hands of the undergraduate, is a beginning, but it is only a beginning. Certainly, liberal arts students don't die; some of them become housewives; some of them become lawyers.

The next question, to me, is: For those who don't become lawyers but who go on into the other social science disciplines, is the introductory course enough to carry them through in the context of a conventionally conceived liberal arts curriculum? I think it *can* be. I am not particularly concerned about the method, although I don't think it hurts students to read either good or bad rhetoric in judicial opinions. I would say that I don't think that the pure case method is any more appropriate to an introductory undergraduate course on law in society than it is to law study; and I hope that my colleagues from the law faculties will bear me out that there is no such thing as a single method of study in the law schools. The case method is being tinkered with, toyed with, replaced, abandoned, re-instated—it's never *completely* abandoned, but you know about Yale, I am sure!

Thus in terms of liberal arts, or general education, the introductory course has a valuable function and one which is desirable. It also has an important function with regard to an initial step for the social science undergraduate majors, some of whom will go on to become graduate students. And I think it has an equally important part in the education of pre-law students. I separate the pre-law students because I am afraid I cannot fully agree with my friend, Bill Roberts, that a liberal arts education is necessarily a good pre-law education because you can waste a lot of time on some liberal arts things that are fine for liberal arts, but are excess baggage when you get them to the law school or to practice. Frequently languages are an outstanding example of that. On the other hand, a liberal arts education, with the addition of some tools which the law student may never ever have the opportunity to get again except in law school, is very helpful; and these tools, such as accounting, specifically, are things that perhaps the law schools shouldn't be doing and the undergraduate colleges should be. I am thinking ahead, you see to a more flexible curriculum of law study.

Apart from these tools and apart from the general liberal arts curriculum, however, courses on law in society—the introductory type course, courses on the sociology of law, courses in, say, institutional economics revolving around the relationships of economics and legal institutions—all furnish what, once again, the pre-law student is likely never to have the opportunity to get again in that form. This calls, of course, for some unusual people in the social sciences, and in philosophy, and even in the sciences—although most natural scientists would be horrified at the thought that a year of law school might help them—it *might*!

Finally, we come to the undergraduate who will end up in graduate study in the social sciences, out of a general liberal arts curriculum or out of a rather specialized social science major. And since it is hardly worth-while talking about graduate education apart from the Ph.D., the M.A. being simply a way-station where it exists, very frequently, especially in the social sciences, considering graduate education as a whole, this is the place, it occurs to me that the feedback can be built in; because what I am concerned with is not trying to break through the vicious circle in terms of the student, but trying to break through the vicious circle in terms of the teachers. We need to have the sociologist, the philosopher, the economist with perhaps a year of law school to furnish a tool for this teacher to relate law as a social science to his own. (Harvard is doing a great thing with their fellowship program for social scientists, for humanists, in bringing them in. It may be true for journalism that you can "learn an awful lot of bad law with one year at Harvard Law School," as Justice Frankfurter remarked about Anthony Lewis; but you can learn an awful lot in one year of law school about the fundamental subject matter which I think will help the teacher.)

From the view of the law school, this is because the compartmentalization that has grown up will pose problems for the law schools and they may be flooded with social science teachers who want to get a few rudiments; but it is a problem that I think the law schools in the long-run are obligated to take up; to face; to deal with. And it will help the law schools in the long-run for two reasons: First, because their students will come to them out of the undergraduate work not only with an introductory course in law and society, but with a partial road-map articulating their professional study with one or more other disciplines. Our failure is not so much within our own disciplines as it is a failure to provide the avenue for articulation with others, law being only one of them, since this is the general orientation of the conference. As someone pointed out in the earlier discussion, you can say the same thing about politics and economics, sociology and economics, and so on around the circle.

I suggest, too, that the Yale experiment should not be entirely washed out as fruitless by the law faculties, and this ties in with what the Chairman had to say about administrative law. It's true, not only about administrative law, but in the upper class levels of law schools of a great many other areas of subject matter. The lawyer needs to go back, not at the same level of undergraduate studies in the social sciences, but at a level in which he can make use of his legal study: specialized courses or seminars in which the law student deals with social problems, not with law problems, but social problems involving law as a social science along with others. These are the sorts of things that I have in mind. And frequently the law curriculum is too jammed with things that might have been done earlier (such as legal accounting for a student without undergraduate accounting) for this type of broadening to take place. I agree with Professor Barkman that this is not the sort of thing that the continuing legal education effort should deal with. Here is where the practitioner has the bread-and-butter advances made available to him in his professional area. I emphasize this because I feel that this is not the function of graduate study in law, but the articulation of law with other social sciences is.

To get to the "second loop" in the spiral—this interrelationship between other social sciences and law—I think the law schools need to pay more attention to the qualifications of legal teachers. And—I am sure that my colleagues in the Law School will start throwing things at me this time!—

I am going to suggest that one of the things that would bear consideration by law faculties is the abolition of the S.J.D. degree as a graduate degree in law; and a deliberate attempt on the part of legal scholars to tie themselves back into the matrix of the other social sciences, the substitution of a Ph.D. (*Juris*) in which law will be an element, but one or more of the other social sciences will be involved. It seems to me that this approach will facilitate bringing back in, at the top level, at the culmination of the law student's career, an appreciation of the things that he may once have known as an undergraduate but has forgotten.

I think the same approach is valid if taken in the other direction: the doctorate in the social sciences. I'm not advocating a field in law as a requisite for every one of the doctorates in social science. But I think it is the obligation of the law faculties and members of other social science faculties who are competent in law, to take a look at the fields that are available to their graduate students with a view to building in fields to relate law with their subject matter. For example in sociology, sociology of law which I think views the subject in one direction, or legal influences on institutions which views the subject from another direction. Of course, having raised all these problems I can shirk the remainder of my responsibility by saying I have no answers other than a few suggestions. But I would submit that we are all dealing with the same problem, and that it needs to be attacked at all fronts simultaneously—the undergraduate, graduate and legal level—in a cooperative effort for which I think this conference is a wonderful beginning.

(4) THE NEED OF ADAPTABILITY

HARRY V. BALL*

I would like just to make three brief points, and then really to get to the teachers in small women's colleges who have no lawyer to teach their courses, etc., to get to talk about their problem tonight, not tomorrow or next week.

The first point is that it's very obvious when one talks about developing this area that there are two extremes—one is to develop a specialized kind of program in which obviously, if you start thinking in terms of kinds of materials that are available today, I think as Mr. Abbott discovered, there is really not much difference between what Mr. Abbott would say he is doing at Carleton and what Mr. Wasserstrom was saying he thought ought to be done as a matter of fact. If you took Wasserstrom's outline and then started looking for the kinds of materials that exist today, you would find that the teacher would be doing pretty much the kind of thing

* Director, Program in Sociology and Law, University of Wisconsin (sociology).

that Mr. Abbott is doing. This is basically it. Now my bias would be, of course, to add a little bit more social science material into what Mr. Abbott is doing.

The other thing is that there is not much point in producing outlines that you are going to give the people to teach, like a third grade teaching outline where you fill out the assignment the night before, etc. Some people teach well one way; other people teach well another way, and in any area, if you've got a good teacher, this person has to develop a format, a method of presentation, that is quite compatible with his work. Ideally, I think in terms of what Professor Roberts was saying and in terms of what Mr. Duff said earlier, that a double-barreled approach needs to be made. That is, obviously in any good school, even in a poor school, the percentage of really top-rate motivated students is not much different as a matter of fact. It may be if you reach the really top. I've never been to those schools, but there may be some.

Now this means that on the whole we've got to develop both kinds of courses. The kind of course you can present to large numbers of undergraduates and the kind of seminar proceeding that Professor Roberts was describing that gives these students something which is much richer, much more intense, but which, obviously as we know, is not going to be the course for every student in the school. My own opinion, as a matter of fact, of so-called honors programs is that you can cut them down a lot lower than most people think you can. That is, you can give a very rich educational experience to students with grade point averages quite a bit lower than where the average school seems to think an honors program can be given, but that's my own particular bias. And I think this kind of experience, this kind of work, in the modern world, is ideally suited for the rich independent study programs, etc., for you've got really good students in small seminars. It is also good for the broader, across the board, general offerings of students.

Secondly, the larger the school, the more specialized, the greater its facilities, its resources, etc. Obviously, you can begin to talk in terms of things like majors, minors. I am actually more interested in terms of the impact on social science and the social sciences, seeing law introduced into all of the liberal arts courses. I really want to see a much greater attention paid to law-government in all American history courses, in history courses generally, in all sociology courses. It is incomprehensible to me how almost any undergraduate sociology course is taught today without considerable attention to law as a variable, just as a variable, if nothing else. I don't care whether it's the courses in the family that tend to be our big money-makers and where law gets ignored totally. Family books have two chapters on law, one where they talk about "You Get Married," and that's some kind of a contract, and there's a small chapter on divorce, which usually has a chart taken out of the Oceana little books on different grounds between the different states. And that concludes the discussion of law as it affects the family. And this is a really tragic oversight. The American social sciences are not going to get going again in terms of any kind of major synthetic integrated work until they rediscover law and they rediscover religion. These are the two major institutions that have been ignored, so I don't deny that in a major large school, you probably can have highly specialized programs, but I am really more concerned with the broad impact, and this means I am particularly concerned with the kind of schools that aren't going to be able to have highly specialized faculty members around to teach these things. We are going to have to rely on training the faculty.

Now, my third point. This is where the Law and Society Association[48] in my great dream comes in, you see, because I don't always see it as providing a vehicle for communication through its bulletin in which we can exchange course outlines, in which we get people commissioned to write articles which deal with specific areas to provide information people need. I am talking about both sides of the fence, that is, specific reviews of social science literature, trying to draw them together in some kind of a meaningful fashion that brings them to bear on major law problems. And conversely, you get specially commissioned articles, etc., written by law people, especially the broadly trained law person, the law-liberal arts person, that begin to make it possible for the people who are going to teach these courses to have some kind of comprehension.

4. Commentary

RACKMAN*—The aim of the one course we give in law on the undergraduate level is to help the student appreciate how unintelligible the judicial process is without reference to philosophy (logic, metaphysics and ethics) and the social sciences (history, economics, political science, sociology, psychology and anthropology.) At the same time the student is made aware of the fact that law is not only the effect of all these disciplines but also a cause conditioning them and an instrument directing their course and movement.

Most of our undergraduate students have some knowledge of Biblical and Talmudic law. Therefore, we deal during the first semester with such specific concepts as the legal personality of corporations—involving history, economics, and logic; contract and tort—involving in addition ethics and psychology; crime—with sociology and anthropology coming into the picture; the state—with political science and political theory receiving another look; legal procedure—with an eye even on statistics. Every concept is examined from the point of view of Stone's threefold classification—law and logic, law and society, and law and justice. During the second semester we attempt a

---

* Professor Emanuel Rackman, Assistant to the President, Yeshiva College (political science).

recapitulation in more formal fashion of most theories of law ranging from the classical to the most radically functional, and discuss in some detail the use of logic in legal analysis, and the roles of the social scientist and the philosopher of values in decision-making by judges and in the process of legislation.

I have not yet found a suitable text but my design for teaching the course was influenced by Morris Raphael Cohen whose experimental edition of readings was published about thirty-five years ago. I refer my students to several text books on jurisprudence and many illustrative cases. It is always my hope that they will glean from the course a better understanding of the relatedness of most learning to the law and the indispensability of law for social existence and improvement.

DOWD*—I am a little confused as to our areas of agreement and disagreement. I assume that we all agree that it would be valuable to conduct inquiries at the graduate level into the relation of law and other social science disciplines. Also, I assume we all agree that perhaps law students should be made more aware of the relation of the other disciplines to law, but, I had assumed that the main problem of this conference was the role of law in the undergraduate liberal arts curriculum.

From the discussion it would seem that at least three distinct approaches to law in the undergraduate liberal arts curriculum in law could be taken. In the undergraduate curriculum one could attempt to describe the nature of the legal process and the particular characteristics of various legal systems. The readings suggested by Dean Wasserstrom would, I think, admirably achieve this purpose. The possible difficulty with this approach is, however, that the student would get merely an antipasto of legal systems and not develop a disciplined approach to the subject.

This suggests a second role, such as I thought Professor Roberts was advocating. That is, the development of disciplined jurisprudential concepts out of the major Western European legal traditions. Such an approach would treat law in its philosophical aspects. This would have the advantage perhaps of being a more disciplined study, but it would necessarily be less comprehensive than the approach used by Dr. Wasserstrom.

The third approach that has been suggested is essentially the "Law for the Layman" approach, or "What To Do Until The Lawyer Comes", a description of what are one's rights in tort or contract or criminal law. I think this approach is unfortunate both from the point of view of the college and from the point of view of the law school. The college is no place in which to suggest legal advice.

As to the role of the social sciences in the law school, I think on the whole we should rely on the undergraduate training in the social sciences rather than attempting to cover practical social science problems in law school. The pressure on the law school to keep abreast of the time and teach courses in water law or SEC law or air law, I think is unfortunate. What we try to do in the law school is to give an approach to law, a method

* Professor Donald W. Dowd, Villanova University (law).

of solving problems. On the informational side, I think all of us tend to forget that our liberal arts graduates and our law graduates do not die when they get out of school. Hopefully they are able to read and hopefully they continue to acquire information.

Finally, I would like to say that within the undergraduate liberal arts or social science curriculum it seems that when law is an element of a problem, that the legal determination should be taken into consideration. I do not suppose that our social scientists or political scientists shy away whenever they see something "legal" in a problem.

ROSENBLUM—I am in very strong agreement with what has been said so far, although I fail to see the alleged irrelevancy between what Dean Wasserstrom and Professor Abbott have been talking about and what Professor Roberts has been talking about in the liberal arts. I think that they are points that have been pertinent to the study of the liberal arts.

CHAPTER IV
OTHER UNDERGRADUATE COURSES
IN LAW-SOCIETY

May law be introduced to liberal arts undergraduates by means other than, or in addition to, a basic course? Family problems, history, anthropology, political science, social ethics and sociology, six courses suggested as possibly adaptable to learning about law, are grouped in this chapter.[1] Another, more experimental, possibility—a proposed course in Law and Poverty—is considered in Chapter V.

1. Family Problems

The papers on Family Problems as a possible course for giving basic elements of law to undergraduates were presented by Professors David Granfield, O.S.B., and Richard Arens of the Catholic University Law School. As in the other courses proposed, it is seen that the element of values looms large.

GRANFIELD—My function on this panel, as I understand it, is to examine the feasibility of using family law problems as a vehicle to help undergraduates learn something about the law in general, its structure and function, and only incidentally about the specific laws governing marriage and the family. Is the area of Domestic Relations a good introduction to law? Aristotle said that man is naturally a social and political animal but that he is by nature even more a conjugal animal. Since we are teaching "conjugal animals" in undergraduate school, a course closer to their own experience than, for example, trusts or negotiable instruments, might enable them to grasp the larger issues involved, to appreciate the basic problems of law and jurisprudence.

Family law has a special pedagogical advantage as an introductory vehicle for it covers a great number of areas dealt with more completely in other courses in law school. If you teach family law, you teach some torts, some contracts, some equity, some property, some taxation, and even some criminal law. The family has many more problems than simply marriage and divorce. In fact, in order to understand the family's legal problems and to propose sound legal measures, one must grasp many areas of non-legal thought. Fowler Harper of Yale was one of the pioneers in this approach. His casebook on the family included almost equal amounts of legal and non-legal materials, primarily psychological, sociological, and anthropological writings. Certainly religion, both as a creed and as a code, has great influence in the life of the family and even on its legal structure. It is operative in the formation of sound family law. Economics, too, is important. Jacques LeClercq made an interesting observation in his book *Du droit naturel à la sociologie*[2] about the relationship between the legal and moral life of the family and its economic status. He said: "One aspect of the question of living in slums, for instance, is that when a whole family sleeps in one room, both girls and boys at times share the same bed, and in rural conditions, cattle spend the night with men in the only room in the house, so cases of incest and bestiality are multiplied, along with the decrease of moral responsibility which is all the more evident because under these conditions, the development of the personality is equally attenuated. For these moral deviations to disappear, all that is required is to improve living conditions. Preaching, on the contrary, has no effect." This mention of the sordid side of family life reminds us that students must be made aware of the fact that human problems cannot always be solved by legislating grand norms of conduct, though they be in perfect harmony with the natural law or some preconceived ideal, and antiseptically integrated into a well-ordered society. Too many legal thinkers and moralists deal with man as a rational being, but as one who is both well-fed and well-housed. Michael Harrington's *The Other America*[3] or Oscar Lewis's *Five Families*[4] and *The Children of Sanchez*,[5] would shockingly but fascinatingly convince the student that poverty is the rule rather than the exception and that family law ought to deal with families as they are.

Law can be called a process of authoritative decision. In other words, it can be viewed as a continuous endeavor to implement the changing needs of society in order to achieve its basic goals. For the student to perceive the function of law it is necessary for him to see how it operates as a distribution of values. Those possessing political power decide about the values that others shall have or shall not have. Thus the law grants or takes away marital rights, custody, support, compensation, authority, etc. Sound law tries to adjust the distribution of values to the exigencies of the situation and the maximization of human values. If the undergraduate learns to view law not as a body of rules, inflexible and sacrosanct, but as a process of approximation in the distribution of values in the achieving of the common good, they will have discovered with a surge of hope the mechanics of making a better world.

There are certain questions that the student must ask himself if he is to move from the specific domestic relations problems to their jurisprudential implications. These are questions which must necessarily be resolved in determining the nature and extent of state intervention with the family. Here are some typical questions. I will quote from the Introduction to *The Family and the Law: Problems for Decision in the Family Law Process,* by Goldstein and Katz.[6] They believe that these questions must necessarily be faced before the more technical, procedural, or strictly legal questions. They are:

1. Considering law and family as processes of social control, what goals should man seek to achieve through law and family in a democratic society? What are the functions of the family and the law?
2. Who, under what circumstances and by what procedures, are to be designated members of what family or families?
3. What consequences, and for what purposes, should be officially authorized to follow a determination of membership in a family?
4. Why, how, and under what circumstances, should and can the state intervene to establish, administer, or reorganize a family?
   (a) To what extent should and can the law create, nourish, or destroy, biological, economic, psychological, geographical, ethical, and historical family ties?
   (b) To what extent can a family relationship be dissolved or destroyed other than possibly by the death of all the members of a family?
5. What alternatives to family could better fulfill some or all of the functions assigned by the state to the family?
6. Who, under what circumstances and at what point in the family law process, should have the official responsibility for formulating questions similar to the foregoing and giving answers to them?

In a pluralistic society such as ours, we have many different and sometimes conflicting principles and value judgments at work. Domestic Relations forms the arena where, in an ecumenical spirit, many of the most personal problems must be worked out. There can be great difference here about the goals and the means to achieve them, about the consequences of law and legal decisions. All the more valuable, therefore, as a laboratory of legal thought and operation, of jurisprudence, is this field of law, so richly human and so politically indispensable.

ARENS*—May I start out with a confession of ignorance. I am not a specialist in family law. I am intrigued by some of the problems that the field of family relations poses and by the inadequacy of many of our legal answers. Very obviously, as Father Granfield has pointed out, it is a field covering many of the legal disciplines, and drawing inevitably upon what little we know of human behavior, to aid us in the solution to the problems that beset us. We note the chaotic state of present family development under the law as it exists at present. Father Granfield has noted the problem of couples who stay together solely because of lack of economic resources to support alternative arrangements. We must note other difficulties as

---

* Professor Richard Arens, Catholic University Law School.

well. Perhaps the most glaring and melodramatic is the phenomenon of fraud, perjury, and connivance in matrimonial actions, so aptly portrayed by Walter Gellhorn's work.[7]

Father Granfield has said that I would address myself to a clarification of a value-oriented approach to the subject matter. I proceed with diffident steps in a field with which I have not worked.

I begin by a statement of my own policy preference, which may or may not be shared. I assume that most of us will voice a preference for the creation and maintenance of healthy rather than diseased family units providing an opportunity for the adequate development of the potential of the individual personalities involved. I voice a further preference for the immunity of the family from unreasonable interference by the state. I object to state action which overrides parental religious belief, e.g., requiring school children to salute the flag, or compels people of all ages to submit to extraordinary medical procedures *sans* due process. It is obvious that men seek values through institutions and resources. A rough check list would include power, wealth, well-being, skill, enlightenment, respect, affection, and rectitude. These values are set forth simply with a view to facilitating analysis of the social process. Instead of studying the *existing law* of family relations in the abstract we could, under such a scheme, address ourselves to the consequences of its administration in the context of economics, political science, philosophy, public health, etc. The basic view strikes me as one which must of necessity be multidimensional, and which cannot conveniently or rationally be packaged into one single undergraduate course. It strikes me as ideally a subject for dispersion over a wide field of discipline, in which the vagaries of the family relationship are taken up in appropriate contexts.

Mr. Cahn spoke of the desirability of sending people out into the field to view reality, and to receive academic credit for the experience. I believe that the subject matter of the administration of the law governing family relations lends itself to precisely this kind of similar approach. Basic questions raised by the students in this field of reality may include the following: Which of our existing rules, by which I mean to include both substantive law and procedural practice, tends to foster and which tends to inhibit the maintenance of healthy family ties? How adequate are present legal methods for resolving difficulties which arise within the marital relationship? One thinks instinctively of the preoccupation with fault in divorce proceedings and the use of the adversary method in the disposal of the question of child custody as approaches calling for field study on many levels. These approaches have been criticized as inadequate for the determination of what is basically a problem of personality compatibility in divorce, and of child welfare in cases involving child custody. This is something that any interested undergraduate is capable of observing at first hand insofar as court proceedings of this kind are open to the public, and many of them definitely are. How adequate, one may go on, are present legal methods for dealing with the so-called delinquent child?

Inevitably in any systematic canvassing of family relations in terms of a multidimensional inquiry, we are bound to stumble upon the handling of the so-called delinquent child by the Juvenile Court, and while the problem of firsthand observation of this particular stage may be a more serious one than in some of the other areas, it is one that can be overcome with the cooperation of Juvenile Court officials who have in the past indicated willingness to engage in collaborative work with interested scholars supervising properly motivated undergraduates. This approach to family relations seems to be replete with opportunity for systematic inquiry in the context of field work which poses, perhaps, the most fascinating challenge to a value-oriented undergraduate curriculum.

MASSEL—May I ask, how far it is possible to go, and how desirable is it to send undergraduate students out on their own to investigate family situations along the lines that have been suggested several times this afternoon, on the theory that they by looking at these family situations by themselves may on the one hand be of some help, and on the other hand, may obtain a fundamental understanding of this whole range of problems?

ARENS—I side with Dr. Hutchins, formerly the Chancellor of the University of Chicago, and credit the undergraduates with considerably greater capacity for advanced intellectual work than they have been credited with traditionally. There are certain instances in which undergraduates certainly ought not inflict themselves upon a painful family scene, and there are obvious cases in which they will be excluded by the courts. Still and all, open court proceedings strike me as singularly useful as laboratories for informed and properly motivated observance.

MASSEL—Are you suggesting then observation of judicial and other proceedings rather than going as far as Mrs. Hostetler has suggested earlier?[8]

ARENS—Since I am a lawyer, I will restrict myself to suggesting observation of judicial and other official proceedings. I cannot vouch for the effectiveness of the observational procedure. I have seen students perform with singular effectiveness in assisting lawyers in a whole range of traditional proceedings, including the defense of the so-called juvenile delinquent.

MASSEL—Has anyone actually experimented with the ideas of sending undergraduate students out into the field to work with families in the kind of problems one ordinarily associates with social workers?

ARENS—I believe many of our legal aid agencies, many of our law school programs designed to aid the indigent, have utilized students. Such law students are, after all, only a year or two removed from undergraduate school.

SPARK*—This is the kind of thing you easily get enticed into when you start by being a little too soft and talk about the kind of subjects that would appeal to anyone's tender side. I had hoped we wouldn't get detoured that way, and opposed the plan to incorporate "Law and Poverty" into the program. I'd rather see "Law and Big Business," or something like that, discussed. Knock that, if you wish, and see where it takes you in the area which is, and should be, properly "law," instead of feeling mushy and getting lost in something which I think is way off base.

SISTER LEONORE**—In regard to Mr. Massel's inquiry I might point out that the social work recruitment program in New York has brought students from the college and junior college level to work with social case workers in summer programs. Some of this work does relate to questions where legal problems in the family would be concerned, but not necessarily so. The program is related to students who might be interested in the sociology and social work area, but not yet interested in it as a profession. It raises the question that there is something else in society other than their academic disciplines, and permits them to see it in actuality.

MASSEL—Does this mean that the student goes into the field with a social worker, or goes into the field alone?

SISTER LEONORE—The student goes into the field with a social worker, and under the direct supervision of the social worker. And where the case might be related to law then the legal aid societies are also brought into it.

MASSEL—Isn't this the type of problem that the sociologists have been facing for some time, Professor Selznick? The question of how far one can go in sending students out into the field for observation?

SELZNICK—In recent years, in my experience, there has been somewhat less of that, and a somewhat greater emphasis placed on the intellectual content of the discipline, with the observation side being somewhat more formalized in relation to some organized research project. There is a fair amount of that going on.

But this business of just going out and participating and observing seems to me to be something we are going to come back to. I don't know how many of my colleagues will agree with me in that. But I do sense a certain lack of the sense of reality on the part of many undergraduate students— and the teachers for that matter. But I think that Mr. Cahn made a very good point when he emphasized that we needed not only to send them out into the field, but also to have an opportunity for reflection. I think if you just send them out without adequate guidance, the most the formalized opportunity and requirement would be is to come back and analyze what has gone on. I don't think there's much to be gained from that sort of thing.

---

* Professor Eli Spark, Catholic University Law School.
** Sister Marie Leonore, College of Mount St. Vincent (social science).

I am a little worried about the suggestion of sitting in on formal proceedings. I think other experiences are probably more rewarding because they permit more access to the materials, closer contact with the people involved, talking to them, and so on. We have at various times had people observing judicial proceedings more or less from afar, or just sitting as spectators. I don't think this has been too useful except in some rather clearly defined situations. We had some rather interesting material develop in connection with the mass trials of some civil rights demonstrators in San Francisco. But that was a very unusual situation, for we knew what the problem was, or what some of the problems were. We knew that the judges in the Municipal Court were under very severe tension, and that they were handling cases in unusual ways, and that they were handling unusual cases, and we were wondering about their responses. But the observation of the routine case—unless you can also have the opportunity to ask questions as to what is going on and why certain decisions were made, and so on—wouldn't help too much. But it might be very interesting, very useful to the student, to be able to interrogate an attorney. To try to get from him the basis of his decisions on *voir dire,* that is, to ask why he excused one juror rather than another, and so on. But if you can't do that much, then you are just guessing.

SPARK—I thought our concern was about bringing legal insights and understanding of the legal system down to the college level. Now this departure about doing experimental work and observing things in operation is fine; but if you are going to observe so as to learn something about the legal environment in which something is happening, shouldn't you learn something about that legal environment first, so you can figure out what is happening when you are in the observation box?

For instance, seeing the judicial performance that involves family law is seeing a play acted out according to formulas and procedures that should first be learned about and evaluated, if we are really to understand the social worker or sociological aspect of it. In every area of learning, quite obviously, it would be nice to have laboratory work to verify facts, or to make us conscious of the vitality and significance of facts and the fallibility of observations.

ARENS—May I make this comment: There are certain features characteristic of family law which are both complex and difficult to put across in any but the most concentrated way in a law school setting. I refer to the law governing divorce by virtue of a series of specific causes, or defenses to divorce such as recrimination, condonation and the like. I do not believe that an undergraduate would benefit from hearing a recitation of these esoteric legal theories, without attempting to view some of their judicial applications in the actual courtroom. I do not believe that such exposure would have to be prolonged. It should be preceded by the proper establishment of theoretical constructs. Appropriate discussion with a properly informed instructor should be afforded at a later stage.

MCDONALD*—I am interested in your laboratory approach to a family court problem—for example, an interrelationship of the various disciplines as they bear upon the problem. Let me give you a short capsule sketch of what happens in the juvenile courts in New York. There is a new law that has only been in force about three years. A petition comes in, brought by the principal of a school, by a parent, by a priest, a minister, or sometimes by a teacher. As a result, a child is brought in and, as the law provides, accompanied by a parent. First, the child goes to an interviewer. This interviewer may or may not be well trained and may be a permanent employee or a volunteer. After the interviewer ascertains certain basic facts, such as the cause of the petition, it may be assigned to a social worker who goes about investigating. At that point, some very interesting points may develop. For example, a psychiatric exam may be asked for and, as you know, under the law of New York if a child has an IQ under 70 he is almost always classed as defective. Regardless of the environment, regardless of education, regardless of reading ability or anything, he may be classified as a defective, sent to a mental institution, and if he is so unfortunate as to have no one vitally interested in him, he may remain in the mental institution almost indefinitely.

In most cases after the investigation if the child is out on probation the report is in the form of a probation report, otherwise as a report of the social worker. Then the case comes on for a finding before a judge. At that time the child is assigned a legal guardian who is usually a member of the Legal Aid Society. The legal aid assigned has about one hour from 9 to 10 in the morning before court opens, to interview all of these children and their parents, and the case load is heavy. The legal guardian is not given the file of the social worker nor can he see the probation report. When a case is before the judge for a finding, even the judge cannot see these reports until he makes a finding. Further, when the children are in a court in which the judge is making findings, there is usually a single legal guardian, and as it turns out in practice very few of the children have their own outside lawyers. For example, there may be assigned to a legal guardian and the judge on a particular day as many as 70 cases.

What kind of a laboratory experiment are you going to have sending out somebody to observe that?

Now you go to the next part after the finding, where the case is up for disposition. At that time the judge has the probation or the social worker's report. And the police prosecutor, as he is called, also has these reports. But the legal guardian does not. He is never allowed to see them but he has to defend his client. This is difficult because he cannot see the file, because of the case loads and because of the procedures. As you know, in the Juvenile Court in New York there is a big question whether the constitutional protections do or do not apply to the child. The so-called integration of the disciplines—social workers, the probation officer (if you call that a discipline), legal guardians and the court—instead of working together

* Robert J. McDonald, member, New York bar.

function apart. Thus, a legal guardian in a New York court almost never confers in advance of a case with the probation officer or the social worker and, instead of pulling together, if the legal guardian succeeds in having a judge make a disposition of the case contrary to the recommendations of the probation officer or the police attorney, the police attorney considers that he has been beaten or defeated. I don't think that while this atmosphere prevails, sending people out into the field to obtain a comprehensive view or an interdisciplinary view of this problem is currently possible.

2. History

The proposal that history courses might be used as a vehicle for teaching law to liberal arts undergraduates was made by a history professor, Rev. Cornelius P. Forster, O.P., of Providence College. His support came, somewhat unexpectedly, from a sociologist, Professor Harry V. Ball of Wisconsin. It is not exact to say that Professor Ball isolates history courses as peculiarly suited to this function, but his remarks add weight to Father Forster's suggestion, by stressing the interrelation between law and history—and sociology, he would add.

FORSTER—I'm sure that most of the deans present will agree that on the undergraduate level we are pretty well bursting at the seams. If you put in another program, or another course, then something must come out. We just can't keep multiplying or adding courses to our general program. I'd like to consider a new approach to the teaching of history on the undergraduate level with a view toward preparing the student for a greater awareness of this problem of Law-Society.

Basically I'm not concerned with the man who is going into law school. The undergraduate program I envision would be for people who are non-law bound. They are looking for a general education and are not specifically looking to law school or graduate school but just for a general liberal arts program. One way that this might be done is by changing somewhat the emphasis in the undergraduate history program. For example, take three great problems that we have in modern European-American History: In the 18th century, take the first break-up of the great British empire, or the American Revolution, depending on how you look at it. Now understanding that particular problem essentially has its roots in a knowledge of the law of the constitutional development. And in teaching a course in which that would be involved, would it not be possible to emphasize in the presentation the legal and the constitutional aspects of that particular crisis? We would also attend to the economic, social and political considerations. But someone who is considering a minor in Law-Society could specially emphasize in that particular course the implications of the legal and the constitutional difficulties.

I think the same technique could also be used in regard to a great crisis of the 19th century, the American Civil War. Analyzing the Civil War roots from the standpoint of a legal and constitutional background, the doubt or the dispute over the nature of the union, the constitutional rights of the sovereign states as compared with the rights and the powers of the federal union. Or in the 20th century, on the question of civil rights, again I think we can teach a course which would give the historical background but which would emphasize particularly the legal and constitutional implications. I think this might be done also in medieval history. For example, the Fall of the Roman Empire, the great contest between the Papacy and the Holy Roman Empire, the background of the Magna Carta, the first Hundred Years' War, the second Hundred Years' War. I think Dr. Arlt has pointed out that in time of crisis we do get legislation which never would have been passed if that crisis had not arisen. I think the whole cabinet system in England must be understood in terms of the coming of the second Hundred Years' War. A presentation of this type might be able to emphasize or orient legal and constitutional development for an undergraduate in such a way that he would have a better appreciation of law, and law and society.

We have a senior year colloquium at Providence College which involves only the top students. It meets once a week for two to three hours and is run along the lines of the Great Books. Each student is required to prepare a paper involving some substantial research to be read at the colloquium. Now in addition to the director of the colloquium, they bring in some outside authority. It may be a visiting scholar in town or someone from Brown University or a legal figure or someone else who has a particular interest and competence in an area. I think that a colloquium of that type in the senior year might be envisioned with a special orientation toward law, toward constitutional development, and toward giving a student, let us say a major in political science with a minor in law-society, or a major in history with a minor in law-society. I think in either one of those cases the student could still maintain the general traditional liberal arts background, but this special emphasis would also give him a peculiar awareness of the development of the legal system, so that he would be better equipped, it would seem to me, to appreciate the workings of law in the modern society.

But I would not be in favor of bringing in a completely new program which would curtail the time and hours spent upon the other general liberal arts programs. I would favor a general college undergraduate program giving to the man a broad general background, and such a seminar and such a treatment of history and perhaps one or two other courses that would acquaint the individual with the workings of law at the present time.

BALL—I don't see what any of the social sciences really deal with except questions of social structure and social change, or I suppose we could call it the ethics of social order and social change, or social statics and social dynamics, and we go through the whole list of social thinkers. These are the only two problems. Almost all of it breaks into one or the other as soon as you analyze them into institutional areas and break them up and put them back together again, and today it's inconceivable to talk otherwise about any process of systematic allocation of values in our society, of the structuring of the kinds of alternatives and opportunities which constitute the major framework within which human beings make their choices, and which probably do more to determine what their choices are than anything else that could motivate them, the simple set of alternatives with which they are presented. If you study this in terms of society as it exists today, you're studying this in terms of the process of structure, you're studying it as it changes, you're studying social change. And I've never been able to figure out why history courses in universities, for example, insofar as part of the liberal arts, why the bulk of their job isn't to study exactly what you were talking about today. If history deals with the unique, it should deal with the origins of the structure, which then continue to direct, guide and channelize behavior for another period of time; and then their next concern should be, what the changes are that are induced in these structures. This should really be the basis for the unique period to which they pay particular attention, when as a matter of fact, new structures are being generated, if you are really talking about what happens to human beings in history. And so it seems to me this is almost exactly what you were saying today when you said you wanted to talk about how these men got together at this particular unique point in time with all these peculiar forces, and generated this old American constitution. What you are actually talking about is the generation of the framework which has turned out to be a peculiarly dynamic framework; it didn't necessarily have to be. There could have been other dimensions of the structure which could have been peculiarly static, which might have resulted in tons of upheavals. But what were the major changes in our constitutional structure? Really the extension of voting franchises and things like that, most of which don't occur in the typical course. Everybody ignores the fact that in U.S. history, how many children know—they are all brainwashed by Vann Woodward and his book *The Strange Career of Jim Crow*[9]—law had no effect on race relations in the United States until 1890.

And you don't have to look at any southern states very far. You can get Leon Litwack's book *North of Slavery*,[10] which describes law and the position of the Negro in the northern states prior to the Civil War, an incredible document. Study the history of Alabama prior to the Civil War. We are told about all these slaves being freed, you know, tons of slaves being freed. All the southerners were going around patting their slaves on the head and giving them freedom. Well, there were 600,000 slaves in Alabama in 1860, and 1200 of them were Negro freedmen. These were a peculiar group of Negro freedmen. They were restricted to their own county, they could not leave the county, they could not become wards of the public without being sold into slavery—that was being a freedman in Alabama in 1860. 1200 of them against 600,000 others. This was by separate Act of the legislature. You can send your students to the Acts of the Alabama Legislature. Let them read them. They can read through all the Alabama statutes from 1820 to 1860 and they will find 130 slaves were freed by name. Now this is powerful stuff, and this is the structure in which these people were operating. To free a slave—how did you free a slave? You had to apply to your county clerk; he made an investigation. If he approved the investigation, you went to county court, and the county court forwarded it to the legislature. The clerk of the legislature would then report it to the legislature of Alabama, and the Alabama legislature by name could pass an act to free a slave. It took all that to free a slave. Now that's a pretty powerful structure. You don't get this in any history books.

What can you say about social structure and social values? We talk about it all the time. Speaking as a sociologist, I can say we, as the best social scientists, know almost nothing about the relationship between social values and social structure, almost nothing. And this is an effort to take an area like race relations in the south, where this thing should be very pronounced and gross, and examine it state by state, looking at Louisiana with its French tradition, Florida with its Spanish tradition, and if we can't find variations between law, social structure and values in those communities, I don't think we are going to find it anywhere, because I don't know by what evidence we're going to claim we can ever make any statements. This stuff is all there, just waiting to be found. As I say, history to me is crucial. If there is any area that we cannot leave to the lawyers—I think we could probably leave sociology to lawyers, and I've met lawyers that I could leave economics to—that is legal history. It's crucial. Legal historians have just done a miserable job, let's face it, and historians have not done any better job on legal history. The historians are needed here almost more than anybody else to really start to get in there and do the work that's got to be done on legal history. This is a very important area and it's the most ignored of all—I don't care whether you call it history or social science or the humanities. Law history in the U.S. is our weakest area, in terms of the work that has been done up to the present time.

3. Anthropology

Anthropological teaching materials used by Dr. Michael Barkun of the Northwestern University Program in Law and the Social Sciences suggest ingredients for an anthropology-oriented course for transmitting an understanding of the legal system to liberal arts undergraduates.

BARKUN—In my dissertation,[11] I am investigating the resolution of disputes in two settings: The first is a group of African societies, primitive societies, that are characterized by segmentary lineage. Such lineage breaks the society up into very nearly equal and very nearly autonomous groups.

The second setting is the arena of international relations. This comparative study generates some questions that I think are broadly applicable to legal studies in general, three of which are: First, how do norms develop? How does a norm grow out of what has essentially been a norm-less or unstructured situation in the past? Second, how are norms perceived by persons within a society? And third, in a conflict situation in which a third party enters to mediate the dispute, what leverage does that mediator have? This is an especially pressing question in the settings I am studying simply because they lack both centralized physical sanctions.

The data is derived principally from social anthropology, on the one hand, and international relations and international law, on the other. As far as analytical tools go for examining the data and patterning it, these come principally from jurisprudence, decision-making theory, and the psychology of perception.

Both the cases of segmentary society and international relations may be considered legally marginal or legally deviant from the standpoint of American law with its tradition of centralization; yet the fundamental questions regarding norms and conflict resolution that exist in the most decentralized and unstructured situations are the same fundamental questions that crop up in the more centralized milieu of American law. And I think it is precisely the marginality of the cases with which I am dealing that makes them peculiarly applicable as entering wedges in undergraduate training. Because of the very surface irrelevance of legal technicality and legal expertise, one is forced to look to other disciplines for the insights necessary to understand these systems.

I tried, for instance, in an undergraduate course to introduce some of the elements of primitive law and social anthropology. This is a course that was mentioned earlier called "The Political Life of Mankind." Despite the cosmic and somewhat overblown title, the simple purpose of the course is to develop some kind of systematic perspective on political experience by using a wide range of cross cultural materials. And in that case, I chose a work which I happened to run across in the preparation of a dissertation, Lucy Muir's *Primitive Government*,[12] which is one of the very few works on political systems directed to the lay reader. The one difficulty in utilizing social anthropology in any kind of introductory course is the fact that the kinship and lineage terminology tends to get rather complex and often seems to erect a curtain between the student and the material. The Muir book happens to be as simple a treatment of the material as one could find.

And I think that in an undergraduate course material that has the exotic quality that much of the primitive material possesses has a certain salutary shock effect. It is so different that paradoxically, it becomes very much the same. It is so different that it enables us to return to the experience of our own system with new perspectives and we can then go back to the experience of American law with a desire to try to rip away the accretions of time and our own prejudices; to try to find some commonality between primitive experience and our own. So I think that it is possible to take exotic and bizarre data from a setting like primitive law and inject it very directly into an undergraduate course that may have as its main focus American law. Jerome Frank attempted to do this in certain sections of *Courts on Trial*.[13] The anthropological material he dealt with was material that was for the most part fairly unsystematic and represented the research of a prior generation. Nonetheless, the same vividness of expression and sharp insight Frank achieved in that book is perfectly possible in an undergraduate course without recourse to semi-professionalization or simulated legal training.

4. Political Science

The undergraduate seminar in law outlined earlier (*supra*, p. 77) by Dr. William H. Roberts of Catholic University is given in the political science department. Professor Victor G. Rosenblum of Northwestern University here discusses his experience with undergraduate law courses housed in political science.

ROSENBLUM—I have been teaching an undergraduate course on law and politics for close to 15 years, beginning at the University of California, and for the last eight years at Northwestern. The content of the course has, by no means, been the same; sometimes I can't even recognize the original structured format with syllabi planned and given out in advance with the more recent formats of the course in which I can only prepare my syllabus after the course is over. I can have some idea of where we have been; I don't have quite the certainty of where I am going when a new course begins.

We have, in short, been seeking to introduce comparative data into the course for our undergraduates, and from the standpoint of the liberal arts, we haven't been so much concerned with the particular amount of coverage in the course as with kinds of stimuli that we provide. At undergraduate level, as contrasted with the graduate level, we view our function as contributing toward the maturation of values of our undergraduates. These are the years of maturing values; these are the years in which students should be able to see not so much the differences among the disciplines as the bridges that there are from one field of knowledge, and we feel that in the area of the law there are particular contributions to be made in a bridging from one discipline to another.

So far as techniques and materials in the course go, in general I have used a multiplicity of kinds of materials, with a heavy emphasis on the case method, but perhaps for a reason which is more a product of my own value system than for any obviously verifiable reason. I think that the case method in an era of mass society is all the more significant in educating the student toward the importance of the individual in society. The answers that we give to questions are very often answers which depend on the questions that we ask; and if the questions that we ask are on the whole: "Does the society function well?" "Does the system function well?"—that is quite likely to produce a different kind of answer than the confrontation that's required when one looks at the particular case and says, "Was this a just disposition of the case?" The need to confront the unique problem, I would maintain, is highly prevalent in the performance of our role as educators, so that we may confront, and compel our students to confront, the crucial issues of the time.

So, I do use a heavy amount of case material, but by no means exclusively. The students are required to read a fair amount of material from people like Cardozo and Pound and Llewellyn, by way of background. Oftentimes, to begin the examination of the role of law in society, they will report on a legal novel, on a legal biography; they will be required to do a report on a visit to the local courts; this may be traffic court, criminal court, family court; and to contrast the image of justice that they had before going in with the view they acquired as a result of the experience; to contrast the perception of the judicial system that they get from reading appellate court cases with the perceptions that strike them when they see a large assortment of defendants, most of them unrepresented by counsel, having their cases disposed of by harried judges, under the most pressing of conditions. And then, from these broader readings and visits and the use of inquisitorial method in class in which they are required to partake, just as law students partake of the Socratic dialog, we then get to the end of the course and the question of what has happened.

And sometimes it works out that this has been a meaningful experience in liberal arts training; and sometimes I feel as though it's been an absolute failure when a student comes up and says, "You know, this has been great! I'm sure it's going to help me a great deal when I go to law school." The entire objective and the entire focus of the course is *not* to appeal to the pre-law student. It is designed to acquaint the student in the liberal arts with some of the roles that law performs in society; but even more so, to acquaint him with his own sense of values; to challenge and test those senses of values; and to pose questions like: "How does one accept the norms of a society without vegetating or decaying?" "How does one innovate in a society without becoming a partisan of revolution or violence?" And it seems to me that the materials of the legal system and legal process are particularly apt for posing these questions and for testing and challenging our students' responses, and perhaps, hopefully, also in creating for each new generation both a faith in and a commitment to the democratic process.

5. Social Ethics

The suggestion that law might be introduced to undergraduates as part of a course in social ethics was made by Professor Thomas R. Peterson, O.P., a philosopher and theologian who is Assistant to the President at Providence College. The proposal met with opposition from Professor Miriam T. Rooney of Seton Hall Law School, the former dean of that law school and holder of a doctorate in philosophy. It was inferentially questioned by Professor John Corcoran, O.P., a philosopher from Aquinas Institute, Chicago, in a comment made later in the conference, but relevant here.

PETERSON—In some colleges there is perhaps already existing somewhat of a minor in law-society. We can say that in many colleges there is stress upon the need of philosophy and one element in philosophical training is the science of ethics. It seems to me that if students are impressed with at least the philosophical disciplines of logic from whence they are taught how to draw principles from conclusions, and if they are also taught a system of ethics which teaches them the rights and obligations of human nature, and that law is somewhat of a guideline for these rights and obligations, and if they are taught as they must be in the science of ethics what society is, that they are already given at least some basis of knowing the relationship of law to society, and at least the tools from whence to draw conclusions. I do not in any way intend to say that this is the be-all and end-all of a law-society program. It certainly is not. It's only a very, very small beginning. But certainly it is some place to begin, in insisting in the teaching of a course in ethics which explains human rights, which explains human society, which explains at least generically the concept of law, and then equipping the students with logic to take this down into the practical, to take this down into the individual, so that the science of ethics would then be completed perhaps through elective programs, elective courses, taught by lawyers, taught by sociologists, taught by political scientists, in which the principles of ethics would now be made very specific, and would now be made very applicable to everyday life. It might be somewhat of a compromise between an absolute program in law-society and the complete denial of one.

ROONEY—I am concerned about putting law under ethics. Law starts originally from the cases and the theoretical protection of human rights, and we're getting back to human rights on the international level, which is just the opposite direction from the political scientist. I am very much afraid that in trying to experiment with just a short course, considered in a limited time, that it may again get into the *a priori* theories of deduction, which is quite contrary to the actual legal thinking, and how we can guard against that. If we are going to train the teachers first, all right, that's a problem. Then we're going to have to get a major in the graduate curriculum to train the teachers first, and get recognition for it. At the present time both the lawyers and the students in the colleges are being deprived of their heritage in not knowing anything about law. If it gets into the wrong hands, we're just right straight back where we started.

CORCORAN—One of the things we arrived at in our discussion of seminary training was that there had been an overemphasis on the deductive method where we had merely a theatrical dramatization of a reasoning process to a foregone conclusion. That was overemphasized, and what we need to see from modern science is the necessity of a research method where we don't know what the decision is going to be until we have weighed everything in the balance. It's necessary for the lawyer to understand the social sciences so that he'll know how to give proper weight to these elements in his balances. It's necessary for the social scientist to know the law so that he'll understand the balancing process.

6. Sociology

A sociological course is already being used by Profesor Harry V. Ball of Wisconsin as a channel of teaching about law to undergraduates. He also discusses here a new course he contemplates in the sociology department called "Social Theory and Social Policy." This proposal leads to a dialog between Professor Ball and Professor Victor Rosenblum of Northwestern, a lawyer and political scientist, on the pros and cons of the actuarial approach.

MASSEL—The question is, is all of your work taking place on the graduate level, or are you doing anything on the undergraduate level, at the University of Wisconsin?

BALL—We are working at the undergraduate level. Herb Jacobs, our political scientist, has introduced a new course in judicial administration at the undergraduate level.

BEITZINGER—Is that a political science course?

BALL—Yes. My sociology and law course is open to undergraduates also. It's kind of funny though, for law students it's very much like the course Mr. Abbott described, and for social science students it's very much like the course Mr. Wasserstrom described. And these are taught simultaneously with them all in the same room.

Then the legal process course, the first introductory course in the law school, from the Auerbach-Hurst-Garrison book,[14] attempts to give a broad overview of law to the first year law student; it is also available to undergraduate students, listed as Law and Society, Political Science 115. It is not broad enough, and a lot of the students today are not really interested in workmen's compensation, you know. Perhaps these books should never be put in hard cover. The central problem just doesn't last that long. You have to move on to the next process.

We're developing a new program in Hawaii[15] which we hope will change the whole character of the school of social work. It begins with an undergraduate course in the third year of college called social theory and social policy. You don't begin with social theory; you begin with an analysis of legislation in terms of analyzing what behavioral assumptions and models of human behavior get built into legislation. You examine these programs in practice to find out what happens at the level of practice. Basically, you are teaching social theory. You don't have to teach models of human behavior by starting out saying you are going to talk about models of human behavior. You can also ask the question, what models of human behavior are we actually using in programs? Then hopefully you move on to the question of an actual empirical-tested program, because law, as I see it, the legislative-administration area in particular, is actuarial. It's just one big mass of experimental programs except we've been pouring tons and tons of academic attention in analyzing how a bill goes through a legislature, and then no one cares.

As a matter of fact I am not nearly as concerned with how a bill got through the legislature as with what happened after the bill got through the legislature. I am not nearly as concerned with how the court reaches the decision it reaches, as with what consequences the decision has. And this is where there is absolutely no conflict. The difficulty in terms of what we talked about earlier, the lawyer being interested in the individual decision, the social scientist taking his actuarial approach, is almost completely derivative of the concentration upon judicial activity.

But if you start looking at legislative-administrative activity, it shifts immediately to an actuarial approach. Legislatures want to know what is the totality of the impact of a program as administered, not what is the impact of every little individual decision. And after you have isolated the cells of possible responses, then you engage in what the social scientist calls latent structure analysis, to try and find out what accounted for the variations in these little cells. But first you try to evaluate the totality of the program in terms of the specified ends of the administrative policy or the legislation. And that's where you begin. So I am arguing that you can teach sociological theory, you can teach psychological theory, by beginning with the legislative-administrative statement. Or a judicial statement, where it's a decision that cuts broadly, then you can actually begin with that because it is there, it's implicit, it has to be there. It's there even if the judge doesn't think it's there, or the administrator doesn't think it's there, or the legislator doesn't think it's there. You find it, and you get the students to dig it out. They produce their own model of what the behavior is. This is sort of Aristotelian teaching, but I am biased because much of my teaching luckily has been at senior seminars where you start off saying,

"You've been here four years, I assume you know a great deal. Now let's see what you know." And so I am saying that we should lower this; let's start at the junior level. What do you know? These students know a great deal, and we repeatedly allow them to forget what they've learned. This is again another function of the process of segmentation. And I am saying increasingly that as students go through the university we have to keep telling them we don't allow you to forget anything you learned in the previous courses. You've got to use it over again. We are not going to reteach it, you've got to use it, use it and think about it, work with it, and finally you are going to come out of here a thinking animal. But right now our own biggest enemy is ourself, and the manner in which we organize these educational enterprises. And these things are natural for liberal arts instruction. This is not a strange and bizarre idea. These are things, again, which everyone has known for years, and we just haven't done anything about it.

ROSENBLUM—I want to be the devil's advocate for the moment, because I want particularly to take issue with the actuarial approach, with the totality approach—

MASSEL—Pardon me, this is Professor Rosenblum acting as the devil's advocate.

ROSENBLUM—I want at least to insist that there needs to be a supplement to the actuarial approach or to the totality approach, because the actuarial or totality approach gives us a picture of what is going on on the whole. It puts us into the scientific observers' category—the social observers' category —but it doesn't put us into the area of giving visibility to the problems of society which may be at an emergent stage, and it takes the particularity of the case approach to give this visibility to social problems that may be only emerging but which may be quite significant if they proceed beyond a certain point.

I'll call it–when we are talking about people moving out of the neighborhood when another group moves in—the tipping point, and this is an important dimension, I would say, of our role as teachers. A preoccupation with an on-the-whole type of view is going to be valuable in giving us a picture of things as they are on the whole. But our role goes far beyond that. It goes toward the point of giving visibility to major problems that are emerging within the community, and I would suggest that there are even some practicing lawyers who have by following the case-in-justice approach helped to provide innovations which are leading us to new eras of on-the-whole. Charles Rhyne, for example, who practices law in the District of Columbia and who was a former president of the American Bar Association, had the sense of justice and the concern to perceive an issue in the status of apportionment in the United States, a problem which was not receiving much attention from us academic people. I except a former and unfortunately bitter colleague at Northwestern named Kenneth Colegrove, who fought the early case of *Colegrove* v. *Green*,[16] and lost, and was very bitter over it; most of us, after the loss in that case, figured that is now a closed area. And we were saying, "but on the whole the system works pretty well." And to Charles Rhyne and to the men with whom he worked, it didn't work very well.

There was a case that was fought with most of the smart money within the law profession and the political science profession saying, "Charlie always was a bit nuts but give him credit for being a good fighter; he's probably going to lose, but good luck to him." And lo and behold, in being able to apply the brilliance of the law practitioner, and detecting the emergence of new legal doctrines, and being willing to put them to test in case format, he sets the machinery going for the totality of reform within the area of apportionment that we are now experiencing with the combination of the burgeoning of court cases and the active compliance on the part of groups within the states, pressured to do so not by indifferences, as predicted by the dissenters in *Baker* v. *Carr*,[17] but rather by, as a result of, the renewed enthusiam for political groups, for achieving the justice of a fairer system of apportionment.

I would say that it is important for us not to immerse ourselves in the detail of what might be the picayune, or the pedantic; but nonetheless the following of a case approach, along with the totality or actuarial approach, is necessary so that we can perform fully our role as teachers. That's my comment.

BALL—I would say I agree completely. I would make two points: one is that it is crucial to recognize the significance of what you can call the kooky individual and how this thing operates, you know, the fellow that picks up this case. I have joined lawyers in several of these cases myself. We've never won yet. We succeeded twice, however, in getting the Wisconsin Supreme Court to review cases which every member of the law faculty told us the court would not review. They at least got reviewed for the first time. They now have a level of visibility that they never had before.

But there are two ways to approach this. One is, as suggested in the discussions today, the reading of biographies. That is, we have certain materials to show how people did this in the past, you see, to keep the individual from being lost, how people got concerned with new problems. Biographies are very good in this area. You pick up some little pocket book like *Profiles in Courage*.[18] Every one of these profiles is about one of these people who paid a price. Very often in the modern world you don't have to pay a price to become famous; if you win—you've got it made. If you lose, of course, you try to find another one.

The other thing is that looking around at the individual problem is still only one way to find out what the emergent problems of the future are. Because I am convinced that an even larger category of future problems consists of the unanticipated consequences of our solutions to the present problems. This is not outside the actuarial approach. It is precisely in any adequate evaluation of any program today; one of the things you have to be looking for avidly, eagerly, and one of the things that pushes your imagination and creativity the hardest, is precisely to ask, what are the unanticipated consequences—and especially those that turn out to be quite shocking because they are the kind of things that, at least in terms of the present values, you don't want. So it may well be, as you say, that in a given program, you are achieving, or you are moving toward the result that you want in 90 percent of the cases. It also may very well be that in the other 10 percent you are not only not achieving the result, you are actually aggravating the problem, or generating a new one. So in a sense it is not the contrast between the individual and the actuarial. You've got to look for this new emergent problem at both levels, and the actuarial approach can produce it as well as the other.

ROSENBLUM—We may unfortunately once again be too much in agreement here—so long as we keep the door open so that a kooky prisoner like Gideon[19] can write to a lawyer like Abe Fortas[20] and can say, I've got a problem here because I've been in jail, and I don't really think that I belong here, and Fortas can pick it up and be willing to invest the time and the energy and the dedication and fight the thing through the Supreme Court, and win it. And who knows, maybe you and I might be involved in fighting a case for a student at the University of California despite the fact that on the whole the university students in the United States are still outside of prison.

CHAPTER V
LAW AND POVERTY

The conference participants gave extensive consideration to the possibility of developing Law and Poverty as the subject of a new undergraduate course in which the law might be studied in action. For this reason, although it is just one among the many possible course vehicles proposed for conveying knowledge about law-society, the theme is set apart in this special chapter.[1] The main paper in support of the idea was delivered by Mr. Edgar Cahn, Special Assistant to Mr. Sargent Shriver, Director of the Office of Economic Opportunity, which administers the federal Anti-Poverty Program. He was seconded by Mrs. Zona Hostetler, an attorney with the Legal Aid Society of Washington, D.C. The chapter concludes with the conference workshop on Law and Poverty that was presided over by Mr. Gary Bellow, who is also with the Washington Legal Aid Society. It will be seen that the proposal there had rough sledding.

1. Brief for a Course in Law and Poverty

EDGAR S. CAHN*

It will be noted that Mr. Cahn's proposal encompasses a course in Law and Poverty for undergraduates, for law students or for graduate students.

I started off thinking about the problem of how to educate either college students or law students or graduate students to the field of law and poverty, and I suppose I found myself taking a step backwards and asking why educate them to these problems at all. Because I think the answer to that will in turn shape the answer to how to educate them. And one answer to that is, "Well, why not leave these problems of law and poverty, particularly law as it affects the poor, to the lawyers, to the professionals and to government officials." Why should this be a fit subject of the curriculum at all? Why is it worthy to take its place along with the study of Beowulf or Herodotus, or of estate law and corporate law?

---

* Special Assistant to Director, Office of Economic Opportunity.

There is right now a real concern about law and poverty, and I don't think it is simply a fashionable concern. I would like to state briefly what I think are the two sources of the concern that underlies law and poverty, because those sources of the concern will in turn determine at least one possible way of approaching how one might teach this subject.

There are two ways of viewing the current emphasis that is taking place on legal rights of the poor. We are all aware that this is a period when the legal rights of the poor have become an area of concern, and that this concern began in the criminal law. One can mention, in terms of recent developments, the *Gideon* case,[2] with its mandate on the right to counsel in state courts, and subsequent cases which have made that mandate even clearer and extended it. Some of you may be aware of experiments in the administration of bail, where we are beginning to find out that in order to protect the presumption of innocence, it's very important that a man be free to go about and prepare his own defense.[3] And in terms of sentencing, it is important that he be able to have a job. And if he is not able to put up bail, statistically it has been proved that he tends to get longer sentences, and he tends to be found guilty more often. And the statistical evidence is pretty impressive that alternatives to bail as we know it will have to be devised.

There are other developments, too, such as the recent Criminal Justice Act,[4] the experiments of summons in lieu of arrest. There are a wealth of developments in the criminal law field which are novel but which also stem from a traditional concern of lawyers for equal justice for the accused. But this concern for the rights of the poor, I would hasten to say, is not restricted to the criminal law. It extends to new areas that have been mentioned earlier, e.g. welfare law, rent strikes, consumer protection. It also embraces new forms of legal aid, decentralized forms of legal aid and public defenders, so that the law offices that serve the poor are more accessible to the poor physically, and are perceived as more accessible.[5] There is the recent *Railroad Brotherhood*[6] case which set forth a new doctrine on the constitutionality of a law which had operated to prohibit group legal services. There are a whole range of developments which are going to have, both in the criminal and the civil area, important impact on the kinds of legal services which the poor have.

There are two ways to explain these phenomena. What underlies the phenomena is important. One can approach it first from what might be called the *Gideon* approach.[7] Many of the developments which are now taking place stem really from a sense of injustice and an unwillingness to subject a person to severe deprivations and punishments simply for the crime of being poor. And this sense of justice and fair play is certainly strongest in the criminal law where the stigma and the sanction imposed is so severe, and where the revulsion at seeing a conviction without due process and full representation is naturally greatest. But I think increasingly we come, as a matter of moral sensitivity, to realize that criminal sanctions are not the only sanctions imposed on the poor simply for the crime of being poor. Termination of welfare benefits, eviction from a public housing project, denial of unemployment compensation, repossession of goods, are all, after a fashion, sanctions imposed by the use of legal process, and they may in actual practice or operation be as severe and harsh as a criminal sanction. And I think there is an expanding recognition of justice, and an expanding sensitivity to the severity of non-criminal sanctions, and that this in part, but only in part, accounts for the developments now taking place in the area of law and poverty.

But there is another aspect of this development which I think needs to be set forth explicitly. The first aspect—the *Gideon* approach—is in a sense a negative one, and legal services approached this way become largely a way of avoiding unjustly imposed deprivations. The forces that are producing the current ferments in the area of the rights of the indigent are not limited simply to a sense of injustice and to avoiding unjustly imposed deprivations. Something else very different is going on. Legal services to the poor are, in fact, a form of enfranchisement. And just as *Baker v. Carr*[8] legitimated the concerns of the underrepresented in urban and suburban areas and just as *Brown* v. *Board of Education*[9] legitimated the grievances and inequities the Negro has been subjected to, I think, so, too, legal services for the poor and concern for the rights of the poor in civil and criminal areas are ways of legitimating the grievances and concerns of the poor and of saying, "You, too, shall be heard." And if we consider legal services a form of enfranchisement, in effect we are saying that by giving the poor representation, we are giving them a voice in the decision-making process, not simply a way of avoiding penalty, but giving them a voice in how public programs are administered and not only how they are administered, but ultimately as to the shape which they take and the efforts for reform and change and alteration which flow from that. When a person fights the proper termination of welfare benefits successfully, he not only avoids punishment, he also contributes to a change of attitude in the persons who administer that program. And he may significantly contribute to the way in which the poor view themselves and the way in which society views the poor. And so I would view this form of legal service and legal representation as not just negative but as a form of franchise—as a new group of voices which, for the first time, have an opportunity to speak and to determine their destiny, not only in the sense of avoiding punishment, but in a far broader sense with respect to the way in which this society treats the poor, treats minorities, treats those who, for one reason or another, have been cut off from opportunity. This aspect of this ferment in the area of legal rights of the poor comes through most clearly if one considers the civil rights revolution. There the drive against second-class citizenship did not take simply the form of a drive to exercise the electoral franchise. It took the form of the right to exercise other kinds of franchises: the right to go to certain kinds of schools, the right to be a consumer of the corner drug store, to be a consumer of the public school system and of public facilities. We are talking about, in a broad sense, the fact that when people entering a school system for the first time or frequenting a drug store that they could not frequent before, that those who administer that school system or store are going to have to be responsive in some sense to the desires and needs of the new consumers of those services. And in point of fact, this is giving the poor—in that case the Negro—an effective franchise as to the shape and nature of education north and south, as to the shape and nature of services and of garments and of food that is available to the whole economy.

These are the two aspects of rights of the poor: the injustice aspect— the feeling that a poor person should not be penalized for being poor alone—and also the enfranchisement aspect.

If we are going to talk meaningfully to students about what this law stuff is all about, it's got to be made relevant. It can't be simply a set of dry rules in a sense, for law students and undergraduates alike. They have got to see it as relevant to functions of citizenship, to their moral and ethical being in a very immediate fashion, and I think that is why one should not approach rights of the poor merely from the point of view of technical rules concerning the point at which representation of the accused is constitutionally mandatory in a criminal proceeding. One has to think here in terms of basic enfranchisement, basic rights of citizenship and a sense of injustice for sanctions imposed for being poor. I think that is one way in which to communicate the significance of the field if it is going to have significance.

I think we are wrong if we treat this simply as a new field of expertise, as a new set of rules, because I don't think that is what's involved. Any law student can—anybody can—walk in and simply learn a new set of rules. When one finds a new set of concerns for the legal rights of the poor something very different is happening from learning a new set of rules.

If this perspective provides a basis for saying why one should educate both law students and college students to this area, I think then one has to ask, in line with this: What flows from this perspective? In terms of what one teaches college students and law students, particularly in the context of interdisciplinary studies, what does this perspective imply?

If we are going to attempt to structure a course that had some meaning I would talk at least about three things. I'd talk about the way that legal service institutions currently operate and ask whether the assumptions which seem to govern their operation in fact make any sense. I made a list of what seemed to me an apt description of the kind of assumptions that underlie the present structure of legal services for the poor. These assumptions are organized in keeping with the following principles:

The first is that because civil and criminal cases differ in terms of procedure and substantive law, separate institutions should provide legal assistance in civil and criminal cases.

The second principle would be that each legal problem is a discrete entity to be dealt with in isolation from every other legal problem of the client.

The third would be that legal problems are separate from non-legal problems and can and must be dealt with in isolation.

The fourth is that legal problems of the poor are basically individual cases to be solved on a person-by-person, case-by-case basis.

The fifth is that the function of legal services for the poor is to extricate them from difficulties rather than to keep them from getting into difficulty.

The sixth is that all legal difficulties must be handled by a lawyer or not at all.

The seventh is that the law has evolved elaborate refinements in order to decide similar cases or like cases alike and different cases differently —this is a basic principle of the law—and that therefore the complexities of the law advance justice and implement the principle of equal justice for all.

It might be profitable if one were talking either to law students or to undergraduate students to ask whether or not institutions organized along these principles to serve the poor in fact do serve the poor. They serve the needs of the profession I think tolerably well. But it might be very interesting to see what happens to each of these principles when one approaches them from the point of view of the poor themselves, as the consumer of legal services. One might find that maybe a person who had legal difficulty should not be dealt with in a piecemeal fashion and that if he has to make a series of complex private decisions as to whether his case is civil or criminal or whether it involves a need for legal or non-legal services then, in point of fact he will never get any of the services he needs, legal or non-legal. We will, in some sense, have outpriced those services in terms of the level of sophistication required. This is something we need to become aware of. Students observing these institutions could bring all this out in a very pointed fashion, and could begin to think through how one might reshape these institutions, and perhaps how one ought to reshape all institutions that are theoretically devoted to service of people but in point of fact serve the professionals rather than the poor themselves. They might begin to find that many problems of the poor are not individual legal problems, although each problem occurs in the context of an individual client, but that many of the legal problems of the poor stem from the status of being poor:— from coming from certain kinds of neighborhoods and from being subject to certain kinds of—you might call them legal epidemics. A list would include: landlord and tenants and slums, consumer fraud and repossession, termination of welfare benefits. These problems are not confined to individual cases and we might begin to reconsider some of the basic premises on which lawyers operate and legal service institutions proceed. This is an area that might very profitably be subjected to question by law students and by college students.

We might begin to think in terms of preventive legal services, in terms of legal education—recognizing the need to disseminate an understanding of rights in a way that prevents people from getting into legal difficulties, rather than assuming that the only job of a lawyer and people interested in the law is to find out what rule you can hook onto to get you out of trouble. And the preventive aspect of law is something that maybe lay persons have a far greater appreciation of the need for than have lawyers, who are accustomed very frequently to operating from the other end.

We need to question particularly the assumption that the legal difficulties of the poor can be solved—or must be solved by lawyers. I think increasingly that the law and the values of the law—the security that the law and legal norms are supposed to provide—are too important and too precious to be entrusted to any profession, including the legal profession. In fact the law is supposed to protect values which are so basic to the privacy and growth and health of every individual that I would hate to see this become the exclusive preserve of the legal profession or any other profession. I think it is a function of citizenship. And unless it is perceived as such—unless there is a dissemination of knowledge about rights on a far broader scale, I think that the legal system won't work. We can't count on lawyers to make sure that people are protected every moment of the day. You can't walk down the street and up the street and into your house with a lawyer, and yet every step that you take is fraught with legal consequences. Whether you go in and buy a bunch of hairpins or whether you buy a house or whatever you do, lawyers are adept at constructing legal problems and for any given moment when one walks around I suppose there is really an infinity of potential legal problems that have to be solved by common sense.

The last thing I would think we would want to question in terms of the way in which legal institutions work is that the complexity of the law is not a luxury which can be afforded only by the rich. In terms of the human cost, the simplification of legal principles and an increase in the workability and accessibility and intelligibility of the law might make a more substantial contribution to the advancement of justice than the accumulation of refinements, technical expertise and the proliferation of distinctions. This would be one area in which both laymen and lawyers would have something very significant to say and which would be a fit area of study in any institution of higher learning.

I think, though, that there are some other areas that could be profitably gone into—and one of them is characterized by the term "advocacy for the poor." I think it is clear that a lawyer is two things—he is an expert, he is a technician—in doing legal research, in distinguishing cases and reading precedents and statutes. But he is also an advocate. And in this latter capacity he performs a function which should and must be performed increasingly by lay persons who become aware of the importance of this function. I think this has important philosophical and epistemological dimensions too. But let me quote from a recent speech by Attorney General Katzenbach. He addressed himself to this to illustrate the principle that advocacy need not be limited to lawyers. He says:

> As an example, let me recall the case on the West Coast of a woman with seven children supported by welfare. A fire destroyed the roof of their house—the woman was too poor to move or repair the damage—the response of the welfare agency was to cut off her welfare maintenance. She was living, they said, in unsuitable housing. It does not take a lawyer to react to such a determination and it did not. A young woman who heard about this case took it upon herself to become an advocate—to go to the welfare authorities and indignantly ask what was the legal authority for the suspension of welfare. And the welfare check was issued immediately. It is this kind of example which we must follow and inspire in others. It is this kind of problem which can be solved without a law degree. Not every injury requires a surgeon, not every injustice requires an attorney. The need is for spirit and a system of legal first aid. We need more people like the young woman I just described. We need what is, in effect, a new profession—a profession of advocates for the poor made up of human beings from all professions, committed to helping others who are in trouble. That job is too big and, I would add, too important to be left only to lawyers.[10]

And this is one area—the implications of an advocacy role in the law and beyond the law, beyond lawyers—that needs to be explored.

I think one of the most interesting aspects of this point of view for a college curriculum or a graduate school curriculm is the aspect that comes home so strongly to any lawyer who has to deal with preparing materials for trial. He finds very quickly that facts are not neutral, and that facts which relate to the needs and grievances of the poor or to a legal case cannot be presented in a neutral fashion as if they were objectively determinable. The fact, at least in the law, operates as a kind of vectoral force in decision making. And the magnitude of the impact it has upon the decision maker—and that means the judge, or welfare administrator or teacher or whoever exercises that function—will depend not simply on the fact alone but on the context in which it is presented, on the purpose for which it is urged, and on the forcefulness with which it is argued. The function of facts in decision making has to be understood more fully by students, both of the law and of our society. The battle of experts, of one doctor saying "Such and such caused such and such" for purposes of an automobile injury recovery case, and the other expert saying, "No, that isn't so at all," is illustrative of this peculiar aspect of facts, and I think one of the most interesting things to question on the undergraduate level, at least for the purpose of law and decision making, is whether any fact can be treated as simply objectively verifiable—as simply lying there cold and understandable, in and of itself. I think it's in the advocacy perspective that this peculiar aspect of facts emerges most clearly. It's not peculiar to law, but I think in the advocacy context the peculiar nature of fact, the relative and subjective nature of fact, comes out. The question of verifiability may be far less important—thus the process of presenting a fact, how one urges it, may be at least as important as the fact itself.

There is a third aspect of law that I would think would be very important to get across to both law students and college students and that is that, although advocacy is important, one must really go beyond advocacy—that rights in our society not only cannot depend upon law and lawyers alone but they cannot depend upon advocacy alone. Advocacy means that you are fighting, that you are urging; that's important. It has very important implications for a person who never realized that he had a right. It can give him a feeling of dignity, a feeling that he is standing on his own two feet for the first time. But fighting takes its own human toll. And if our system of rights, if our legal system, is dependent either on legal fights or on advocacy alone, then I think we as a society are in real trouble. Karl Llewellyn once sat down to describe what we really mean when we say a person has a right to damages if a contract is broken. He said,

> That right could rather more accurately be phrased some-
> what as follows: If the other person does not perform as
> agreed, you can sue, and if you have a fair lawyer and
> nothing goes wrong with your witnesses or the jury, and
> you give up four or five days of time and some ten to thirty
> percent of the proceeds, and wait two to twenty months, you
> will *probably* get a judgment for a sum considerably less
> than the performance would have been worth, which, if
> the other party is solvent, and has not secreted his assets,
> you can, in further due course, collect with six percent
> interest for delay.

If rights really come down to this, if this is what a poor person or really any person has to do every time he has a fight with the landlord or welfare officials or the principal of his child's school or the merchant who sold him a TV set, then he really has no rights at all. And, we cannot elevate litigation, or advocacy in the broadest sense, to the status of being an end in itself. It is a means, to shake off helplessness and dependence, to insure that all sides of the story are heard, to prevent indignity and manipulation and exploitation—but ultimately advocacy and law and litigation must advance the cause of justice and there are times when the price of winning, of securing a just result, can be too high in human terms of the distortion it works on one's way of viewing other human beings. I think this is a fit area of inquiry and concern for every person in this society—and certainly for institutions of higher education.

There is one last area. How does one teach people about law and poverty? I am sad to say that there are very few materials, virtually none. I think to a certain extent that the case method that has been developed in law schools—that is, approaching individual cases and exploring their ramifications and then reflecting on the various materials from the social sciences as to the kinds of insights or kinds of policy assumptions that a rule of law makes, is a very important and very useful instrument. Because of my background I compare it to the value of the new critical approach in literature, particularly for students—for young students who don't have a sense in literature of whole traditions, of whole systems of metaphor, or of conventions, of dramatic patterns developed through the ages. The idea of taking a poem as an entity in itself or a piece of literature as an entity in itself, exploring it fully and then having implications radiate out from it is a very important pedagogical device. And I think the isolation of the legal case involving a particular problem—such as that of a woman who has been cut off from welfare, or a man who has been charged with disorderly conduct because he has been fighting with his wife—can be useful pedagogically. The fact is that he has been laid off from his job and that, in turn, is tied in with automation and with bankruptcy problems. When one begins to explore the ramifications of a particular case it is evident that they expand outward and radiate outward and give one a kind of complex sense of how legal and non-legal problems interact. And I think this is a very important way in which one could begin assembling materials for teaching students. To a certain extent this has been done at least in one case book I am aware of, put together by Professors Donnelly, Goldstein and Schwartz in the area of criminal law.[11] It is a massive tome but I think a very exciting thing to read, and in a way it is a work of art. But I would be unhappy if we thought in terms of teaching people about law and poverty from materials in case books alone. I think that they have to be involved in reality. Reality involves more than observation. The nature of fact, the nature of legal institutions, the nature of our society, is best understood by involvement—maybe guarded involvement, maybe protected involvement for students—but by active involvement. Simply looking at an institution is not enough. One must identify, one must participate and then perhaps one must draw back and consider. Isolated study by itself which assumes the neutrality and the objectivity of what one sees is basically inconsistent with the nature of fact, the nature of law, and the nature of hardship as it affects human beings. I think that if we want to teach the people about law and poverty, we have to send them out into the community, into the slums; we have to cast them in the role of advocates; we have to cast them in the role of helpers, in the role of people who assist the poor, and then we have to say, "All right, you've done that for a number of hours a day; step back, and let's look at your understanding of what you did, at what you thought was wrong in society." Because I think ultimately we ought to be giving academic credit for people's ability to understand and cope with the reality about them. And I don't think that understanding comes necessarily best from isolation from that reality. I think that isolation is necessary; I think drawing back is necessary. I don't think one gets perspective by eschewing involvement altogether.

I would very much hope that when we think in terms of teaching subjects like law and poverty to law students and to undergraduate students, that involvement plus understanding, plus perspective, would be what we would be thinking.

HOSTETLER*—I would primarily like to second Mr. Cahn's last comment about the need for what might be called laboratory work as a part of the study of social science, particularly in the area of law and poverty.

As a legal aid lawyer and consultant to various private welfare agencies, I have observed that most professional persons, including lawyers, have little grasp of the multiplicity of legal problems that affect the poor. And there is even less cognizance of the part that law plays in the problems of the poor among the educated community generally. If the poor man needs a lawyer, for example, it is just assumed that he can obtain one through the court or through a legal aid organization. What few realize is that both courts and legal aid organizations have many qualifying rules and regulations which often operate to preclude assistance in a particular case, or make it unavailable as a practical matter. As an example, it is almost impossible to obtain a divorce without paying court costs and lawyers fees. Most legal aid organizations will not even handle divorce matters. This means that rich persons in the community may obtain a divorce when they are legally entitled to one but the poor may not. Inaccessibility to courts in turn becomes an integral part of the much publicized statistics on illicit relationships and illegitimate birth among the poor.

As another example, if a poor family needs welfare assistance, the community generally assumes that it will be taken care of by the public welfare authorities. Seldom does the community realize that the application of a myriad of legal rules and procedures may have the effect of denying a poor family assistance. A family, for example, that has just moved to a community will find that it is not eligible for assistance because it has not lived within a defined area of land for the prescribed period of time—usually a year, and in some cases, five years.

An understanding of the practical socio-legal problems that the poor face should be an important part of one's education. And I think it can be best obtained by involvement—by walking through the steps that the poor person must walk. Laws cannot be fully understood by reading the statute books but only by seeing how they are actually administered in practice. Moreover, I think all students, whether they are going to become professionals or not, should experience this kind of involvement in the legal process as a part of their education. For it is important that ordinary citizens in the community be attuned to recognize and react to injustice and to use

---

* Mrs. Zona Hostetler, Legal Aid Society, Washington, D.C.

the legal process to right wrongs. To do this they need some understanding of law and of the legal process, particularly how it works for those persons in the community who are poor and powerless to challenge or change by themselves.

2. Workshop on Law and Poverty

MR. BELLOW*—Let me begin by briefly outlining what our purpose is today, and then, we will open the discussion to the panel. Most of you here have dealt with Law and Poverty on a practical level. The purpose of this meeting is to discuss the possibility of constructing graduate or college level courses of interdisciplinary dimensions in the Law and Poverty area. This raises two questions at the outset: 1) Should there be a course on the undergraduate level in the liberal arts curriculum; and 2) What form should this course take?

Mr. Caplan and I have prepared an outline of course materials[12] which might prove useful in such a course, and we would like to offer it to you for criticism and comment later in the discussion.

MR. CAPLAN**—I think that most of the materials in the outline are being taught now in one course or another. Many of them I have studied myself as assigned materials in courses in political science, psychology, etc. As I see it, the only novelty here is bringing them together in one syllabus. To take an example, in the literature of political science, there is a large literature on political participation—who votes and who doesn't, who becomes active in local politics and who doesn't. This area has never been viewed or treated as a "poverty" problem; rather it has been placed within the framework of political participation, a traditional category in the discipline. So I am really raising the fundamental question here as to whether it is useful at all to lump materials now being taught in various disciplines together. Do we gain anything by stamping on them the single label, "poverty?"

MR. BELLOW—If I understand you, you are really questioning the utility of interdisciplinary work per se, because in any interdisciplinary program I think you rarely find any single component that has never appeared elsewhere under another heading. The whole utility of the interdisciplinary approach is its juxtaposition of previously familiar material, because through the juxtaposition new relationships are perceived and developed.

---

* Gary Bellow, Legal Aid Society, Washington, D.C., consultant, Ford Foundation.
** Gerald M. Caplan, Assistant United States Attorney, Washington, D.C.

MR. CAPLAN—I agree. I just wanted to raise the issue.

MR. BELLOW—Going back to the bibliography, I would like to ask Earl Johnson [Neighborhood Legal Services Program] what types of materials he feels would be useful; that is, what would he recommend for one of his neighborhood lawyers to read, in order to analyze better the legal problems of the poor.

MR. JOHNSON*—What I would like to see in law schools across the country is a course that would emphasize the particular problems faced by the poor. Our law courses tend to concentrate on corporate law, anti-trust, on wills, estates—matters which are of concern to the wealthy, those of upper-class incomes. Now, what I have in mind is a course that would focus on problems such as landlord-tenant relationships, particularly as they exist on the low-income level, rather than the rent of the Empire State Building. Another important area, heretofore virtually ignored, is that of the public welfare agency and the welfare recipient. There are many legal problems here that are demanding research and litigation.

MR. BELLOW—I gather you would consider it very important that there be substantive course materials dealing with specific legal areas affecting the poor. But shouldn't we also be concerned about sociology and psychology and the social sciences in general as they affect the legal relationships shaped by poverty?

MR. JOHNSON—Yes. And, I think there is room for both and a need for both. However, I would think the students should get their social science background in the undergraduate curriculum so they would come to law school already familiar with social aspects of the legal problem. Frankly, I am not at all sure what materials I would recommend, or on what level of education these courses should be offered.

MR. CAPLAN—Or, if they should be offered at all?

MR. JOHNSON—Perhaps a little explanation on what you had in mind in preparing the bibliography would clarify things.

MR. BELLOW—Mr. Caplan and I started with two primary focuses. First, that any course dealing with the legal problems of the poor must be sufficiently broad to cover the reading material and the learning from several related fields, but be sufficiently specific so that one could focus on definite problems. Secondly, that such a course should not be organized around the typical divisions such as civil and criminal, used in law schools. We were very interested in opening up new approaches both in organization and methodology. For example, we explored the idea of using some sort of case method approach organizing legal, factual, scientific and other types of materials. Such an approach would, for example, take a particular low-

---

* Earl Johnson, Jr., Neighborhood Legal Services Project, Washington, D.C.

income family and analyze the inter-relationships between the problems they faced. The materials would, therefore, have a report from a doctor, a statement from the clinic, an evaluation from the social worker; there might be included a legal suit they are involved in, a copy of the contract they signed regarding their lease and so forth.[13]

Of course, such a course could not be taught to college freshmen or sophomores; it would have to be taught, at the earliest, to those who have had the elective courses in the various disciplines of the social sciences. The bibliography assumes a background of minimal exposure.

MR. FREEDMAN*—I am a little puzzled. My difficulty here is that I do not know what the purpose of the proposed course is. I suspect that each of us has one or more purposes in mind. We could be planning a college curriculum that would make people better citizens and more aware of the society around them with some emphasis on poverty . . . or we could be interested in specifically making college students aware of the problems of a very important segment of the community, that is, the people in the community not living as well as others, and you could focus on their problems in order to create a degree of sympathy and awareness of the need for a better social, legal system, particularly with regard to them. And that is a different kind of course, and a different kind of bibliography.

MR. CAPLAN—It seems to me that if your main objective is to make the members of the upper-classes aware of the problems of the poor, to make them aware of certain changes that will probably occur in their lives if the poverty program achieves some success, and to make them more receptive to this kind of change, then you are going to have a much broader type of course than this is—not one for a small, hand-picked seminar, but something that can be given to the general student body at the first and second year level; and if that is what is wanted, then the course, I think, should not be on law and poverty, but on poverty. And law is only one aspect of the poverty problem, only one small part, one chapter in the book, so to speak. I am thinking of a course which takes up the political, the economic aspects of poverty—as well as the legal dimension—and puts the works into an integrated course on poverty.

MR. BARKUN**—Mr. Caplan, your course would aim at providing a basic map of what the terrain looks like in all its dimensions—each dimension could then be explored more fully in a separate course, or within the larger, introductory course. In other words, your course is one way to cross-

* Professor Monroe Freedman, George Washington University Law School.
** Dr. Michael Barkun, Program in Law and the Social Sciences, Northwestern University.

section the materials in the poverty area. I think the general area of poverty, and the changes that are being wrought in that area, is something that could be put into a beginning course that would have a broad enough interest to attract a large portion of the student body.

MR. JOHNSON—I think we ought to throw into this discussion some assumptions as to what kind of students we are talking about. Are we talking about a big city college where the students are pretty much off the street anyway, going to night school part-time working part-time, or are we talking about those who come dressed in Harris tweed jackets?

I think we have several dimensions going here. We have first of all the undergraduate, the course for junior and seniors, where we are less concerned with introducing the student to the broad scope of the poverty problem than getting him deeply involved in some of the major issues, philosophical issues of the whole problem and what remedies, if any, can be provided. Now the problem is how to make this meaningful to the student, whatever course you decide to provide. The student who is right off the street himself, if he is coming from a slum area—his exposure to the problems is quite different than an undergraduate at Princeton who lives in an exclusive suburb, has gone to an exclusive high school, and sees only poverty when he is on a train that happens to go through the slums on the way to the better shopping center or better homes. You have to focus really more on who it is you are trying to teach. I think that will help determine exactly what kind of course you would want to teach.

MR. VIHON*—I wonder if part of our difficulty in this discussion doesn't stem from the use of the term "poverty." It is, after all, a very loose concept. Are the problems of the poor really analytically distinct from the problems others in our society face? For example, motivation is commonly spoken of as a problem of the poor. But, aren't middle-class people sometimes lacking in motivation? And, if they are, is it because they are middle-class?

MR. BELLOW—I think we tried to face this definitional problem and I agree with you that it is the initial problem. The bibliography makes an attempt at definition or more precisely at dealing with some of the components of such a definition. This is reflected in the divisions that are made. Any definition of poverty must be seen in part in economic terms. Poverty, at bottom, is an absence of wealth compounded by limitations of economic mobility and employment opportunities. However, economics does not define poverty totally. Poverty is also a racial problem, at least in today's metropolitan areas. The Negro's lack of access to housing or education forces him into poverty ghettoes. Now I recognize that there are differences between groups independent of socio-economic class. The Negro and other

* Charles Vihon, Washington Planning and Housing Association.

groups adopt practices in such areas as child-rearing, for example, independent of income-level patterns. Nevertheless, the large number of Negroes who are the poor of our cities cannot be ignored in defining the problem. There are, of course, other dimensions of this problem of poverty. One of the political scientist's concerns relevant to poverty is the problem of non-participation. The poor are not active politically; they do not vote, and so on. There are many other components of poverty, but I think that those I cited are part of the definition.

MR. CAPLAN—I gather your point is that poverty cannot be defined exclusively in economic terms, but that we must also talk about an impoverishment in values and in mental health in general.

I think that is true to some extent that the poor have a unique psychology. The personality structure of the poor, which is not of course a monolithic entity, is nevertheless a cultural by-product and is therefore shared to a large degree. Therefore, it is useful to talk about, at least for some purposes, the psychology of the poor as a group—as opposed to the psychology of individuals in the group. Of course, for certain purposes we must also distinguish between certain types of poor people. Mr. Bellow indicated that the white ethnic poor may well be significantly different than the Negro poor. And similarly, the rural poor and the urban poor differ. Mr. Harrington in his book, *The Other America,* identifies in rather broad strokes, different categories of the poor, each with unique characteristics.

MRS. HOSTETLER—I think that taking what has just been said, I see here an enormous amount of very excellent material descriptive of various facets of poverty. Also, there has been listed a variety of techniques for analyzing and understanding the various components of poverty, ranging all the way from the economists' approach to the psychiatrists' approach. These are very different methods of looking at the topic and I wonder if this, at least to the undergraduate student, wouldn't be confusing to understand, not only as to the actual subject matter, but also the methodology which differs so tremendously? Unless we ask him to accept their findings and not try to evaluate their research techniques, how can we expect the student to jump from the economists' approach to the political scientists' approach?

MR. CAPLAN—The problem with an undergraduate course for freshmen is that it must be out of necessity confined to presenting the findings of what studies have been made. There is no time for depth analysis and there is no time to assess how the researcher went about organizing his data. And, of course, the freshman lacks the tools to make such an evaluation. He must accept the findings as a matter of faith, unless there are contradictory findings, and then we are all in difficulty.

MR. FREEDMAN—Let me play devil's advocate. You asked the question, at the outset of this workshop: "Is everybody certain that there should be a poverty course?" I am not. The more I listen to this discussion, the more it seems to me that there is no place in the college curriculum for this course. What we have been doing here is attempting to take pieces out of a number of other courses and making artificially a course that has little justification in any college curriculum. I don't think that those who want to tamper with the status quo have sustained their burden of showing why we should throw a new course into the curriculum.

MR. CAPLAN—Let me tackle that. I am an Assistant United States Attorney. I handle a number of problems daily that my undergraduate training did not prepare me for in any way. I am in the criminal division, the section that handles citizens' complaints and tries, among other things, all the misdemeanor cases in the District of Columbia. I can't recall any courses I had that would help me know what these people look like, what their problems are, what their values are, etc. The poor are, in so many ways, a mystery to the middle-class. Let me take a typical case, an assault case. In the District of Columbia, assault with a deadly weapon is a felony. It is a very common occurrence. I had no idea, prior to entering the office, of just how frequently violence occurs. It is a routine way of settling common disputes. Guns seem to be everywhere, despite the severity of the law. And the people who get involved in these cuttings, and stickings, and shootings, often don't view them very seriously at all. They don't want to prosecute at all. And when they do prosecute, it is often very reluctantly, and early in the game—when they are still just out of the hospital. In short, their way of viewing the problem of force is to accept it. This is an entirely different perception than that of the middle-class. How we handle it poses some tremendous problems. When do you treat the cutting as a felony? As a misdemeanor? When do you ignore prosecution altogether because everybody is back together again, one, more or less, happy family?

We are taught in school, especially law school, to respond to problems in terms of middle-class bias. This is no help in my job. I need courses, somewhere along the way, that give me insight to people different than myself.

MR. FREEDMAN—If a two or three hour course in poverty had been offered, what is the likelihood that you would have taken it, and, if you had, what reason is there to believe that you would have any greater understanding in these problems than you now have picked up in a few months, and, thirdly, if it had been given directly to you, how many other people might be interested in the course who would have gotten nothing out of it because of the focus on the specific kind of problems you are talking about.

MR. CAPLAN—I think it is likely that I would have taken such a course. People recruit themselves into electives, and, a course like this would have sounded exciting, interesting, I think.

MR. VIHON—Let me give an example from the civil field. In housing, the housing regulations sanction the failure of the tenant to maintain a decent and habitable residence. Why is it, I would like to have learned in undergraduate school, that a woman who works five days a week from six to ten hours a day as a domestic in other people's homes, keeping these homes beautiful, is willing to come home to a pig pen. I'd like to be able to understand that so when it comes to enforcing or counseling with respect to the housing regulations. . . .

MR. FREEDMAN—You know as well as I do that you aren't going to give an undergraduate student, or even a graduate student, an insight into the answer to that very complex question in a two hour course, much less a two hour course in which you need to also explain the difference between ethnic groups, and who uses knives under what circumstances, and whether Negroes raise their children differently regardless of economic background. Each of these questions in itself is a major or at least a minor subject of study and is not properly the subject matter for a single two or three hour seminar.

But I think that these problems we have been discussing today are being taught in the colleges. In the separate disciplines. The problem stems from attempting to fuse it all together, all the various disciplines into one course.

MR. BELLOW—I must confess I disagree with the theory that because we can't do a lot, we should not do anything. I personally feel we should have a course at the graduate level which deals with the problems of law and poverty. And by law I mean law in its broadest sense—law as all the attempts of society to solve and control its problems through institutional, administrative or even coercive methods of change. Such a course would have several values. First, it would provide an excellent vehicle for the use and understanding of interdisciplinary materials. The problems of the lower-one-fifth of our society are certainly rarely talked about at all in our educational curricula. Insofar as these problems are dealt with, they are dealt with in isolation from one another. It is my feeling that it is valuable and important and necessary that psychologists talk to the economists and that the economists talk to the sociologists and that the problems be illuminated in multiple lights. Poverty, of course, is not the only area where interdisciplinary work will yield results. But poverty is a good vehicle for all of the various disciplines since no single discipline can really, as we pointed out, fully define the problems of the poor in its own terms.

Secondly, and I must admit that this is what attracts me most, I don't think we have begun as a society to prepare ourselves to fully deal with the problems of the poor. I realize, of course, that our generation as is sometimes suggested did not discover poverty. This country has faced the problem for a long time. But new approaches are being tried—approaches that will involve a commitment of many, many more of our population than are currently involved in this area. There are countless non-legal jobs to be done—important jobs—and unless we begin to get new definitions of what must be left to the lawyer and what can be done by others, we will have far too few people performing tasks that must be performed by many.

Finally, I think poverty is in many ways the central social issue of our time and one which has to be faced and discussed in our educational experience. The changing status of one-fifth of our population will have enormous ramifications for the rest of society, especially when this changing status has militant revolutionary dimensions. If this revolution is to be absorbed into the legal system, there must be a growing understanding by the population, and not just lawyers, of its nature, goals and contradictions. A course on law and poverty—at least using law as has been defined, offers an opportunity to cope with these isues.

I, of course, recognize that what I am saying doesn't answer the question of whether a single course would suffice. Perhaps it would be more appropriate to have this area dealt with in each of the several courses in the curriculum. What I am concerned with is reflecting this area of concern in the curriculum. I think one course is a beginning, but not the only way to approach such an effort. The real issue is whether the university will search for new issues to add relevance to its course content, will seek new methods to broaden the impact of such courses, will open up new questions of those of us who are so hell-bent on molding society along new value premises and approaches.

MR. VIHON—Assuming we are going to have an interdisciplinary course, I have an inquiry that has not been touched upon. And it is a very practical one. Everytime we get in a room with psychologists, political scientists, sociologists—in front of students—we always find that no one knows enough about the other's discipline to really intelligently have a dialogue with him. When a person is in the Department of Psychology, he has over one, two, three years developed a vocabulary he assumes, and when we try the interdisciplinary approaches we have difficulty there because everybody is coming in with a different set of words. How do you overcome that?

MR. CAPLAN—My answer is not a totally satisfactory one. It is one I have wrestled with for a long time. Perhaps at bottom, you need people who are trained in two disciplines, and not just two people, each of whom is trained well in one area. The notion that we, as lawyers, or political scientists, can pose a problem which then can be handled by somebody in the appropriate discipline is naive. It just doesn't work that simply. For example, it is by now obvious, in the area of insanity in criminal cases, that the lawyers have had a problem in posing a question that psychiatrists can answer. And it is the same way when the lawyer poses a question for the sociologists or for the economist. Language is a great barrier. The other man is always tempted to say, "I can't answer the question the way you have asked it." Or something even more basic: "I am not interested in that question. That question is just a small part of my range of concern and why don't you quit using me as your lackey, as your intellectual servant. I will be happy to talk to you about some of the things I do, and see if you as a lawyer can give me some of the mechanics of it." I think lawyers are more guilty than other specialists of using others as raw sources of data or of viewing them as IBM machines who can crank out answers at will. This, perhaps, stems from the fact that many lawyers do not basically hold the social sciences in high esteem, say, compared to the natural sciences, or the professions. But, primarily, lawyers are in the business of making decisions, quick decisions on data which they feel they can assimilate in a short time. I don't think that there is any good lawyer who doesn't think he can master somebody else's problem or discipline in a week or less. But, if the answer is having people with double skills, then we are moving in that direction. There are more people wearing two hats now than ever before.

MRS. HOSTETLER—It seems to me from the last comment that interdisciplinary study on a really sophisticated level probably could be done only on the graduate level by pretty accomplished students who have spent a lot of time in study. But I think there should be something in addition to that which the student could perform at the outset of his undergraduate years. Something with appeal and some excitement about it. It can't be done just by reading materials. Some schools require you to join an extracurricular club. I don't see why it can't be required, perhaps in the sophomore year, for the student to join a group, the whole class could be required, under the guidance of one person, or a panel, to actually work with people, to assist professionals in the community. You could use your bibliography and sit around with these professionals and discuss the materials on a sophisticated level. Students are anxious. They are going down South by droves all on their own. The poverty program is going to pay for college students to work in the community. I don't see why this can't be combined with some sort of intellectual guidance from the university. It is just a beginning, but you get a feel for it, some excitement, some challenge, just like the students feel when they go to Europe. When they come back they sign up for many more international courses. It is more meaningful to them.

MR. BELLOW—It seems that in looking at the purpose for introducing a new course into the law and undergraduate curriculum, we have dropped out the law and focused on poverty. As I said, I see real value in a concern for the problems of poverty. Nevertheless, I think there is also need in a liberal arts curriculum to give the student, whatever future he envisions, something of an understanding of the role of law in society, and in view of that purpose, it probably doesn't matter too much whether we deal with family problems or international problems or poverty problems. I think that we might focus on poverty in light of the present concern that has been stimulated by the Administration's policies. However, I think our real problem, and somewhat the whole focal point of the conference, is whether we can incorporate legal materials into the undergraduate curriculum so as to strengthen and broaden that curriculum. This involves finding the right vehicle so that the student will deal not just with abstract theories but with enough practical situations, enough facts, to get a realistic appreciation of the relevance of legal learning. Perhaps in light of this discussion, poverty as a subject is a little too big and too unwieldy. If we are going to do a good job with it, maybe we should narrow it down some way.

MR. FREEDMAN—Poverty is not the vehicle for getting law into the undergraduate curriculum. I would not want to teach college students initially what a tremendous failure law can be. I don't want the first exposure to the awareness of the problems of legal structuring, of the importance of law, of the various pulls and strains of law to be in the poverty area. . . .

MR. BELLOW—It seems that we have raised far more questions than we answered which is a very lawyerly role to have played. My thanks to all of you.

SUGGESTED BIBLIOGRAPHY ON LAW AND POVERTY
By Gary Bellow and Gerard Caplan*

PART I—THE ELEMENTS OF POVERTY

I. *General Considerations*
Bagdikian, *IN THE MIDST OF PLENTY: THE POOR IN AMERICA* (1964)
Conant, *SLUMS AND SUBURBS* (1961)
Conference on Economic Progress, Washington, D.C., *Poverty and Deprivation in the United States; The Plight of Two Fifths of the Nation* (1962)
Elias, Gillies and Riemer (ed.), *METROPOLIS: VALUES IN CONFLICT* (1964)
Handlin, *THE NEWCOMERS* (1959)
Harrington, *THE OTHER AMERICA: POVERTY IN THE UNITED STATES* (1962)
Humphrey, *WAR ON POVERTY* (1964)
Hunter, *THE SLUMS* (1964)
May, *THE WASTED AMERICANS: COST OF OUR WELFARE DILEMMA* (1964)
Miller, *RICH MAN, POOR MAN* (1964)
Morgan, David, Cohen, and Brazer, *INCOME AND WELFARE IN THE UNITED STATES* (1962)

II. *The Politics of Poverty—Non-Participation in the Political Process*
Alinsky, *REVEILLE FOR RADICALS* (1946)
Lane, *POLITICAL LIFE* (1962)
Lipset, *POLITICAL MAN: THE SOCIAL BASES OF POLITICS* (1959)

---

* The reading list presented at the conference by Messrs. Bellow and Caplan was considerably expanded by Mr. Bellow for a course to be taught at Georgetown Law Center on "Poverty and the Administration of Justice" in the Fall of 1965. The readings listed here constitute an abridged version of the later list. A further expansion and updating of this bibliography was published as an Appendix to the Proceedings of The National Conference on Law and Poverty (1965), pp. 177-200.

Miller, *PARTICIPATION IN ELECTIONS: THE PROB-LEM* (Michigan Industrial Relations Research Association) (1960)

Miller, "The Politics of Poverty," *THE NEW SOCIOLOGY,* Horowitz ed. (1964)

Moore, "Social Deprivation and Advantage as Source of Political Values," *WESTERN POL. Q.* (June, 1961)

Rossi and Dentler, *THE POLITICS OF URBAN RE-NEWAL: THE CHICAGO FINDINGS* (1962)

Schattschneider, *THE SEMI-SOVEREIGN PEOPLE* (1963)

III. *The Psychology of Poverty*

Caplan, *PRINCIPLES OF PREVENTIVE PSYCHIATRY* (1964)

Duhl, (Ed.), *THE URBAN CONDITION* (1963)

Duhl, (Ed.),*URBAN AMERICA AND THE PLANNING OF MENTAL HEALTH SERVICES* (1964)

Gans, *URBAN VILLAGERS* (1962)

HARLEM YOUTH OPPORTUNITIES UNLIMITED, YOUTH IN GHETTO: A STUDY OF THE CONSE-QUENCES OF POWERLESSNESS AND A BLUEPRINT FOR CHANGE (1964)

Langer and Michael, *LIFE STRESS AND MENTAL HEALTH* (1963)

Lewis, *THE CHILDREN OF SANCHEZ: AUTOBIOG-RAPHY OF A MEXICAN FAMILY* (1961)

Myers and Roberts, *FAMILY AND CLASS DYNAMICS IN MENTAL ILLNESS* (1958)

Riesman, Cohen and Pearl, *MENTAL HEALTH OF THE POOR: NEW TREATMENT APPROACHES FOR LOW INCOME PEOPLE* (1964)

PART II—THE LEGAL PROBLEMS OF THE POOR

I. *Housing*

Anderson, *THE FEDERAL BULLDOZER* (1964)

Editors of Fortune, *THE EXPLODING METROPOLIS* (1958)

Fossum, "Rent Withholding and Improvement of Substandard Housing," 53 *Cal. L. Rev.* 304 (1965)

Friedman, "Tenement House Legislation in Wisconsin: Reform and Reaction," 9 *Am. J. Legal Hist.* 41 (1965)

Jacobs, *THE DEATH AND LIFE OF GREAT AMERICAN CITIES* (1961)

Levi, "Problems in the Rehabilitation of Blighted Areas," 21 *Fed. B. J.* 310 (1961)

Meyerson, Terrett & Wheaton, *HOUSING, PEOPLE AND CITIES* (1962)

New York City Rent and Rehabilitation Administration, *PEOPLE, HOUSING, AND RENT CONTROL IN NEW YORK CITY* (1964)

Schorr, *SLUMS AND SOCIAL INSECURITY* (U.S. Department of Health, Education and Welfare, Research Report No. 1, 1963)

Weaver, "Housing and Community Development Act of 1964," 43 *Title News* 2 (1964)

Weaver, "Housing Our Low Income Population: Federal and Local Powers and Potentials" 10 *N.Y.L.P.* 459 (1964)

II. *Consumer Protection*

Black, *BUY NOW, PAY LATER,* (1961)

Caplovitz, *THE POOR PAY MORE,* (1963)

Crown, *LEGAL PROTECTION FOR THE CONSUMER,* (1963)

"The Loan Shark Problem Today," 19 *Law and Contemp. Prob.* 1 (1954)

Note, "Small Claims Court as Collection Agencies," 4 *Stan. L. Rev.* 237 (1952)

III. *Deprivation of Liberty*

Allen, *REPORT OF THE ATTORNEY GENERAL'S COMMITTEE ON POVERTY AND THE ADMINISTRATION OF FEDERAL CRIMINAL JUSTICE* (1963)

Freed & Wald, *BAIL IN THE UNITED STATES* (1964)

Goldstein, "The State and the Accused: Balances of Advantage in Criminal Procedure," 69 *Yale L. J.* 1149 (1960)

IV. *Social Welfare*

Greenleigh Associates, *REPORT TO THE MORELAND COMMISSION ON WELFARE* (N.Y. 1963)

Keith-Lucas, *DECISIONS ABOUT PEOPLE IN NEED: A STUDY OF ADMINISTRATIVE RESPONSIVENESS IN PUBLIC ASSISTANCE* (1957)

Lester, *THE ECONOMICS OF UNEMPLOYMENT COMPENSATION* (1962)

Reich, "Midnight Searches and the Social Security Act," 72 *Yale L. J.* 1347 (1963)

Sparer, "The Welfare Client's Attorney," 12 *U.C.L.A. Rev.* 378 (1965)

V. *Family Relations*

Mandelker, "Family Responsibility under the American Poor Laws," 54 *Mich. L. Rev.* 497, 607 (1956)

Note, "Aid to Needy Children: Liability of Cohabiting Male for Support," 9 *U.C.L.A. L. Rev.* 261 (1962)

Weyrauch, "Informal and Formal Marriage—An Appraisal of Trends in Family Organizations," 28 *U. Chi. L. Rev.* 88 (1960)

PART III—THE ORGANIZATION OF LEGAL SERVICES

Cahn & Cahn, "The War on Poverty: A Civilian Perspective," 73 *Yale L. J.* 1317 (1964)

Carlin & Howard, "Legal Representation and Class Justice," 12 *U.C.L.A. L. Rev.* 381 (1965)

Hostetler, *THE NEED FOR STAFF LEGAL COUNSEL: A REPORT TO THE BOARD OF TRUSTEES OF FAMILY & CHILD SERVICES AGENCY OF WASHINGTON, D.C.* (1964)

Katzenbach, "Extending Legal Services to the Poor," 23 *Brief Case* 148 (1965)

Lewis, *GIDEON'S TRUMPET* (1964)

PROCEEDINGS OF H.E.W. CONFERENCE ON THE EXTENSION OF LEGAL SERVICES TO THE POOR (1964)

Silverstein, *DEFENSE OF THE POOR IN CRIMINAL COURTS, A PRELIMINARY SUMMARY* (1964) (American Bar Association).

SUMMARY OF WORKSHOP ON LAW AND POVERTY PRESENTED TO PLENARY SESSION OF CONFERENCE BY GARY BELLOW, WORKSHOP CHAIRMAN.

The topic of our discussion was the materials that might be used in a course on law and poverty. The first question and the one that really consumed much of the time was the most basic one which is whether such a course, in fact, should be taught. Those who had reservations about such a course being taught quite validly said that a course of this nature involves a problem so large that it might be beyond the capacity of undergraduates to deal with it. That the number of interdisciplinary materials that might be used in such a course might tend to be confusing because students would not be familiar enough with the methodology of all those courses. Thirdly, that such a course ranges across problems that should better be left to the individual subjects and that if schools have any important role to play in the problems in poverty it should be by the faculty opening up these problems to students in their individual courses.

On the other side there were expressed views that such criticism is really an attack on interdisciplinary discussion of any kind, that poverty as a subject matter is peculiarly amenable to interdisciplinary approach; that it is a problem of great interest that might absorb the interest and ideas of the students; that there is also an obligation on the university to prepare people for meeting problems in this area in the future and perhaps for participating in them.

Those were the two sides of the discussion; it was capped by another discussion which dealt with the whole problem of law and the social sciences in which it was suggested the concern for teaching an interdisciplinary approach to poverty in the law can best be tested in the question of whether law should be brought into the undergraduate curriculum at all. That, I understand, is the general subject of the conference. I think many people agreed that although poverty is an interesting subject it is not one that should be given the only place where the problem of legal process is brought into the undergraduate curriculum, but that it would be useful as part of an overall approach to law and the undergraduate program.

We then touched on problems in teaching such a course. They included whether or not if it were an interdisciplinary course it should be taught by one professor or professors of related disciplines working together; whether it should be geared differently from first year students as against third year students; whether or not the type of school the course is being taught in makes a great deal of difference. Whether it is being taught in a night school or in a day school, in a school which has a tradition of having had exposure to this kind of thing, as compared to schools in which most of the students have had no exposure to the problems of poverty.

There was also a discussion as to the content that such a course would have, and a bibliography (which is preliminary) was prepared which the members of the committee have agreed to look over and submit additions and other suggestions.

CHAPTER VI
NEW STRUCTURES FOR THE LIBERAL ARTS CURRICULUM?

In Chapters III and IV the conferees showed interest in the basic general course in law, and in the introduction of law themes in other liberal arts courses. This chapter is concerned with their reaction to more drastic proposals. The agenda for the conference proposed considering the introduction of law-society as a departmental major, or as a minor theme of concentration, in the undergraduate liberal arts curriculum. The law major proposal had been advanced at the 1954 Harvard conference on Teaching of Law in the Liberal Arts Curriculum by Dean Carl Spaeth of Stanford University Law School. Although law had for centuries been a "major" area of concentration for undergraduates at English and French universities, it was almost totally untried in American education. Lack of enthusiasm at the conference for this proposal was not unexpected; from a more central place in an early draft agenda it had been reduced to a muted note in the conference program. But correspondingly little interest was shown in a law-society minor, although this approach had already been initiated at some universities, including Wisconsin and Indiana. Are there any steps intermediate to the major-minor possibilities and the introduction of single courses that appeared feasible to the participants? This is a third question answered in this chapter.[1]

The first topic treated here is experience from foreign universities. Professor Michel Villey calls attention to the flux in undergraduate legal studies at the French universities, where law has long been a subject for an undergraduate degree. Professor Abbott tells of an experiment at Carleton University, Ottawa, Canada, with an undergraduate law department which does *not* offer law as a major or minor field of concentration. Attention then turns to the proposed law major and minor, which the consensus rejects without opposing an arrangement that would offer several courses in the undergraduate curriculum in which law-society themes might be developed. A fresh proposal is made by Professor Thomas R. Peterson, O.P., of Providence College—a composite year's course involving law and (by quarters) individual social sciences: economics, history, political science and sociology.

1.   Some Foreign Experience

(1) UNDERGRADUATE LAW TEACHING: EUROPEAN EXPERIENCE (PARIS)

MICHEL VILLEY*

What can the experience of continental Europe, and especially that of France, bring to us on the subject of undergraduate legal studies? First of all, before beginning I should like to point out that in Europe's distant past the general public of educated men was not at all ignorant of law the way it is today. In ancient Greece a Plato or an Aristotle knew the law of their time very well. This was still true in the Rome of a Cicero, a St. Ambrose, or a St. Augustine. It was still true to a great extent in 17th century France. Perhaps this historical fact merits some reflection. For an historian, the public's ignorance of law is a recent phenomenon.

However my purpose is not to speak of such far-off things, but to speak of the teaching of law in France today. I don't think I am mistaken in thinking that our juridical teaching reaches a much wider and more varied public than yours does, and that it includes a larger and more liberal course of studies.

I should like to investigate the *causes* of this state of affairs; to give you a summary *picture* of our French system; but to be less incomplete, to point out to you in concluding, that our system is at the moment in the process of evolving and perhaps of losing its most original characteristics.

I. We might consider here the way in which our system of law differs from yours—but I shall only stress the fact that our French universities are of a very different type than American universities. Our universities are government institutions. In their present state they are creations of Napoleon I, who built them according to a uniform type with identical programs of studies and with an identical organization throughout all of France. In the other continental countries, the universities are also creations of princes, or formerly of the Church.

This fact certainly leads to great differences between your system and ours:

It isn't that we professors, who are government officials, enjoy less liberty. I think that in France we professors have an almost perfect liberty of thought and of expression with respect to the political power. In some of our law departments there are even quite a few Communist professors, and

---

* Professor of Law, Faculté de droit et des sciences économiques, University of Paris.

no one disturbs them. Just as nothing prevents a Catholic professor from professing his faith.

But this gives us a great liberty—perhaps too much liberty—with regard to legal practice, its needs and its exigencies. We are chosen as professors by an examination, which consists in four lectures on theoretic subjects, after a morning of preparation, before a jury of professors. This *concours d'agrégation* makes us professors, proprietors of our office. From this moment on, no one can take our teaching status from us, nor make any great changes in our salaries. We are extremely free, with (in principle) only three hours of class a week. We may orient our courses toward very theoretic subjects, and we address students of the most diverse vocations.

II. For my second point, I want to give you a very quick picture of the characteristics of our teaching system. I will address myself to two questions: (1) the public which our law faculties teach, and (2) their programs.

1) Our *facultés de droit* certainly reach a much wider and more varied public than your American law schools. Relatively few of our students become judges, lawyers, barristers. We don't have precise statistics, but certainly less than a quarter of the total number of our students pursue juridical careers properly so-called. The greatest number are preparing for careers as government officials: as officials in the ministries, in the different public services such as the tax department, in international organizations. Others are preparing for business. Still others will do something entirely different. For example, the French poet Victor Hugo, the French novelist Balzac, the musician Berlioz passed through our *facultés de droit*. One of my cousins got his license[2] in law in order to become a farmer. This results from the fact I already mentioned, that historically most of our *facultés de droit* are institutions of the state (after having earlier been institutions of the Church). It was from among the old pupils of the *facultés de droit* that the kings of France recruited their officials. And this was even more true in 17th and 18th century Germany when the princes established law faculties to train their officials and even to train men who would be capable of directing the public economy.

And then this also results from a still older tradition, which goes back as far as the Middle Ages, which gave the *facultés* of law almost as much dignity as the *facultés* of the arts, and even the *facultés* of theology. The law *facultés* of this tradition gave their students a true culture.

2) And this wide audience also results from the programs of studies of our *facultés*. They are very vast, though they have not always been. For Napoleon really only wanted to create narrowly specialized schools of law in France. But tradition overcame him, as did the example of the German universities, which the French imitated in the course of the 19th century. In 1808 Napoleon's law schools were restored to *facultés,* and various subjects beside courses in private law were put back into the curriculum.

First of all, there was Roman law and the history of law, which until recently held an essential place; then public law, constitutional law, the general theory of the state and of political liberties, administrative law, international law; finally political economy arrived in 1896; my grandfather, who was dean of the *faculté de droit* of Caen in Normandy, was the first professor of political economy in France. But political economy quickly made a place for itself that was at least equal to that of public law and of private law, and its importance has become even greater.

And up until a very recent date all these studies were common, that is, a French jurist would receive the same training as a public lawyer or an economist.

Within the past 20 years the number of subjects taught has grown considerably. This chiefly results from the influence of sociological ideas in the world of the professors of law. A part of the professorial body was persuaded that the art of law requires not only a knowledge of public law and of political economy, but also a knowledge of sociology. In France sociology is a disputed field between the *facultés des lettres* (arts) and those of law. Several meetings have been held in the past few years between sociologists and jurists, chiefly at Strasbourg and at Toulouse, and these conferences have produced important publications.[3] And in the *facultés de droit* numerous courses have been recently created in the political sciences, the sociology of law, the history of political ideas, and the history of social facts. Sociology has certainly made a massive entrance into the French *facultés de droit*.

Various other courses have also been created in recent years: in history, in comparative law, and in the philosophy of law. The *faculté de droit* of Paris has four courses in juridical and economic philosophy. You see that all this appears to give our *facultés* a more and more theoretic style, and a rather general interest.

III. The picture that I gave you earlier which shows our *facultés* offering a general common culture to a large public, would have been true a few years ago. But it is true no longer.

The multiplication of courses that I have just spoken about which has occurred in the last twenty years, has *split apart* our law *facultés:* they have been divided since 1956 into three specialized *sections*: private law, public law, and political economy. Instead of the four years that were required for the *licence* in law, we now have only one or two years of studies that are common to all our law students. And even they are not entirely common. The separation is even more drastic in the higher studies that we call the doctorate. I myself, an historian, had the same general formation as my colleagues in private law, public law, and political economy. This is no longer true of the present generation of students.

Besides, our *facultés* have felt the weight of what we call the democratization of education, the call to the university of an immensely increased number of students, and which in practice leads to a *devaluation* of education. Now that everyone wants to be a student—contrary to tradition—the pressure of the demands of a professional preparation grows stronger and there is less time for a disinterested theoretic study.

And so, in each one of the now separate *sections* of the *faculté de droit,* we have not only offered the theoretic courses of which I have just spoken, but also an increasing number of specialized courses adapted to it, such as courses in air law, insurance, and nuclear law.

In the midst of all these new creations, the theoretic courses, such as those in history or in Roman law, are bit by bit losing their importance. Most of them are no longer obligatory. And many of them are not well attended—even juridical sociology, for example. In my course in the history of the philosophy of law I have but 20 students; and there are more than 20,000 in the *faculté.* That is the present truth.

Under the pressure of the same factors, as our teaching becomes more specialized, it tends to become less theoretic. We tend to diminish the place of lecture courses (which correspond to the tradition we inherited from the Middle Ages) in order to increase the place of what we call "practical works." In private law this corresponds to the pragmatic legal method of studying law cases. The truth is that for the past few years we in France have been turning our back on our tradition; we are becoming somewhat Americanized and—on this point—I am very sorry for it.

As I said in my lecture on "Law and Values,"[4] I believe in the desirability of theoretic studies in law that can interest other people than practitioners, of disinterested studies that do not seem useful, and yet are useful in the long run. It seems to me that the proper way for a university to be useful in the long run is to be disinterested.

I hope—I am not alone in Europe to *hope,* but are we right in this hope —that even if we ourselves are temporarily unfaithful to it, you Americans will take the relay of what is most sound in our European university tradition.

(2) AN UNDERGRADUATE LAW DEPARTMENT: EXPERIMENT IN CANADA

RICHARD D. ABBOTT*

I want to make a proposal which lies somewhere between the Law-Society graduate program which was described yesterday and the Law-Society minor which has been described this afternoon. I will describe the administrative set-up in my own university for the study of law, and suggest it as a workable alternative. I am engaged in teaching an Elements of Law course and administrative law. Furthermore there is another law man at Carleton teaching constitutional law and international law. I don't think there is anyone here who will disagree that these latter courses, administra-

---

* Professor of Public Law, Carleton University, Ottawa, Canada.

tive law, constitutional law and international law are courses which can be taught effectively in the liberal arts curriculum. However, I have heard it suggested by Professor Duff that it is difficult to find lawyers who will become members of an Arts faculty and take on the job of teaching these courses. And this is true—unless you give the law man the autonomy of a separate department.

In my school we do have a Department of Law which is quite autonomous. It has the same sort of autonomy as the Department of English or the Department of Philosophy except that we don't have a minor program; we don't have a major program. In other words we have no integrated set of courses. Our courses are piecemeal. They are bits and pieces. Now this sounds unsatisfactory. Yet my colleague and I find it rewarding. We find it interesting, engrossing and a sufficient challenge for us in the strictly law school type subjects such as administrative law, constitutional law and international law to warrant our continuing with the department. When you have a separate department with two law men in it, it is then possible for other departments in a university to find the links, the interrelationships, between their disciplines and law. They don't need to go to a law school, which is apparently a closed corporation that will not provide the interrelationship that is needed. They have a department right in the Arts faculty whose members are willing to meet with them. The measure of the interrelationship which occurs between my Department of Law and the other departments is in my role, and the role of my colleague, as supervisor of graduate theses. This is a valuable role. As soon as a student in another department finds an area which involves a heavy interest in law, we may become the supervisor of that particular student in his graduate study.

Now I wanted to mention the topics which I am working on with my students this past year and in this coming year. For instance, the rights of federal civil servants. The particular topic for the thesis involved working with civil servants themselves. Another topic was the commerce power and its application to insurance companies in the United States and Canada. A very large topic, granted, but it was done by an economics student who wanted to do her M.A. in this particular field. She would not have been able to do it had there not been a law man on the liberal arts faculty. Another one from last year concerned Crown privilege in the law of evidence by a civil servant who is deeply concerned to see how the law of Crown privilege may influence the effectiveness of the administrative machine. How much can be put down in memorandum form, how much must be done by telephone, and so on.

This coming year the areas that my students will be working in for thesis work are: firstly, on the disciplinary proceedings in the civil service, the military and the mounted police and the organization of our tax appeal board, and lastly, administrative responsibility in the federal disallowance of provincial legislation. You can see in these topics that I have mentioned there is a necessity for at least an advising function by a law man, and preferably actual supervision by a law man. And my colleague and I are available for this. This is the advantage of having the public law department right within the Faculty of Arts. I feel that this sort of approach being used at Carleton answers the problems of teacher recruitment. There is a sufficient academic satisfaction for my colleague and myself in this sort of program. It answers the difficulties of interchange of personnel between a Faculty of Law and a Faculty of Arts. At Carleton there is no need for this interchange—we are right in the Faculty of Arts. I would suggest this to you as an alternative proposal for any sort of minor or major in Law-Society.

2. Some Drastic Restructuring: Law-Society Major or Minor

The original proposal to transplant the European tradition of an undergraduate degree in law to American education as made at the 1954 Harvard conference by Dean Spaeth of Stanford, and as replied to by McGeorge Bundy, then Dean of Harvard College, was included in the preconference materials. Their exchange is worth repeating here:

SPAETH—"I am aware that all quarters, Presidents, Deans and faculties, will view with alarm, but I maintain that we should give consideration to a possible major in law or a B.A. in Jurisprudence. . . . Each of the law courses in the undergraduate major would include much more of other disciplines—history, economics, philosophy, psychology and anthropology, wherever appropriate—than we are able to include in our professional law courses."[5]

BUNDY—"I would suggest that you should decide. . . that you are not attempting to introduce the law as a field of concentration. . . . The difficulty here is not so much that you could not do it, because it is quite clear that you could, but rather that those who took it in the main would be pre-law students. . . . You would not attract into an undergraduate B.A. jurisprudence major a very large number of persons who would then go on and do something else than law after finishing college."[6] ". . .There are really only two obstacles to all changes in the university—one is the argument of the entering wedge and the other is the argument of unripe time. You will be exposed to both of them and by men whose energies are stimulated by a sense of rivalry and in some cases by a sense of superiority. . . . I suggest to you that if you do wish to proceed by the method of the entering wedge, you should be careful not to make the kind of statement that Dean Spaeth has made about the future introduction of a field of concentration;

. . . Make it clear that your ambitions are limited; that your territorial claims will soon come to an end. Adjust yourself gently to the notion that college faculties are composed of people who are used to fighting fiercely for fragments of undergraduate time. . . ."[7]

Although the Spaeth-Bundy audience was largely made up of law teachers,[8] and the Catholic University conference was not,[9] the following dialog makes clear that here too the Bundy view against the major prevailed, and the minor was swept off with it:

MASSEL—Would you mind explaining why you would be against starting a law and society course, or a law-society minor or major at Wisconsin?

BALL*—My reasons are really quite simple, and that is that as soon as you do this you tend to move toward setting up a separate department. As soon as you start to do that, you then end up with a group of political scientists, sociologists, and those of us who went through the traumatic days together all become like minded, we're old buddies, we're all friends and what not, etc., and you immediately reduce your impact on the economics department, the political science department, the sociology department. I don't want this to occur. I don't want a major or a minor. I want the role of law given a proper place in every course in the social sciences.

BEITZINGER**—Well, then, there's no reason why these people can't try to develop some of this within their regular departments?

BALL—Absolutely. And they are.

MASSEL—Does anyone else on the panel feel this way about the possibilities of developing a course or a minor or a major in law-society? Does anyone see the need for or the advantage of developing a minor in law-society? Professor Abbott, do you think there is a need?

ABBOTT—I don't go out on a limb and say "No, I don't think that there is a need." But, on the other hand, the approach that Professor Ball has suggested is one which I had felt was part of the concept of my own department. I am surprised to hear that you feel that it should be fragmented into other departments rather than being concentrated in one department. I like to feel that my department is a law department, providing a service or an appendage for various other departments. On the other hand, I don't conceive of my department ever producing a minor or a major in law or law-society.

---

* Professor Harry V. Ball, Program in Sociology and Law, University of Wisconsin (sociology).

** Professor Henry Beitzinger, Catholic University (political science).

BALL—But the pressure on you will come as Carleton grows. Now that you are a three man department you can view yourself that way. But what happens when you are a ten man department?

The real pressure, if you start with the department or the major and the minor is to put yourself back in a cocoon—that's the danger. And I think in terms of the problem you discussed there, in the Canadian educational system, at Carleton you made an excellent beginning. Now I would like to know what has happened at British Columbia, for example, where I know they have two sociologists of law, but they also don't have a law department, as to what has been their comparable experience. And I don't know what is happening. I do know that the sociology department in British Columbia has written the sociology and law program at Wisconsin asking if we have any more men. We are getting letters from everywhere wanting law-social science trained people, for research directors in action programs, top level people in areas of welfare.

MASSEL—Any other comments or commentaries or questions with regard to this issue of whether there would be any advantage in setting up an undergraduate minor in law-society?

BEITZINGER—Has anyone seriously suggested it?

MASSEL—It has been seriously suggested if you will just look at our program.

BEITZINGER—I haven't been here for all of the discussion so I don't know.

MASSEL—I meant it was suggested in writing. It's on the program.

BEITZINGER—What is the consensus of the gentlemen on the panel with regard to this—I think that's the answer many of these people want to get.

MASSEL—We shall start taking a consensus. The question is, what is the consensus with regard to the desirability of having an undergraduate minor in law-society?

FORSTER*—I would be personally opposed to it.

MASSEL—On what grounds?

FORSTER—Chiefly, I think, because I haven't been convinced there is a need for it.

MASSEL—Professor Ball?

BALL—I want to make it clear though that I am not opposed to those programs in a Machiavellian sense, that is, I can conceive of a campus situation in which it might be a very good intermediate strategy. What I am saying is that I personally would be very disappointed if it were viewed as the ultimate goal. That is, I think it is very, very far short of heaven. As

---

* Rev. Cornelius P. Forster, Chairman, Department of History, Providence College.

far as my own particular biases are concerned. I want something bigger, broader and that has a much greater impact, but that does not mean that I don't think, that as a matter of fact, they have used it as a device for making a tremendous beginning at Carleton. I think one of the things before you start, anyone would start out exactly repeating the Carleton procedure is, they should visit Carleton, and analyze why it worked at Carleton, why it is a good idea at Carleton, but basically pay as much or more attention to examining their own situation, their own resources, where they want to end up, what their present positions of strength are, and then you start to build, and always begin to build in your position of strength, but don't assume that's just where you are going to end up. And be very aware of what the pitfalls will be, where you are building at the start, because the point of strength may turn out to be a runaway horse. You've got to have controls built in. The major control in Wisconsin was my promise to myself that I was going to leave after four years, and I refused to become a vested interest in the program. And this was one way of guaranteeing that if it failed, it would end. I am leaving, and the program is continuing. I take this as sort of a vote by the institution that the program has been a success.

MASSEL—In all due justice, I think that Professor Abbott's description of what he is doing at Carleton does not involve a minor but rather a department.

ABBOTT—That's right.

MASSEL—Therefore, I take it that you were speaking about a department and not about a minor.

BALL—I was saying that as their program grows, Professor Abbott is going to find very strong emergent pressures to have some kind of a specialized program which may result in actually reducing their interaction with other departments. And this is something they are going to have to guard against as they develop their program.

MASSEL—Does this mean, then, that you are against both a minor and a department?

BALL—I would say I am really opposed to the idea of a minor. I am not opposed to a department in the proper circumstances.

MASSEL—Professor Abbott?

ABBOTT—You already know my position, but I am against both the minor and major concept and what I am most in favor of is an autonomous law man on campus.

MASSEL—Is there anybody who will add to the consensus in the group in terms of raising any questions that would be in favor of establishing a minor in law-society program, or do we have a consensus not only on the part of your panel, but also on the part of the people in the group, which is a consensus that is a combination of abstention and disagreement with the law minor program?

It seems to me in all due justice that none of the points that have been made against a law-society minor was made on the premise that there was not substantial room for a law-society course, or even a number of courses which would deal with issues and problems of law-society, for the issue that came up really was, should the law-society field be set up on a so specialized basis that it would provide room for an undergraduate minor or an undergraduate major, along the lines of taking law-society, in effect, not merely as a department, but as a department which offered a minor or which offered a major. But as I have heard the discussion, it has seemed to me that there has been no point made at all against the desirability of having a law-society program, and indeed of raising questions and developing issues about law-society in a number of courses in various fields, including, although not necessarily including, a specialized course which might review a number of issues in the field. However, as I understood the consensus on the part of your panel, there was nothing in the consensus which would be against a law-society course. The issue that was developed was whether there was room for, or a need for, a minor in the field, so that it seems to me that there was no conflict in the last point that was raised and the discussion on the part of the panel. Does anyone on the panel differ with this?

FORSTER—I think I do, to a degree. If you say there is room for one or several courses in this area, it seems to me that you have *de facto,* at least the equivalent of what would be a minor in the ordinary administrative set up on the collegiate level.

MASSEL—What would happen, for example, if you had a course in the law-society field which would be given as part of a general program in the area of sociology, one that would be given as part of a general program in history, one that would be given as part of a general program in economics, with each course being developed in such a fashion that you would have the law-society approach, which would be developed in such a way that it would add to the understanding of the specific disciplines that an undergraduate was majoring in, in an individual department? Again, this goes back to some of the points, it seems to me, raised by Professor Ball, when he raised a question about whether you would have a department in law-society, and suggested that instead of having a department, you would bring these subjects and these areas into focus on a departmental basis. Now I take it that while he was demonstrating and illustrating his point with sociology,[10] that he would not by any means imply that the only way to approach problems of law-society would be along the lines of sociology, but rather that he was developing the possibilities of what could be done in this area taking the field of sociology which he knows best.

3.   The Non-Structural Approach—Adaptation of Law-Society Program to Local Resources

A go-easy approach was urged by Professor Rosenblum, and with it his advice to adapt the mode of introduction of the law-society theme to the resources of the particular college or university.

ROSENBLUM—I don't think the objective at this stage is to change fundamental thrusts. I think that the objective of the conference will be served if there is simply a greater awareness of the role that law plays within our society and of the importance of that being a dimension of our teaching. I don't think it's a question of whether we get a law and society minor or law and society department, or how it is structured. Rather, it is that it be feasible to treat it; whether it be treated in economics, or be treated in history, or be treated in sociology or political science, may vary depending on the institution, its resources, the kinds of people who are teaching within the institution. But, I would think, the recognition of the fact that it should be a dimension of our teaching is significant enough in itself, and I would think that with just the groups represented here, anyone of the men from this university or from any of the others who are here who are connected with such teaching, who would have a chance to write a letter or to visit a campus, or to give a lecture, or to say here's what we've been doing, and to do it in terms of the particular situation with which you are faced in your particular school, and on the basis of the particular resources that you have, that this would mark this as a significant enough venture to have made the whole thing more than worth while, and that the establishment of new structures are things to be faced only as, if and when they need to. I don't know who my sponsor was on that one!

BALL—I don't either.

But I think one thing LSA[11] wants to avoid is precisely the kind of situation that you can get into, say when massive government resources are poured into an area, you get a three year grant, you hire lots of new people, and the grant is cut off after three years. In a sense, even though we have had money at Wisconsin, the thrust of the program has been to help Wisconsin to help itself, that is, the reason I am leaving is that Proposition 1 in the Wisconsin program was that no additional man would be hired at that university to carry out this program—not one—that was the thrust of the program, that was the challenge. Can you retrain the people you've got to do the work that ought to be done. And more and more this is where, at least at the upper educational level, to keep up with changes that occur, funds have to be committed. The funds have to be for training and retraining, and not for hiring lots of new people, where everyone goes running in to immediately hire them, whether they really have figured out what they want to do or not, whether they have stuck their foot in the water and got burned, or they have had a chance to explore a little bit. The effort has to be to give people time to explore. Sure there are problems where you've got to pour in lots of money and generate new structures, and so forth and so on. But there are also a lot of universities in the United States that are in incredibly bad shape today because they accepted the first grant from Ford on the belief that they were going to get the second. And they are desperate right now. And right now they have no more control over their own developmental policies than the man in the moon. They'll buy anything and the kitchen sink, if it can bail them out some way with some money, and this is precisely the kind of thing we want to avoid. We don't want to generate more problems for the schools than we are solving. We want the schools to define their problems, and we'll try to help them solve them, but we don't want to leave them in worse shape than they were found in in the first place.

PETERSON*—I have in mind a teaching program in which someone from political science would teach a course in law and political science, but teach it for one quarter. Someone else from the sociology department would pick up the notion of law and society and teach it for six weeks. Someone from the history department would treat the influence of law in the development of history, and do this for six weeks. And someone in economics would show the relationship of economics to law. It seems to me that we would have the benefit at least as a pilot program that could implement what has been discussed here. It could begin almost immediately, or certainly by September.

It would take some doing to coordinate the efforts of four men and also to bring in the practical side of the legal profession. This might possibly be done through a series of seminars between practitioners who would be available and interested in the program and the professors who are actually going to teach the course, in which they would prepare themselves for the actual teaching of their students along the lines of the program we have discussed here. It would certainly bring in the practical side of the law; it would take it out of the realm of theory since it would stress the case techniques and the problem approach. The various difficulties that lawyers have with the social sciences and the various problems the social science professors have with the practitioners could be prediscussed in this series of seminars. When the program was ready to go, it could be run on a pilot basis for a year, perhaps with selected students. If there is an honors program in the college this might be a natural place for it to start. Perhaps after having gone for a year in this particular way, it could be

---

* Rev. Thomas R. Peterson, O.P., Assistant to the President, Providence College (administration and theology).

expanded through the rest of the college. The time might come when one man would be able to take over the whole thing, but meanwhile there would be a definite program already organized. As far as expense is concerned, there simply is none because you are using the faculty members that you already have available. Any individual professor might hesitate to take on a whole new course and do it alone immediately; but, if it were merely a case of his being a specialist in one given area, and simply orientating a series of lectures toward law and society, he might be much more willing to do this and do it well on a one quarter basis. Furthermore, this plan would give the students the opportunity to see in a practical way, in various areas, from various approaches, and in the course of a year the relationship of law to several social sciences. And perhaps this might stimulate interest which could later be further expanded. Although there are problems and difficulties with the idea, it seems to me that it might work.[12] I feel very strongly that there is no single way of putting law into the curriculum. On the contrary given the differences in size, given the differences in faculties available in the teaching, I would think that it is only on the basis of each person knowing the strength and the resources of his own school that the proper kind of introduction of the subject matter can be made.

ROSENBLUM—It seems to me that what is being proposed represents a gradual start which can then be implemented further, which doesn't represent a deep plunge but initially a set of planning sessions putting the big toe in the water to see how the water is. I would say that this sounds to me like a good way to get going geared to the particular organization and faculty size and faculty needs of the university.

Part Four

THE WIDENING INTERDISCIPLINARY
HORIZON IN LAW-SOCIETY

CHAPTER VII
ACTIVITY IN RELATED DISCIPLINES

Throughout the conference the notions recurred that the social disciplines are interrelated, and that in each of them the factor of values is involved, explicitly or implicitly. Are the social and value factors present and interconnected in other educational spheres? This question was faced at the conference in the context of theological and religious training—and in an area so traditionally remote from general education as the formation of future priests and religious sisters—in a workshop on Social Studies in Religious Education. The question was also raised with respect to the natural and physical sciences, but reserved for full consideration at another meeting.[1]

1. Social Studies in Religious Education Workshop

In this workshop leaders in Catholic university education, in adult education and the Catholic action movement, in seminaries for training of future priests, and in the formation of religious sisters, discuss the role of social studies in their work.

The dialog that follows was edited from the full transcript of the workshop by Rev. Anthony D. Lee, O.P., editor of *The Thomist*. Chairman of the session was Professor Ralph Powell, O.P., of Aquinas Institute, Chicago, where Dominican seminarians of the Province of St. Albert receive their training in philosophy. The other participants, in the order of their appearance below were: Rev. Richard McSorley, S.J., Georgetown University; Mr. Matthew Clarke, The Religion and Labor Council of America; Sister Maria Eucharia Meehan, C.S.J., Brentwood College, Brentwood, Long Island, N.Y.; Mr. John Kenna, National Catholic Welfare Conference; Very Rev. Walter J. Schmitz, S.S., Dean, The School of Sacred Theology, The Catholic University of America; Rev. Richard Murphy, O.M.I., Seminary of the Oblates of Mary Immaculate, Washington, D.C.; Sister Mary Gabriel Hobler, Maryknoll Sisters Motherhouse, Maryknoll, N.Y.; Sister Felice Shumway, C.S.J., College of St. Rose, Albany, N.Y.; Very Rev. Ferrer Smith, O.P., Regent of Studies, Dominican Province of St. Joseph; Rev. Alban A. Maguire, O.F.M., Holy Name College (Franciscan), Washington, D.C.; and Rev. John Corcoran, O.P., Aquinas Institute, Chicago.

FR. MCSORLEY*—Georgetown now has a course in the morality of socio-economic life. *The Social Conscience of the Catholic* is the textbook—it has 40 cases in problem form. It's being used at Marquette University. In fact two Jesuits under the direction of Father Everett Morgan have been putting a course together at Marquette for about three years, and this text is the result of their work—it's still being evolved. I think that it's the best for American college students and it's better than any seminary moral theology course at least in reference to group morality.

It is a three credit course, undergraduate for seniors, accepted for credit in philosophy, theology, foreign service—genuine foreign service credits—and business. It's still being considered by some of the other departments —political science, economics and sociology. Besides being what the Popes have asked for during the last 50 years, it is a unifying course. I have convinced the Provincial and Georgetown that it should be a full-time undergraduate credit course and institutionalized into the obligatory field of the curriculum. I am in the theology department now; I was trying to get it into the philosophy department but failed, so it is included in theology. Some of the theology faculty object to its inclusion. The general objection is that it's not theology.

I have run into a similar difficulty with the philosophy department. This department considers even special ethics to be ridiculous for philosophy because there is so much to be discussed in general ethics that you never really get to particular ethics. When you do have particular ethics, it's not really philosophy—it brings in so much influence from theology that it becomes theology. It looks as though the dispute will never end. Philosophers, it seems, are often more content to fight and disagree than to solve things.

FR. POWELL**—Thank you, Fr. McSorley, for the discussion of the problem at the university level. Now may we ask Mr. Matthew Clarke for his observations on the level of adult education and the Catholic action movement.

MR. CLARKE***—I will speak of adult education of a specialized sort. My work is to organize seminars with The Religion and Labor Council of America. I direct their program which is aimed at clarifying basic socio-economic issues in the light of religious values and religious principles. For three years I have been organizing seminars on topics such as "The

* Rev. Richard McSorley, S.J., Georgetown University.
** Rev. Ralph Powell, O.P., Aquinas Institute of Philosophy and Theology, River Forest, Ill., Workshop Chairman.
*** Matthew Clarke, Religion and Labor Council, Washington, D.C.

Cooperation of the Public Interest," "The Humanization of Work in Labor," "Industry and Religion in the Community Power Structure." Last February, we brought Father John Maxwell from England to Washington. We had a seminar on Father Maxwell's proposals for corporation law reforms.

I would like to call particular attention to an article by Father Maxwell, "Should Christians Press for Revision of Company Law?" It is a very specific application of encyclical social teaching, of natural law doctrine. Father Maxwell makes a kind of breakthrough here, giving us a critique of essentially what is the basis and root of the capitalist system from a natural law and encyclical point of view. This article was published in the October, 1962 issue of the *University of Detroit Law Journal,* and the following issue had a symposium by American experts on the subject.[2] David Bazelon and a number of others contributed essays commenting upon Father Maxwell's work. This is an ideal text for what I am doing, i.e., it is an attempt to establish a social dialog on a basic economic issue with contributions from people in government, labor, management—everyone concerned with the issue—and Father Maxwell is someone who deserves attention here. More directly related, this is the topic which, in a disciplinary way, relates to law, society, and the Church's social teachings. The new work which I recommend to you has not received due consideration, but it's valid and is something that should be and will be more important in the future.

I would like to focus on how indirectly to relate Catholic social teaching and seminary education. I recently did some notes for Father Dennis Geany, who is doing a chapter of a book on the reform of seminary education—the chapter was entitled "Social Action in Seminary Education." The key consideration of the chapter was how principles of social action could be made an integral part of seminary experience. Here are my observations.

We first need to show that the principles of the encyclicals are from enlightened experience. This probably must be assumed as we cannot question here the values of the Church's social teachings. However, I think the adequacy of the Church's social teachings can be questioned, certainly in application to particular areas. Often they are not relevant; they are too general; the implications have not been developed. Father Maxwell, for one, is working at developing these, but we need much more of this development. We simply can't assume that the principles immediately solve all problems; we have to clarify the general teachings in reference to particular areas.

Next, we must consider what kind of experience can make social principles a part of seminary experience. This is almost a contradiction if the seminary is the only place seminarians go. If seminary experience is considered a time period of the training and seminarians are allowed beyond the walls, then they begin to get experience during their training period. But it has to be experience; it can't be just the academic side of it. Inside the seminary, of course, they must be familiar with the best literature currently produced, with the history of the Church's engagement in social issues, and with the guiding principles of social theory. This is a minimum. In history, for example, they should be aware of the social movements in the United States, and more specifically of American Catholicism and social action since the Civil War, and they should have a general historical consciousness of where the Church has been in social movements in relation to European experience and American experience. In other words, they have to be conscious of a tradition, and such knowledge is seldom imparted. I went through a Catholic college where no one had ever heard of American Catholicism and of the history of Catholicism in the United States. Recently I met a girl from the midwest who is very active in the Catholic social movement. She was in the Young Christian Students in Davenport and elsewhere; she is now in the Peace Corps in Brazil. She was being questioned at one point by the Director of the Peace Corps about some experience she had, and he had reason to talk about past history and he referred to Father Charles Coughlin. She had never heard of Father Coughlin. Although relatively trained in social science, she was completely uninformed about the history of Catholic social action. A young man who had attended a Catholic college came to Washington from one of the specialized movements in the midwest of the Young Christian Workers. He wanted to find out what the National Catholic Welfare Conference and Young Christian Workers required. He didn't know where to go. He didn't know who Monsignor Higgins[3] was. He just didn't know there was a department, what it did, where it came from; he didn't know anything about the Bishops' program; he had a complete blank of historical consciousness. The only way something can grow is to have a group of people with this historical consciousness. That has to be emphasized.

The other point is that the seminarians not only have to gain this historical consciousness in seminary training, but they have to be engaged with the people who are doing social action work in the city. Their experience in seminary training must involve active participation in the movements which have developed independent of official sponsorship; they must enter in and be able to relate their academic training to this kind of experience.

FR. POWELL—Thank you very much, Mr. Clarke. Now we will have Sister Maria Eucharia give us a resume of what is being done in her community.

SR. MARIA EUCHARIA*—Brentwood College was established about ten years ago for the education of our own Sisters (and now for other communities as well.) In 1961 I was selected because of my training and experience in economics to set up a social science curriculum for majors

---

* Sister Maria Eucharia Meehan, C.S.J., Brentwood College, Long Island, N.Y.

in that area. I have studied ways to incorporate the social doctrine of the Church within the courses offered. The major consists of six credits each in the following: economics, government, sociology, and geography. Courses include the requirements of New York State for teachers in the elementary and high school.

While the immediate problem under discussion in this meeting is the possibility of offering a separate course in the encyclicals, it is my belief that the principles and materials of the encyclicals should be incorporated within actual course content. This requires knowledge of social doctrine on the part of the college professor. Last summer I met Fr. Morgan of Marquette University where they offer a social doctrine institute program. Father is anxious that Sisters know of this offering. He mentioned the formation of ten-day institutes at the various colleges and motherhouses as a means by which Sisters could receive adequate training in encyclical materials. I would like to make a bargain with him to teach the economics part of his social doctrine program and in turn attend courses in theology and social philosophy.

FR. POWELL—I would like to offer at this point a few words about the program at Aquinas Institute in Chicago. We have in our philosophy section three basic courses which relate to the social field. In second year philosophy we have a reading course which I conduct. The course requires about 1800 pages of reading material in sociology and anthropology. This provides a good look at primitive society, treated in the anthropological method of investigating the diversity of social structures and social values. Of course, this method shows very clearly that primitive society is radically different from our ideas of Christian values and life according to virtue. The principal idea communicated to the student in this course is that life according to virtue should not be conceived of as a universal prescription for human beings, that is, life according to virtue is only a particular type of social realization, social ideal. Aristotle, in writing his *Nichomachean Ethics,* deliberately excludes from life according to virtue the vast majority of mankind whom he says are incapable of appreciating or even understanding the meaning of virtue. I think that most Catholic social teaching makes the gross error of attributing to the common man—I mean to everyone, in every circumstance, in every type of society—an ideal which Aristotle deliberately restricted to the Greek aristocracy, people who had a complete philosophical and liberal formation, who were freed from economic necessity. It seems to me that until we correct this particular error our training will indeed be miserable. So we have a reading course which brings out the distinction of social values and ideals—a distinction which corresponds roughly to the sociological distinction between *gemeinschaft* and *gesellschaft,* or between primitive society and civilized society.

In the second part of the second year of philosophy, Father Benedict Ashley gives a survey course in the encyclicals. This is also a three hour course for a semester, as is the reading course. It is intended to give the student a realization of the problems which the Church faces throughout the social field. It is not just a reading course. Father Ashley brings all the problems before the students, making them aware that this is a world in revolution with very great problems indeed.

The third regular course is given in the third year. This is a graduate course because our students come to us with at least two years of college. It is a theoretical course in problems of natural law philosophy, designed to build on the materials already laid down, and trying to show how the human conscience evolves according to social conditions. The basic message is that, if you look at the facts, the origin of all moral conscience consists of a very bare minimum which St. Thomas can call the absolute natural law. It comes down to group solidarity, kinship piety, and an effort to explain the world—not that the term is reached, but it is a loyal searching. It's a motion; we must get the idea of conscience as a process of being and thinking. And being is not just thinking, the whole man must think out his socially determined circumstances.

Another mistake which I think our social teaching incarnates is the neglect of the category of social determinism. This is a very important concept. You can't touch the social sciences today without first considering social determinism. Anthropology and sociology are basically about social determinism. They are value free for the very simple reason that what a man does under social determinism, he is not responsible for. It seems to me you cannot understand social conflict unless you see that each group is thinking from its socially determined category. Not that this social determinism totally destroys transcendence of the social situation. On the contrary, the social determinisms should be conceived of as the enemies of the voluntary—according to scholastic tradition, *hostes voluntarii*—in which there is always some freedom, some ability to transcend determined group interests. But if social study neglects the socially determined world view out of which each group is thinking, it seems to me the study degenerates into talking intergroup justice in terms which are totally outside of the reality. It must be understood, for example, that for the Jewish community the basic social determinisms are religious and such a world view is fundamental to all subsequent moral thought. For a Jew, Christianity is defined in terms of a system of persecution, that's all. And until you realize that, you are simply not talking to Jews.

In other words, the complexity of society comes out of small groups which have their inculturated socially determined world views and values and structures, and the effort of social justice is to bring these together. In complex societies the more primitive groups remain and are the condition of all social group inter-action. Such is the message of the third year course.

Finally, we have some special courses, seminars for those writing M.A. theses. Here there will sometimes be a course in social subjects, for example, a seminar on state and religion was given one year.

FR. MCSORLEY—One observation concerning Sister Maria Eucharia's presentation involves the problem of specialization. Perhaps my point could be illustrated in this way: a Jesuit, already older by the time he is ordained, who gets a doctorate in political science, in economics, in sociology, or something else, will find it very hard to give up the academic prestige of being in the sociology department, and perhaps being the head of it, to teach social encyclicals or theology, where his special competence is not really given its proper place. We constantly run into the impossibility of resolving this difficulty in the Jesuit order. I suspect that it is true for this general synthesizing course anywhere. You can't get the people to teach it. The reason we haven't been able to get it in seminaries is simply that we do not have the teachers. Everyone thinks he is incompetent to teach it, and if he has a doctorate he feels very confident in his field and wants to stay in it. The argument I get is that no one is competent enough to teach this kind of course. My own solution to the problem is to have competent specialists as guest speakers every week. I have had the Undersecretary of Labor, John Henning, who has lectured at San Francisco University, discuss Pope John's encyclicals with regard to a labor question, unemployment in the United States, and international aspects of unemployment; Leon Keyserling, who was an economic adviser to President Truman and is one of the national figures in economic analysis, illustrated from his analysis what is wrong with the economy. This program is designed to meet the objection of specialization. The one who organizes such a course is really managing and supervising the interdisciplinary experts, and providing it with relationship to moral teaching.

FR. POWELL—I would like to suggest a problem concerning the fact that now the great majority of members in our American church are solid, satisfied, well-fed bourgeoisie, whereas in the 30's the Catholic population was generally lean, hard, ill-fed, and felt underprivileged whether they were or not. This makes a difference, for example, in the race question today. As long as we were fighting for good solid Irishmen who were dishonored in the plant, we could talk about the necessities of union organization on a mass scale. When you talk about the rights of Negroes who are Protestants and who don't follow the Christian ideas of marriage, a totally different problem arises. It seems to me that we've got to get at the implicit world view, the socially determined position of our Catholics. Mr. Clarke asked for historical awareness, and obviously, this would contribute toward a solution.

On the other hand, there is one thing I think we left out of the discussion: a very real factor in the American situation is the power of the Catholic hierarchy. It seems that Mr. Clarke's approach might be setting up exactly the sort of thing that frightens about 75% of Americans. In the presentation of the encyclicals, the impression may be created that the word goes out from Rome—here is what is to be done—and Catholics merely apply it to their particular circumstances. You tighten a bolt here, you shine up some other part of the mechanism, and 50 million American Catholics spring into action: the word from Rome goes into effect. Well, this is, after all, a managed conception of society.

First of all, it will appear thus to non-Catholics, and to show that I am not talking nonsense, when *Mater et Magistra* came out, it was widely criticized in Germany on this score. Secondly, it does not take into account the doctrine of *Ecclesiam Suam* which is trying to de-clericalize. One of its real messages is the de-clericalizing of the power structures within the church: that the ecclesiastical authority will only function in terms of dialog within the community. So we have to discuss this sort of thing—the ecclesiastical power and the Catholic power within the community. If the encyclicals are taken as a sort of blueprint for America, the way the Catholic social movement did in the 30's, once the program begins to be realized it is going to meet a formidable resistance from terrified non-Catholics.

MR. CLARKE—My point would be that past experience has to be criticized and a more adequate theory of present conditions would have to be developed. In other words, if you think Catholic social experience in the 30's was nothing more than a labor priest going out to fight for his boys— some of them were indeed very narrow and parochial—then the social determinism has to be examined, people have to be made aware of this, and a way of coping with it has to be developed. That's why I suggest the method of social dialog and realistic dialog between opposing groups. In a seminar, on labor, industry and religion in the community college structure, we utilized the work of two sociologists, Delbert Miller and William Form. We had Miller and Form give papers on the whole study of community power structure, as it has been developed by sociologists since about 1951, beginning with Floyd Hunter. They study community power structure by going into a community and investigating who can veto a program which is begun, or who can initiate a program to get it through a community. From such an inquiry they know what forces are operating there.

How important is the church? An example is their study of Archbishop Lucey's attempt to get another union in place of the Mine, Mill and Smelter Worker Union in the southwest. It was found that when priests came from St. Louis and elsewhere to tell the workers not to vote for the communist union, the workers didn't listen or at least didn't agree because the priests were not part of the community. It was ineffective. This is one little example of what we are talking about, but what is needed is a wider awareness of the forces of social determinism. This is the reason I took up the idea of power structure in the community.

The only studies we have which are worth going into in some detail are studies of local power structure. National power structures have not yet been studied sufficiently. People like C. Wright Mills have addressed the subject but there is not enough known to talk about it adequately. It's such a wide field of controversy and opinion you can't do much. The church and the community, and the way in which the church is engaged in social problems, is certainly part of it. But the way in which the church is related to social problems has not been critically analyzed to date: for example, there has never been really an adequate criticism of the labor school experience. The labor school experience was not based on a theory. There were people grabbing from here and there. Richard Deverall was one of the more active participants who started a magazine called *Social Justice,* a few years before the name was taken over by Father Coughlin. He became a labor organizer and got five bishops or so to accept the idea of the CIO within about a year. He went with John L. Lewis, doing public relations for the CIO. The point is that the movement grew out of practical experience, not from theory, and that the whole area of labor experience has not been criticized, and no new approach or new way of looking at the world has been developed. The only way this can be done is, it seems to me, by more and more attention to it in a structured way. It has to be done on an inter-religious basis also.

FR. MCSORLEY—Another example, about which I have had some personal experience, is the Civil Rights Bill. In general, the Catholic has looked upon his social involvement as limited to the Catholic world. The Catholic world has been looked upon as the whole world and the only world because of the social determinism created by Catholics living in the Catholic ghetto all their lives. If social determinism is in effect, and I think it is, the Catholic answer to it is not just to study it or not just to know that there is social determinism, but to meet the world as it is and to realize that this Catholic world, the formally Catholic world, is just a small part of the world. It may even be deforming to the Catholic to be restricted to the formally Catholic world of thought and activity.

I myself found that you couldn't do very much for the Civil Rights Bill if you stayed in Catholic organizations. The Catholic influence was at its greatest when it was exerted outside of the structured organizational work of the Catholic Church. In fact, they were looking for bishops and priests for their influence in the civil rights organizations. They were looking for them in the public sphere. I think that the Catholic social teaching program has to present the idea of the Catholic open to the world and the whole world as being part of the Catholic idea. I think this is just what Mr. Clarke is doing. He's trying to convene social dialog, not just between members of the Catholic religion, but between religion and the structured working forces in the United States. Apparently he's meeting the same sort of formalistic objection and difficulty that I'm meeting on a different level: the labor unions don't think this is labor, and the religion groups don't think this is religion.

MR. CLARKE—There is a constant overlap with all of these. The difficulty is that large groups are aware only of their own set of values. I meet it all the time. They find our program interesting, but beyond their immediate concern. In other words, there is an area of overlap which is just a little bit in everybody else's domain, so they say, "Well, that's really just a marginal concern for us. We can't spend much time on it." Yet this is the implication of the whole thing.

FR. POWELL—Do you think that the basic ghetto character of American Catholicism and the formidable power which the Church has within her ghetto, is the reason for this failure, or is it the unwillingness of these other people to look on Catholic social efforts seriously? I know when Mr. Deverall was working on the Auto Workers Newsletter in Detroit, he was expelled by the communists who organized a demonstration of 6,000 people shouting, "Down with Deverall, the fascist!"

MR. CLARKE—The history of the whole thing is written in the careers of people like that. You can see from where they have been. Recently, I introduced Father Calvez, S. J., of *Action Populaire,* Paris, to Mr. Deverall and a few other people, people working in international development and community services for the American Institute of Free Labor Development. We discussed where these people meet, what is their organ of communication and opinion. *Social Order* was an attempt at such an organ but it has gone out of existence. Mr. Deverall said the only place they meet is in small groups in various cities. They know each other from across the country from experiences in the past., That is the sociological level at which this activity goes on. It doesn't go on in any organized fashion. What I would argue for is a commitment of resources for development of something like *Social Order* where you have a magazine devoted particularly to social discussion. Father Calvez is the editor of *Action Populaire.* He has a circulation of 7,000 or 8,000 and the whole magazine concerns social issues and Catholic thinking.

MR. KENNA*—I am officially in the ghetto now, as I work for the National Catholic Welfare Conference. Like Mr. Deverall and Mr. Clarke and others, however, I have spent a good part of my life out of it, too, so I can see, I think, from both sides of the fence.

I would like to make an observation on our stated problem here about seminaries. I recently attended the Airlie House meeting in Warrenton, Virginia, organized by the government for religious leaders, clergy and laity, from all over the country. About 250 were there, of which 40 or so were Catholics. The Catholic group took the occasion to hold its own junior ecumenical council. The general conference concerned the Civil Rights Act and the Poverty Bill, so our rump meeting discussed the relationship of the Catholic community to this legislation—what contribution we could make, and how we could participate most effectively in its implementation. Of course, we got into the very thing that we are talking about now. I was greatly impressed with reports on the advances that the nuns have been making—the coordinated, determined efforts of the sisters to become more socially aware and to enter more meaningfully into the life of the broad general community—and equally concerned about reports of the utter lack of seminarians who are able to do the same thing. I gather

---

* John Kenna, National Catholic Welfare Conference, Washington, D.C.

that whatever can be said about the Catholic ghetto in this country can be raised to the third power as far as the seminarians are concerned. These future priests will be expected to assume the position of leadership in the general, as well as the Catholic community. The nuns are beginning, even in the early years of formation, to see the community dimensions of their vocation. Seminaries could learn a great deal from what the sisters are doing in regard to the social aspects of their task.

FR. MCSORLEY—In reference to our own seminaries, we have done nothing. The last rector of Woodstock tried but couldn't do anything because the faculty was not in agreement. They either couldn't see that the encyclicals were theology or didn't think them important enough. This is emphasized by the decision of the Jesuit Provincials—ten Jesuit Provincials—who, two years in succession, decided unanimously to kill *Social Order,* the magazine Mr. Clarke mentioned, because they couldn't get $15,000 a year they were losing on the magazine. It seems to me they didn't have enough priority value given to the magazine to get the $15,000. That amount is allotted for many other things. This illustrates the Catholic difficulty: priests in general are not going to believe this is really part of the Gospel or part of the faith if they don't get it in the seminaries.

FR. POWELL—Are we not merely assuming, and it seems to me something we could question here, that the priests should be leaders in every field? It seems to me that what we see in Europe, and to no small degree in the United States, is the appearance of a new type of man, namely, the lay theologian. I think of the birth control discussion in this country as an example. We have laymen like Georgetown's Professor Dupré, people who are competent, who can treat in depth the details of the question, who are not just talking to make themselves heard, but who know their field. In Europe also this is true. Europe has many good lay theologians like Le Bras of the University of Paris, a canonist, who is also a real theologian. But we have attached the notion of ordination to that of theologian and this is not necessarily the case. I do not mean to infer that the clergy should not to be introduced to the social dimension of the apostolate, but I question that they have to be the leaders.

FR. MCSORLEY—The difficulty of specialization is that the priests are often not interested in theology because they are interested in their own subject. I can't see Jesuits teaching the course that is started now at Georgetown, unless, of course, the Provincial decides to prepare somebody for it. Obviously, so many other specialized fields require long and careful preparation, but I don't think the priest has to be an expert in many things. He doesn't have to have anything more than a basic philosophy and theology to teach the Gospel as it applies to the group aspects of the world today, or at least to manage the course.

MR. KENNA—I think your point is excellent. I wasn't assuming by any means that the clergy would necessarily be leaders in carrying out all the ramifications of the social apostolate personally. But they have to communicate, and this is an important role. They have to be able to communicate with the people who do fully carry out that role and, given their sociological dimension as persons, they also have to live in society. They must reach and in some way be accessible to society. What is happening, I think, is that in many areas of the United States priests find themselves pastors or assistants in parishes in which perhaps a sizeable minority or even a majority of their people are better educated and more aware of the realities and issues of life and society than they are. Now this is a tragic thing because it reduces the importance of the role of the priest even in relation to his primary responsibility. I wasn't talking about equipping priests to be primarily social leaders, in fact I think that is a mistake.

FR. POWELL—I would suggest in line with this that Father John Courtney Murray has done a work which is very proper for the priest to do: to show that the Catholic ghetto is false on the political level, that the medieval idea of a confessional state is false theologically, that the Catholic community has its obligations to the whole community at the civil level, that there is no such thing as a Catholic group within the community. The Catholic faith is invisible from the point of view of the civil order. What has really held us in our ghetto is a loyalty to the medieval order wherein the only obligations in justice were to Catholics. The non-Catholics were defined as serfs, people who could not be citizens, and so all obligations of justice were due only to Catholics. This, I think, goes into the thinking of the hierarchy and the priests all the way down the line. But here a theologian says to Catholics, "This is an error, get out of your ghetto. In the civil order you are just like anybody else." I think also of the theological implications of realizing that non-Catholics are members of the Mystical Body, something which medieval theologians never fully realized.

MR. KENNA—Mr. Clarke brought up the particular question of social experience in the seminary. I wish he had gone into it a little more because I thought it vital to our topic. If seminarians want to participate in some community action, whether a demonstration of Christian concern, or a series of lectures, there are times when they can't go because the event is on Monday and their day off is Wednesday. Though this situation is not as common as it used to be, seminarians tell me it still happens too often, and in some situations regularly.

FR. SCHMITZ*—I will have to disagree with you. It sounds too much like a recent article in the *Saturday Evening Post*.[4] I resent very much what was published there, because they generalized on a few instances, and then we get statements like you made right now. I think it is terribly unfair. The article in the *Saturday Evening Post* talks about the seminaries in Wash-

---

* Very Rev. Walter S. Schmitz, S.S., Dean, School of Sacred Theology, Catholic University.

ington. If you read the article carefully, I think you will find there was one seminary concerned, the Paulists', but many of the statements were generalized. The fact is that many of our seminaries are perfectly willing to adapt themselves according to the opportunities they have of doing so. Last week at The Catholic University of America the students of theology attended lectures at Georgetown University. We've used other opportunities, and we give the students all the freedom they need. I feel that you might also be generalizing a bit. We priests nowdays have a terrific problem with seminarians, you just can't let them run loose at every whim. They just want everything without discretion; you give them an inch and they take a yard.

FR. MCSORLEY—I agree with you to some extent, but not entirely. In the Jesuit seminaries, about which I can speak with more experience, we are losing men, we have the smallest number entering, and the largest number leaving in our history. They even have the Assistant General of the Order for America saying that maybe the day has come when the Jesuit order has to decline. I think that a big reason for this has been the failure of our seminaries.

For the first time, under tremendous pressure from the men leaving and objections at Woodstock, we have optional class attendance for all, and this is a concession that is direct. Our men are ordained generally from 31 to 33 years old, and they have grown all through this period from high school on without meeting their youth. They have three years of teaching, but they haven't seen the effect of their personality or themselves on the world. What they have really lost is both an appreciation of themselves and for the world around them because they are so kept out. This will not be solved unless they are going to be let out in the summer time, unless they are going to receive many more concessions, concessions like that made last year by the seminaries in Washington to help in the civil rights vigil. These concessions are being made reluctantly, and sometimes not made at all. The idea of a vigil going through the night, even for something like the Civil Rights Bill, was objected to formally on the basis that seminarians are not out at night. Protestants were coming from New York, coming every day and going back every day, and providing their car for this at their own expense. During this period Catholic seminarians weren't even able to get a telephone call after 9:30 at night. On a phone call I tried to make I was told to contact, or go to, the superior, and the message would be, "We don't take phone calls." This is small, but this is cumulative, and it affects the personality of the seminarian by the time he is a priest.

MR. KENNA—I am not blind to the difficulties of deciding how far you let the leash out. However, I think that the more we can build within candidates for the priesthood a sense of personal responsibility, and give them the freedom to exercise it, the more they will operate accordingly. This could be encouraged, I believe, more than it is at present. Furthermore, the directors and faculties of seminaries could benefit a great deal by having an equable percentage of lay faculty members. Perhaps seminaries need boards of trustees, or regents, in order that professionally competent lay people, particularly in the areas of communications, social sciences, etc., would be present and give a layman's slant on the relevance of the curriculum in regard to the dimensions of the life of the priest that touch the issues we are discussing.

FR. SCHMITZ—The seminarians probably have an advantage here at The Catholic University of America. Our students attend classes with lay students and they're better adapted to meet this lay situation.

FR. MURPHY*—I think all of us who are in seminary work recognize the need for reevaluation of curriculum. That will gradually come and the Council will help to accelerate it. I think Sister Formation has gone far ahead of seminaries in this effort. What we have done in the past is simply multiply courses. When somebody suggested the need of social studies, a course on social encyclicals was added; when someone else recognized another problem, the need of the liturgy, another course in the liturgy was forced into the curriculum. This accumulated curriculum is the result of the past. But I seriously question much of the clamoring to free seminarians of this tremendous burden. I think some of the people criticizing seminaries today are criticizing seminaries which no longer exist.

The more basic problem is that we have to get a unifying principle and coordinated program in seminaries in theology, philosophy and humanities. It's pretty difficult to find anybody who will tell you what philosophy is supposed to do in the formation of a priest except in general statements from *De Scientia Dominum* or *Sedes Sapientiae,* and that's it. Many of the problems we are facing in social action, social problems, I think, will be helped a great deal when we get a better appreciation of the Mystical Body, which I don't think we have as yet, and when we get a better appreciation of theology and wisdom on the supernatural-natural level, the humanities. We still have a collection of courses that are thrown together, and we don't have the unifying principle. My only experience is in seminaries; I can't talk about colleges or universities, but I think we're working towards a better curriculum in seminaries and a better unifying principle, and a lot of these problems will be clarified. Seminaries are really not the ghetto that they are sometimes made out to be today. They are much more open than people sometimes realize.

FR. POWELL—I would like to summarize the discussion so far. Several participants have presented what they were doing in their respective institutions. Sister Eucharia raised the specific question as to whether we need a special course, a special new course in encyclicals, or in social doctrine. And since this is the point that we are discussing here, it's worthwhile

* Rev. Richard Murphy, O.M.I., Seminary of Oblates of Mary Immaculate, Washington, D.C.

recalling that in the Law-Society Conference there seemed to be a general consensus that we do not need new courses. What we need is to build concepts into the existing courses, and so I think this fits with what has been said here. Academic time is already apportioned as tightly as can be; there is no more room for other courses, but there is plenty of room for new concepts (as Father Murphy has just said), a new way of looking at things, and especially the social dimension of modern life; the social dimension of the apostolate and of the citizen in the modern world.

SISTER MARY GABRIEL*—I would like to present the program we have in a small women's college. Since it is for our own sisters, it may suffer from a ghetto mentality. We have prepared an Associate in Arts degree, for those working towards a Bachelor of Arts degree. Presently we have a Bachelor of Science degree in education, which was the next step beyond the simple B.A. We would like to liberalize as much as we can, and have always kept two or three basic minimum methods courses because we felt the need. Liberal arts is of course much more useful to our sisters. But because of our work as a missionary congregation, we have been very conscious of the needs of knowledge and understanding brought by a cultural anthropology. So now we have anthropology which is a two semester course, three credits. To provide introduction to this and to missiology we incorporate mission encyclicals and other encyclicals that deal with social problems.

Since our students come to us from varied backgrounds—some have already been prepared by their college programs, and some are totally unprepared—we do have to cope with special programs. We need, of course, to bring the history of American social activity into the college of the sisters. We have also a program and a department which is called the missionary education secretariat. The director's work has been social service training. Our need to prepare sisters for the missions demands the social services department. We do a great deal of medical work also. As I think through our courses, I realize we have done much of what has been discussed—not that we could sit back and say well done. We can do very much more. We do have the advantage, I think, of filling the needs of the sisters because of our work, and for this reason the picture is a little broader for us. But we can use this advantage to do more in the direction suggested here.

SISTER FELICE**—In our provinces, the sisters have three years at the novitiate during which they begin the regular college program. A juniorate period of two years follows. During this time, the young sisters attend

---

* Sister Marie Gabriel Hobler, Maryknoll Sisters Motherhouse, Maryknoll, N.Y.
** Sister Felice Shumway, C.S.J., College of St. Rose, Albany, N.Y.

classes in one of the institutions conducted by our community, the Sisters of St. Joseph of Carondelet. In some cases, if these junior sisters constitute a large group of 35 or 40, which itself comprises a class, it is taught separately; otherwise, junior sisters form part of the regular session classes. The majority major in education, history, social studies or English; a few select the other more specialized majors. Majors are chosen after an interview with the Academic Dean, according to the interests and abilities of each sister. In New York State we have a social science requirement of two courses which the sisters fulfill in their sophomore year. For this, economics, political science, or sociology may be chosen. Education majors take geography to complete this requirement. Girls who enter with previous college work may be given special courses; this past year a course in social principles and economic life was taught for them. I believe they used Father Cronin's book on *Social Principles in Economic Life* as a text. The work on the encyclicals is incorporated into the subject matter of the various fields.

FR. SMITH*—I would like to present three observations on seminaries for your criticism.

First, the most informative remarks for me have been Father Murphy's—especially about the unifying principle of the seminary. Years ago the people who put out the Minnesota Multi-phasic were striving to find a profile of a priest. To my knowledge they have never succeeded. Do we know, does anybody know, what we are trying to do in the seminary? We seem to be operating on about ten different levels, acting as if one moment everybody in the class is going to be a sacramental technician, with obligations to individual souls. And this takes time, it takes a good deal of effort, it takes a good deal of self-discipline to become an adequate technician, as Father Weigel used to say, let alone even dream of becoming a theologian or a philosopher, or a liberally educated man. But simultaneously in our seminaries we are striving to be liberal arts colleges, trade schools, productive of leadership, productive of administrators. Back of it all we have the constant refrain from the saints, the Holy See, and tradition, that we are trying to develop a spiritual life. We are trying to do too many things at once. And I don't know of anybody who is quite sure of what we are doing.

Secondly, it has always been a mystery to me why young men of 21, 22, up to 26 (we ordinarily ordain at 26 or 27) are treated as children. What kind of a course have we organized, or has been organized for us by Rome? It takes the same amount of class hours per week in the fourth year of theology as it takes in the first year of theology. To me this is ridiculous. We have accomplished nothing—there has been no development, no per-

---

* Very Rev. E. Ferrer Smith, O.P., Regent of Studies, Dominican Province of St. Joseph, Washington, D.C.

sonal grasp of what we are teaching. They are in the same position as fourth year theologians as they were as first year theologians, with five hours of dogma and five hours of moral per week. Their contemporaries in the world are already in postgraduate work, they are adults, responsible human beings. We prolong adolescence. We turn them out and they stay adolescents, as far as I can figure out, until they become pastors, and then they become senile. I am exaggerating, of course, but it brings out the point that Father Murphy made about responsibility—there is a lack even of academic responsibility.

We definitely have a problem, as Father Schmitz pointed out. As far as our students are concerned, they would be out all the time. They'll go to any lecture except the ones we hold in the House of Studies. They'll listen to anybody except our professors. They are in accordance with anything except what we teach. I am exaggerating again, but I am just trying to make the point. Father Mailleoux pointed out one time at the Institute of Mental Health up at Collegeville: "I stayed in my room for 16 years, and then I had something to say, and I went out and said it." Our boys want to go out and start talking right away—whether they have anything to say or not. So they add their ignorance to everybody else's ignorance and we have a right to get worried.

To me the key is Father Murphy's suggestion. We have to make up our minds what we are doing. Surely just adding courses, e.g., introducing social sciences to the seminary, is not the answer. It is absolutely necessary, but it must be done, as Sister Eucharia pointed out and Father Murphy pointed out, within the existing structure. But we must also start treating them as adults, and demanding adult responses. This is a time of transition and in the process we are going to have to go through torture as far as I can see. Just telling them to act like adults—they can't do it. We've given them nothing to train them to be adults, to be personally responsible, and to be mature. We treat them, are treating them, have treated them as children— not to the extent that we are accused, not by far—but maturing is not an automatic process. It has to be planned. If we don't know what we are doing or how to do it, then how can the students feel that they are being adequately trained and formed.

Thirdly, we can't be run from a desk in Rome. But this change is going to take time. As long as our curricula are set up for us by the Jesuit order or the Dominican order, or the Secretariat of Seminaries and Universities, or the Secretariat of Religious, we have to find out how we can move within this structure. And there is a lot of movement possible.

I don't know exactly how many seminaries we have in the Washington area, but my conviction is that these seminaries could be a thousand miles apart. I have been here for 22 years. I get together with Father Schmitz, with Father Murphy, with Father Gene Burke, and so forth, but it's only in recent years that we are really, I think, beginning to get somewhere. The communications have been non-existent. This whole problem of communication, and this big word nowadays "dialog"—we're just beginning to find out what it means. Through local, or regional dialog we must find our own solutions to our local problems within the structure set down by Rome.

FR. SCHMITZ—I know that Father Smith, Father Murphy, all the priests here, will agree that there is a tremendous gap between the life in the seminary and the life work as a priest. The White Fathers of Africa at one time had a very good plan. They sent their seminarians out for a year before ordination, sort of an apprenticeship, to see how they could do with cathechizing, and how they could fit into the picture of pastoral work. The Church is now using the deacons to a greater advantage, and this strikes me as opportune. Father Vieban, who was in seminary work for over 45 years, has said many times that he felt we weren't preparing seminarians for actual priestly work. You just lift a seminarian out of the seminary and dump him. He is on his own and he has to reorganize his life completely. We have been interested in sort of an academic thing and not the practical and how he is going to face up to it.

One thing that we could do to help a great deal, I think, is to use to a greater advantage our various seminaries and schools, exchange professorships, and the consortium. In Washington, Father Bunn has created interest in the consortium, but I think the religious houses could use it to a greater advantage. For instance, at St. Mary's Seminary in Baltimore, we have Father Raymond Brown, who is one of the outstanding scripture men in this country. Why not let him go to one of the other seminaries for a period of a month or six weeks, and exchange with somebody else from another seminary. Colleges do that with nearby institutions and use all their resources to mutual advantage. I heard recently that there is a plan for some of the smaller schools in Louisville—where they probably have only four and five in a class with one teacher—to bring their faculties and students together in Chicago.

FR. POWELL—I know of similar moves in Chicago, for example the Passionists, Servites and Benedictines are coming together to form a theological school on the campus of the University of Chicago.

FR. MCSORLEY—Here in Washington where there are 65 houses of religious men, we could do this to a much greater advantage. There would be other areas away from Washington, as the sisters were telling about up in Albany. Even if it does cost a little money for commuting and things like that, why not use what we have? We are not tapping our resources—the idea of the consortium and exchange professors.

I want to add a thought to what Father Murphy said about a purpose for the priest or a purpose for the seminary. It strikes me that part of the reason for the difficulty is that we have had a purpose which was established a long time ago at the Council of Trent. A structure was set up from a kind of a static world view, as though the world of the Council of Trent (and this is exaggerated) is the world as determined for all time. The program for seminaries then had nothing built into it allowing for a dynamic change or for the change of times. When a younger person suggests something to a superior, the ordinary reaction is "Well, we never did that when I was in the seminary." I propose that in the ideal of the seminary—whatever it's going to be or whatever the priest is supposed to be, or whatever the structure is supposed to be—something be incorporated allowing for changes in the seminary which are going to come at an even faster rate in the next ten years. The world has changed more in the last 15 years than it had changed in the 50 years before, and the prospect is that it is going to change more in the next ten years than it has in the last 15 years. We are not only in a transition, but we are never going to get to a static state. Let me just add this—I know about the Jesuit order. It has been looked on as disloyalty to the Jesuit order to talk reform. Now that might change because the Church is talking reform.

FR. POWELL—We have an interesting situation here where a Dominican father is sitting next to a Jesuit father; and the Dominican father criticizes the Dominican situation, and the Jesuit father the Jesuit situation.

FR. MCSORLEY—This is a problem for the Church. I just see it for the order. We can't reform ourselves right now. It's built into our constitution, we can't change—and as a result we are losing out.

FR. POWELL—Everyone is doing public penance—the Church in the Council is doing public penance, confessing what she did to the Jews, and no longer blaming the Orthodox and Protestants exclusively for the schisms in the Church; and now the orders themselves have to take on this same role, realizing that there are many things that need to be corrected.

MR. CLARKE—I would like to pick up a number of comments of Father McSorley. What we are looking for is a way of establishing flexibility in the Church and ability to deal with change. And we talked about the unifying principle of seminary education. The Church is in a way having an identity crisis. The priests, the laymen—all are having the same kind of problem, i.e., understanding the relationships in the past, discerning the great events and crises which have changed all these relationships. There has to be a unifying principle. There has to be a new clarification of what we are doing in all areas. Then there has to be institutionalization of the new approaches.

One of these in the local community, as Father Schmitz mentioned, is consortium in the graduate schools. This is one institutionalization, a new institutional form. Within Protestantism there has been a lot of discussion of new institutional forms of the church, and I am in contact particularly with the people in the area of Protestant social thought who have created these new institutions.

One such new form in the area of relating the church and economic institutions in modern industrial society is an industrial mission. It began in Sheffield in England with the people in that industrial area. Here in the United States the Detroit Industrial Mission and the Cincinnati Industrial Mission have taken their cues from the Sheffield Industrial Mission in England and the priest workers in France. They read Congar and they read the experience of the priest workers. They are attempting to research what the relationship of the church should be to the powers in the world, particularly the economic powers. At the Detroit Industrial Mission, they have had about five to eight ministers working on this for nine years. They have had what they call a total approach: a method of dialog in which they talk with the heads of the corporations, the heads of the unions, middle management in the corporation, middle management in the union. For several years they had minister workers on the assembly line at Cadillac. That is, they went to talk to everyone there to see how the religious institutions could be related to the economic institution. In other words, this is not ministry to the individual, but to the powers of the world, particularly economic institutions, because they consider the economic institutions to be central.

Within Protestantism Gibson Winter has focused the attention of the Protestant churches on the urban scene, through the book *Suburban Captivity of the Churches*,[5] and through another one he calls *The Metropolis as a New Creation*.[6] In the Detroit Industrial Mission, Hugh White, the director, and Robert Batchelder collaborated on a book on the morality of bombing Hiroshima. They have recently published a paper called "Mission to Metropolis" which is available from the Detroit Industrial Mission. In it they talk about the new restructuring which is necessary, particularly in the area of social power. They believe that the churches now have a certain concern for urbanism. They are speaking for Protestantism when they talk about urbanism and the urban church and the inner city.

They would like to see an emphasis upon the economic institutions and engaging people on the basis of where they work, where they spend the major energies of their lives, and examining what they do in this area.

This is hardly a developed thing in Catholicism, but now Catholics are adopting these terms. When I was active in Chicago in the Catholic Action group, during the 40's and early 50's, there were several specialized movements, CFM, YCS, etc. They used to discuss "the problem of the downtown communities," the suburbs, and family, but no one thought about the man on the job, and how this thought affects the powers in the world, particularly economic powers. This is what the Detroit Industrial Mission is attempting to do. They are calling for new institutionalization, particularly in the area of the economic order. They want research and study agencies and more of these on a wider scale, ecumenical if necessary, and preferably ecumenical. They began under Episcopal sponsorship, became interdenominational Protestant, and now would like to have Roman Catholic cooperation. In this latest pamphlet, "Mission to Metropolis," they call for attention particularly to the economic order, not just the urban one. They think those churches will pass which are concerned with urbanism and a false notion of the problem of the future, e.g., concern with leisure, or concern with liturgy; rather they want particular and quality examination of the relationships within the economic order, since the political order, the city, is just a product of what goes on in the basic economic order. They want attention to this primary area, because they consider this to be the primary institution in American life. In America, business is business. The corporation is the unifying institution of the entire society, and this is what they want to engage. They don't want to go from one fad concern to another, which is not addressed to the basic issue. So they are now attempting to call a halt to what they think may be a movement from urbanism to leisure or something else, and saying, "Look, we have to take stock of ourselves, this is the direction in which we should go, and what we need is more attention to this." And I think we can take the same cue, though the discussion within Catholicism has hardly developed at all. We are just nibbling at the problem.

FR. POWELL—There is something in the way social doctrine is taught in the seminaries which is relevant to Mr. Clarke's point here, and that is the notion of property. We conceive natural law principles as sort of immutable atoms (preferably the Democritian variety which are solid, round, and fall in only one direction), and this cuts off the possibility of real moral commitment in a social order. Father Duff, in an article in *Social Order*, in January 1959,[7] raised the question of property, and he said very frankly the way the notion of private property is taught out of *Rerum Novarum* has no connection with property as it is in the United States today. And this incongruity exists because we do not distinguish the natural law notion of property from its particular socio-cultural realizations. Consequently in the name of natural law we try to analyze present American economic reality with concepts which patently do not fit it.

We are in a situation similar to that of the 15th century princes related by Huizinga.[8] The princes of the time were political representatives of organized national states that gave them a public role quite different from that of a private knight as defined in feudal terms of private individual valor. But respecting warfare, the princes had only feudal terms with which to conceptualize their role. And according to feudal concepts, every knight including the prince must fight opponents on a basis of equality. Consequently, a prince frequently offered to settle conflicting national claims by single combat with his rival prince. And the challenged prince had to accept although such duels were constantly postponed and never carried out. And this was so because their real situation, that of a national organized state, did not enter into their conceptual pattern. They had to think their real situation with concepts that simply did not fit. Now in the same way we have difficulty with the notion of property. We are trying to analyze the American economic system in terms of the property analysis which we find in *Rerum Novarum,* based on the principle of small agricultural properties, and this does not fit our present situation. It is essential to isolate the real natural law notion of property from any particular cultural realization of it. Property is economic power.

Again going back to the 15th Century period, they had continuous litigation in the 15th Century because they were using feudal concepts of the 11th and 12th Centuries in analyzing a 15th Century property structure which was based on private peasant ownership. The same is true here. The real definition of property is economic power, and if you're going to determine what property really is in the United States, you have to determine where the real economic power is, where the power of decision is. For example, in the corporation, they say the real decision makers are the managers of the corporation. Hence the stockholders have property only in a derived and secondary sense. In other words, to talk about the natural right of property, without the capacity to isolate this from particular social structures, seems to me worse than useless. And this is part of the false notion of stability that you build into the seminarian's mind.

FR. MCSORLEY—You could take your example of the military and apply it to the seminary. The director of the seminary has to deal with the young seminarian in the framework that makes his mobility so limited and his options so small that he can't actually deal with the real situation.

FR. CORCORAN*—I think that if you were to try to find one point in which outsiders consider themselves distinct from Catholics and especially from the approach of the Catholic seminary, it would be in their use of the research method as against what they consider use of the deductive method in Catholic seminary training. We hold a scholastic disputation, for instance, like a communist trial, where you can drink to the death of the defendant before the trial is held. There is never a doubt in any one's mind about sustaining the thesis, and as a result the impression is created that there are no real open questions because there aren't any open minds in the Catholic church. I think we could solve a lot of these problems, if we would, by a course of apprenticeship, gradually wean away our seminarians from the reliance on the deductive method, which is necessary in the earlier expository kind of teaching where the pupil has to receive the traditional knowledge through a direct pedagogical approach, even as in undergraduate physics. The student would reproduce experiment and demonstration to a foregone conclusion to show that he has received the traditional knowledge; but then he would be apprenticed to the research method where he demonstrates his ability to address himself to an open question and find an answer that perhaps no one has found before.

FR. POWELL—This seems to meet with much of what Father Ferrer Smith said. The unfortunate characteristic of the typical seminarian is that he is immature whereas his colleague of the same age in the university has a highly critical mind trained in what Father Corcoran called inductive method and problem-solving method. We need then a more critical teaching of philosophy in the second and third years of philosophy, and perhaps in the later years of theology.

---

* Rev. John Corcoran, O.P., Aquinas Institute of Philosophy and Theology, River Forest, Ill.

FR. MAGUIRE*—This discussion is coming at me from so many levels that I don't know where to begin. I would agree wholeheartedly with everything that Father Smith and Father Schmitz and Father Murphy have said. We are in this thing together and we are all trying to figure out, if for the present only in a tentative sort of way, some solutions to our multiple problems beginning with the curriculum.

At Holy Name College, a house of theology, we do not study sociology because the students have already had the course. They have also studied social problems. The point made by Father Corcoran has been obvious for some time. Unfortunately, I am afraid, our weakness in this field shows up in parochial work. Our approach is completely theoretical; we study Catholic social principles and we study social problems from a book, but we rarely study the concrete reality.

How to bridge the gap from the theoretical to the practical, I think, is an almost insoluble problem in the seminary situation. At Holy Name College we have had for some time what is called The Pius XII Discussion Group. Run entirely by the students themselves, this Group tries to meet the problem by studying social questions from both the theoretical and practical angles. After they have studied and discussed a subject among themselves they will invite guest speakers to address them on the topic about which they are presumed to have practical knowledge. For example, just recently they invited four married couples to discuss marriage. After going into a question as thoroughly as possible they usually come to the conclusion that there are many things that they do not understand. And this, I think, is a good result.

Added to this is another level of activity—the level of social work. For more than 20 years our students have been engaged in an organized system of apostolates. There are six of them at present: the Franciscan clerics of Holy Name College go to 1) D.C. Village, which is for old people; 2) Junior Village, for orphans and abandoned children; 3) the Receiving Home, for delinquents; 4) Children's Village at Laurel, for exceptional children; 5) Glendale, for the tubercular; and 6) St. Elizabeths, the mental hospital. There is also other social work which they carry on informally.

This social work is fairly well organized now. About 15 years ago there was a danger of it getting out of control; so much was undertaken that the apostolates tended to become more important than studies and so they had to be curtailed. The overall good result of all this activity is that by the time they are ordained the young priests have had experience with the actual living human beings who are considered social problems. They are very much aware of the actual situation of these people, of what is on their minds, of what is bothering them, and the like.

As valuable as this experience may be, it deals only with individual social problems. How to approach community social problems is a question that is almost too complicated to be answered. We can begin by trying to open the minds of the seminarians to the existence of these

---

* Rev. Alban A. Maguire, O.F.M., Holy Name College, Washington, D.C.

things. In this we need a great deal of help from the outside and from one another. As Father Schmitz said we should employ the faculties of the various houses of study in the neighborhood. There are something like fourteen full faculties of theology in the neighborhood and until recently they might just as well have been on the other side of the moon.

FR. CORCORAN—I think that part of the trouble of one generation against another has to do with the notion of authority and freedom. I was with a Jesuit once who was here from Canada making a television film and we were visiting his relatives. They hadn't met a Dominican before and they said, "Well, what's the difference?" And while I was formulating a theological answer in the back of my mind, he blurts out, "The Dominican order is a democracy, they elect all their superiors. In the Jesuit order we have totalitarianism mitigated by the insubordination of the subjects." But there is a changing notion of authority which eventually will solve a lot of these problems because authority is connected with authorship. A person is given authority to the extent that he has a mission as an author in the growth of someone else's life or his own, and the notion of authority held by too many of the elders and seen by too many of the younger is a static one of a position which you maintain by keeping others in their place, like the Apostles who were going to chase the children away. But authority is really a work to be done by drawing your children or pupils into collaboration with you. When Cardinal Suenens was in Chicago, he said that collegiality doesn't mean the substitution of an oligarchy of bishops for the monarchy of the Pope, but rather that in some way every Catholic is a colleague of the Pope. I think if that spirit of collaboration were communicated, there would be more of what Cardinal Stritch used to call a "creative obedience" on the part of subjects, and collaboration with the leaders rather than this feeling that they have to go separate ways in order to achieve the ideals of their life.

MR. KENNA—Yes, I certainly agree on that. And as one of the Pope's colleagues I would like very much to suggest that distinguished seminary professors regularly consult appropriate laymen on the very things that you are talking about. We have some ideas to relate to our priests who serve with us in Christ's cause. We even have some ideas on the training of our clergy. We, naturally, applaud the consortium and other projects allowing seminary professors and rectors from various faculties to meet more often. I simply suggest here that a few competent laymen who are in touch with some of the social realities be brought right into the very center of the planning and discussion. Laymen have some worth while things to say. They have interesting views, and valid, constructive criticisms, and at least they ought to be heard. I believe you'll agree that, by and large, they are not now being heard.

We have been nibbling at what Father Murphy originally laid out, namely, the whole matter of understanding the priesthood and its relationship to the Mystical Body and the laity. Lay Catholics, many of them quite knowledgeable, can help the seminaries just as they can do their part in every element of Church life. To try to solve seminary problems, or problems of sister formation, or anything else of importance to the Church —the People of God—without direct reference to the laity is a tragic error in this day and age.

FR. POWELL—There is in *Problems of Authority*,[9] edited by John M. Todd, a very interesting article by Congar, and I rather suspect that it is behind *Ecclesiam Suam*.

Father Congar brings out in that article the very interesting notion that since the 12th Century one of the most decisive factors in the history of the clergy has been the formation of the clergy as a separate social class, having its own way of feeling, acting, living, whereas in the early Church, the clergy was not even allowed to have distinctive dress. The Rule of St Augustine says that you should not be distinguished by your dress. This seems to mean that you are forbidden to wear a habit. We read that rule every Friday during community meal and we are all there, sitting in our habits. But there is a letter written by Pope Innocent I, at the same time that St. Augustine was writing the rule, in which he is forbidding the Archbishop of Narbonne to impose a specific dress on his priests. And so it seems to me that this enters very much into the formation of a seminarian, making the clergy a separate social class, having its own way of feeling and acting, set off against the laity, which, of course, is what hinders dialog. In fact, it is a very great obstacle to dialog to maintain a class distinction.

MR. CLARKE—How do we institutionalize the feedback principle? This is the question we are trying to get at when we talk about "creative obedience." The way I first came upon this was in an article in *Cross Currents* by Frederick Heer. He talked about the positive side of obedience, and the obligation of the person in the subordinate position to make the authority give a rational command. Now that's the issue. How do you get feedback from the experience of the laymen; how do you get feedback from the lower clergy and upper clergy. What are the institutional forms by which this is accomplished? We don't have these, and the reason we are in this crisis is that we haven't had them. We are still working with the structures of the Council of Trent, and this is vital to the whole issue. How do you get an institutionalization of flexibility, so that people with a certain degree of collegiality can get this experience communicated, criticized, analyzed, and have adaptive measures taken by the rest of the body.

FR. POWELL—Isn't this the great challenge which the Council is putting before us. The papal commission on birth control includes many lay experts to help the theologians. The Council is building up these very institutions that you are calling for. In other words, collegiality is going to be institutionalized, and right down to the laity. And what has already been suggested here, i.e., that lay professors be brought into the seminaries, is another way of institutionalizing this. We are moving out of the feudal order of the clergy as the dominant social class into a democratic church. We might even go back to the Irish 7th Century where the hierarchy were just monks in a convent, and a layman, the abbot, says, "You ordain that man. We need another priest." Now that's a little too radical, and not too much in contact with 20th Century industrial society, but it does show the marvelous adaptability of Catholicism to social orders which are almost indefinitely heterogeneous.

FR. SCHMITZ—I think that in seminaries and in universities we have to revamp the entire curriculum in theology. We are working on this at the university now. I am thoroughly convinced that apologetics should not be taught until the last year. Father Bernard Häring says the students get the conclusion the first year and then try to find out what is supposed to fit into that conclusion. I am convinced as well that the study of marriage and canon law related to it should be incorporated in the matrimony course. The same can be done all along the line. Then the bare norms of canon law would not have to be taught three or four times a week. It would be treated in the perspective of the proper subject.

Along this line, St. Meinrad's Seminary has made quite a departure in its theological program. I don't think it's ideal; I think it is a step forward. One professor takes over a class and teaches for six weeks or two months, another takes over and complements the work of the first. The programs are worked out in cooperation with the whole faculty. Father Gene Burke went out recently to examine it, and reports that they are very pleased with what they have. They feel they are getting good results. He noted particularly in research and library work an improvement over the work done before. One of the difficulties with the program is that the poorer student just can't keep up with it. But I think the innovation is a worthwhile approach and deserves attention.

I know that many in seminary work are engaged with a self-evaluation in their own seminaries. They are trying to determine the needs of their institution, not only the academic, but the disciplinary, the pastoral—their whole program. I think it's true that all of our training has to be rethought. We can't go along with it the way it has been. For instance, one thing we have to drop, if we could, is the requirement of Hebrew (two hours a week for two semesters) in order to earn a licentiate in theology. We also have two hours a week for two semesters in Scriptural Greek. What if those of us who have degrees in theology were asked to give any of our Hebrew now? Well, it's just a stupid requirement, that's all. With Scriptural Greek, we can depend on the people that are specialists in that line. They know what they are talking about, and if I have to do some research I'll go to the Scriptures. But we have that awful problem of meeting the demands of Rome and meeting the demands of our American educational associations.

MR. CLARKE—Could I ask a question? I don't want to make any other comments, but about 25 years ago or more, I guess, George Shuster was raising the question in *Commonweal* about the education of priests in normal liberal arts colleges, Catholic colleges, presumably. He was suggesting that this be done. Father John A. O'Brien was looking for an institute to be formed at the University of Illinois. He opened up a New-man Foundation there and built a big plant in the 20's, before there were many Catholics there. I would like to ask the question, when is it, and by what form, and how soon can we expect serious consideration given to the education of priests in ordinary Catholic liberal arts colleges (which are still part of a so-called ghetto) and then going beyond this to education of priests in public institutions and state universities. Is this within the foreseeable future? Is it possible in five years, ten years, and if not, then it seems to me we are still talking impractically.

FR. MAGUIRE—There is a considerable amount of work being done already. You may have received a letter from the NCEA[10] recently about the Catholic colleges open to situations of this kind. At Duquesne the semi-narians of the Holy Ghost Fathers are going to college with the rest of the students. So it is already in existence at Duquesne. The Augustinians have built at Villanova a big house of philosophy, a four year college actually.

MR. KENNA—What would be the relationship between these Catholic seminaries and the Divinity School at the University of Chicago, that is, with its four Protestant faculties?

FR. POWELL—Apparently they would only hope for some sort of friendly relation, an informal relation at the beginning, maybe later being developed into a recognized branch of the university.

MR. KENNA—The cross-fertilization of Catholic seminarians with some of the minds there at the university would be really interesting.

FR. POWELL—Most people are aware that one of the basic problems of the seminary is that it is isolated. Another problem that was brought to the fore was the immaturity of the seminarian. The difficulty of overcoming this is very closely related, of course, to isolation, but perhaps even more to the way in which philosophy and theology are taught. After all, these remain the principal intellectual disciplines of the seminary. Besides, we have the difficulty of composing the intellectual training of the priest with his technical training as a dispenser of the sacraments, and his spiritual life. I think the danger which Father Schmitz mentioned, and which would appear to me a danger in St. Meinrad's program, is that we come to think of the priest only as intellectual which, of course, is not the truth. This always has to be balanced against the fact that the priest is basically a priest, and not an intellectul, not a theologian, not even a community leader. So this certainly brings us back to a more full consideration of the problem of the seminary.

SUMMARY OF WORKSHOP ON SOCIAL STUDIES IN SEMINARY EDUCATION AND SISTER FORMATION PRESENTED TO PLENARY SESSION BY RALPH POWELL, O.P., WORKSHOP CHAIRMAN.

From the outset our group was not concerned with the problem of legal studies as were the others. The reason is that the seminaries are more remote from the social sciences as a whole than the average college. Hence, what we discussed was social studies in seminaries and Sister Formation. But the problem of legal studies did come up.

In general, the group agreed that no special course be added to the already overburdened seminary and Sister Formation curricula. We found, among other things, that the Sister Formation programs are more advanced respecting social study than are the seminaries.

This brought us into a critical examination of the structure of the seminary, perhaps more negative than was quite just. It was pointed out that seminaries were set up at the time of the Council of Trent; their structure had been determined in Canon Law since that time. And now there is a decided cultural lag between the present needs of clergy formation and the seminary institution of formation. However, most of us expected the present Council to revise the structure of the seminary. The group found the seminary confronting the knotty problem of integrating formation for the multiple roles expected of the priest. These roles are namely: the role of administrator of the sacraments; the role of intellectual, especially in theology; and the role of man of, and counselor in, the spiritual life. It is very hard to put together these three components of seminary training. Specifically, the seminary faces the problem of isolating the students sufficiently to give them a spiritual formation, and on the other hand the contrary need of having them participate in social action. However, the seminaries are more open to social action than in the past, but it causes difficulties.

A more general situation was indicated relative to formation of sisters and priests in understanding social reality and social action, to wit, the ghetto character of the Catholic community as a whole. It was felt that this condition was breaking down, especially through the present council with its conception of religious liberty and the consequent non-confessional character of society and state. It seems that this is the critical breakthrough for the whole formation of the clergy because the isolation of the Catholic community and of the clergy in particular stemmed from the enduring Catholic commitment to the medieval ideal, where the only people in society were Catholics. Consequently, in the post-medieval centuries, the Catholic was obliged to withdraw from a society which was not specifically Catholic. He had no commitment to non-catholics according to the medieval ideal, since a non-catholic was defined as a non-citizen. Hence, as society acquired its modern definition as non-catholic, society itself became a non-object for Catholics. In contrast to that rejected medieval ideal, our group agreed that seminarians and lay Catholic actionists must be trained to cooperate with Protestant, Jewish and other social action groups in solving the common problems of society.

As regards clerical and lay relations within the Church, the laymen were eager to vindicate a role within the decision making process of Catholic social action. The clergy were quick to admit that they were even incapable of giving the seminarians the social formation which they required, and that they would need to bring in laymen to help in the training of the clergy in the social disciplines. So also the group foresaw that the laymen must have their proper role in implementing social action, and that this role was destined to increase.

The group was very conscious that the Catholic community was moving to a dialog situation wherein the ecclesiastical authority will be only one element, an important element certainly, in a dialog of a community in which the laity will have voice. Here Father Corcoran introduced the notion of "creative obedience" whereby what people do is not pre-defined by what the ecclesiastical authorities may think, though the authorities retain responsibility for ultimate judgment. Provision for dialog within the Church between hierarchy and laity is made in Pope Paul's encyclical *Ecclesiam Suam*[11] and in the *Constitution on the Church*[12] of Vatican II, but so far these concepts have not been institutionalized.

At the practical level, we proposed more interchange of good teachers among our several institutions. Moreover, it was thought that several neighboring institutions could pool resources to obtain either courses or single lectures from competent scholars and lawyers in the area of law and society. This would include having laymen as ordinary teachers in seminaries and Sister Formation institutes.

Finally, strong support was accorded the view that decentralization within the Catholic Church as between the Roman Curia and the U.S. hierarchy is also an important thing which tends to a more adaptive formation of the American clergy; because as long as the seminaries here are held to the norms layed down in Rome, there can never be a full adaptation to American life. Such decentralization is implied in collegiality, but once again it is not yet institutionalized.

So we ended up, I think, with an optimistic view towards the future, not however without considerable public penance for the past.

2. Natural and Physical Sciences

Aspects of the problem of interdisciplinary education that are common to natural and physical sciences and to the social sciences and liberal arts, were touched on earlier in the remarks of Dr. Gustave A. Arlt, President of the Council of Graduate Schools in the United States (*supra,* p. xvi). The conference returned to this theme in an exchange in which Mr. Massel, Professor Rosenblum and Sister Catherine Therese took part, but only to underscore its significance. This subject was not on the agenda and it was reserved for another day.

MASSEL—What about the natural and physical sciences. I've heard in several quarters that there is an interest on the part of some of the people in the natural and physical sciences. They are concerned about what is going on. Their concern is not only with regard to the law but also to the whole social science area—of where we are going. I have the feeling, at least looking at the scientists around Washington, that many of them are getting concerned about social problems in a way which they never have before and many of them are developing the feeling that something ought to be done in the education of natural and physical scientists. I have heard in several quarters about great distress on the part of medical faculties. They say that the law faculties are much better off than they are. That for some reason or other the high proportion, in fact, almost all, of the students going to medical school now go in because they see a chance to make a lot of money. And this is all they are interested in. This is not true on the part of the faculty, but true on the part of the medical student.

ROSENBLUM—I wish we had representatives of the medical and of the other faculties here, but where is the appeal to idealism in pursuing medical education today, if the battle is a battle in which every public image of the leader in the medical profession is one of saying "no, no, no, we're against this, we're against that, we're against something else." Where are the affirmatives for which medicine has always traditionally stood? I think the difference between the leadership of the medical profession and the leadership of the legal profession is that the leaders in the bar acknowledge the many areas of inadequacy in lawyer services and are anxious to get things organized so that plans can be developed to improve the situation, whereas you don't get that kind of affirmative leadership coming out of the medical profession.

MASSEL—It's because of this that there are people in the natural and physical sciences who are very anxious to do something with the development along these lines. As a matter of fact, they are beginning to become aware in some of the Washington scientific circles that we really have to take a look at many phases of where and how science fits into the whole structure of American life and many phases of the relationship between science and law, and science and economics.

ROSENBLUM—With respect to the inner humanism of the profession, I was in Dakka in East Pakistan several years ago, and one of the most unforgettable persons I met was a doctor who was a member of the Sisters of Mercy who had spent ten years in the jungles of East Pakistan practicing medicine. This is a story that ought to be hailed by the medical profession, that ought to be used as a means of attracting young people to medical careers, and it isn't. So that when you look at the structure of leadership there, it's no wonder that its greater appeal is to young men who see this as an opportunity to earn a respectable or better than respectable living, rather than the inherent idealism that medicine offers a means of curing people, helping people, or leading people.

MASSEL—People who have those ideas probably include many who go into public health and are just uncomfortable working in other fields.

ROSENBLUM—In a way it is unfair to dwell on this because there is no confrontation, no one here to speak for that profession.

MASSEL—May I say in response to that, I think that the reason that the scientists were not brought in was because of the fact that the program was pretty filled just by bringing in the social scientists. But if we are going to think of developments of this type in terms of taking some action, it might be better to bring in natural scientists now rather than wait for later, partly because of the need and partly because of the practical reason.

ROSENBLUM—One of the problems, medicare for example, would be a perfect example that the three have to be put together, law, society, and medicine.

MASSEL—And medicare involves a number of rather interesting economic problems.

SISTER CATHERINE THERESE*—Go back to the very beginning of Blue Cross and even that was against their wishes. And everything they've done since is only because they've been pushed toward it.

MASSEL—Then are we in agreement that it would be desirable with respect to any future planning to make mention at least of the natural and physical sciences.

---

* Sister Catherine Therese Knoop, C.S.J., College of St. Rose, Albany (social science).

Part Five
PROPOSALS OF IMPLEMENTATION

A dominant concern at the conference was what next steps are in the order of practical achievement with respect to the introduction of the law-society theme into the general liberal arts education of undergraduates. A sharp focus was given to the immediate needs of faculty training, area planning, and servicing the small colleges, and to the role of a central co-ordinating institute to further these steps with efficiency and dispatch. Chapter VIII takes up the conference discussion on these needs.[1] Chapter IX sets forth specific proposals derived from the conference deliberations.

CHAPTER VIII
FACULTY TRAINING, AREA PLANNING, THE SMALL COLLEGES

1. Faculty Training

The 1954 Harvard conference heard doubts voiced as to the possibility of getting enough law men to do the undergraduate law teaching it recommended. Sheer disinclination, lack of professional incentive, cost in scholarly time—all these were suggested as obstacles. And yet no enthusiasm was expressed for the idea of non-lawyers giving courses involving basic legal elements.[2] At the Catholic University conference the view was expressed that, even were they available, law teachers may not be best suited for the task of teaching law-society to undergraduates. The Chairman, Mr. Massel, had called the attention of the conference to the fact that "the roles and functions of government which lie outside the conventional field of law are becoming more important," citing social security, regulations concerning safety and minimum standards, a wide range of government licensing functions that escape judicial review, governmental activities in purchasing, research and development and antitrust. In an era of great change "much of the work in the law schools of the United States suffers from a substantial cultural lag." In this posture, he added,

> . . . the social sciences, through sociology, political science and economics may, because of the areas with which they are concerned, actually help to throw more light upon an understanding of law and our society than if we develop liberal arts courses which are left entirely in the hands of people coming from the law schools.[3]

We have already seen the emphasis put upon training social science men in the law in earlier statements at the conference. But this still leaves a significant role for law teachers in the task of transmitting to undergraduates a general learning in law-society. This was developed by Professor Harry V. Ball of Wisconsin in his discussion of faculty training, and of the need for lawyer consultants:

BALL—I am not just talking about the possibility of organizing summer institutes, but also of the possibility that a small number of law schools will at the outset organize special one-year programs for social scientists. I have become convinced now from kicking around law schools for seven years that it does not take three years to learn what a social scientist has to learn about law. A bright social scientist can learn it in six months, generally. Now this means any particular area of the law you've got to work in. But you have to work at it just like the lawyer works at it. For the average Ph.D., it will take a year to become as competent in the general approach to law as the average lawyer. Now note, I didn't say as the average law professor. I said as the average lawyer. Let's not make too many demands on these poor social scientists. But then if they become really interested in a given area—and they've got to reach the point that they can continue to develop and adapt their own course materials in terms of those areas of the law which are exciting, pressing, which constitute the basis of generating real student interest and motivation—then you have reached the point that by gum you are really ready to go on one of these things. Now this will take a little time.

In regard to filling these positions, we also have the simple fact that it is estimated that in a very short time, a matter of a very short number of years, there will be openings in American colleges and universities for 37,000 Ph.D.'s. In the same period of time we will produce a total of 21,000, of which one-half will be taken over by industry. Now we are down to 10,000. What this means is that as a matter of fact there are an awful lot of very bright young men who've gone through law school who really don't want to be lawyers, who did very well in their undergraduate work, who did middling well in law school, who probably when they come out of law school are the closest thing to the liberal arts lawyer that Professor Roberts was talking about. They're not law review. They are bright, intelligent, motivated, with good undergraduate backgrounds. Some of them were Phi Beta Kappa. We've got to be able to produce to fill this void since everyone is getting interested in saying we've got to have teaching programs which are less than a Ph.D. This becomes a huge reservoir of people to tap in on, because with one year, again of specially developed programs, one year, just like we must develop special one year programs of social science and law, I want now special one year programs in the social sciences for these lawyers. And it is out of this group that we can fill the teaching voids in history, political science, economics, sociology, in many of the colleges across the country. When you start to get these people you begin to get a law resource. You've got it, you've got the lawyers you need on your faculties to help you, consult with you, assist you, work with you. He is also at least a semi bona fide social scientist.

But you've got to change the orientation of the administration, too. You know, the fact that this man doesn't have a Ph.D., you can't let it kill him. You've got to say he's got four years of professional training. He's filling a position that we really need, and he's got to become a specialist in the teaching and curriculum development. Now while this is taking place, we've got to fill this void in between. While we're pushing social science teachers into this area—they're going to come out, they'll come out to a summer institute, they'll go back home—they'll be completely incapacitated. They've got all excited on this first eight weeks exposure to this thing, they're ready to go; they suddenly get back, nobody else in the place cared what happened to them, they suddenly don't have any confidence about the thing. Someone says *Brown* v. *Topeka*,[4] and they say yes, *Brown* v. *Topeka*, that was an interesting case, very interesting. And then the first student comes to them and says, "I'm having trouble with my landlord," because he heard they went to a law institute. And they have to learn how to resist saying, "Well, now, landlord and tenant law says. . . ." You just say, you know, go see a lawyer. You have to reach this point but now we aren't stopping here. From here I go to Chicago to another conference to try and tap lawyers, and then I go to the American Law School Association meetings and get more lawyers.

We have to set up consultant lawyers out of law faculties. If these schools can't get their lawyers right away on their faculties, there are at least enough law schools scattered throughout this country where we can find liberal arts lawyers who I am positive will agree to consult these social science teachers during their initial innovative work. In other words, what I am saying is we need a great leap forward. You can queue up for so long and then you have to make a move in terms of the manpower demands, competition demands, and the need for introducing law into our liberal arts curriculum across the board. If we don't move fast, if we don't develop a communication network such as has never been developed in the academic field, if we don't make use of law professors, we can't develop consultive framework. We need to get a man here at Catholic University to agree to service, and I mean in a consultive capacity, to find these legal materials that these teachers need, to go out and give an occasional lecture, but also to make the teacher give the lecture, and to listen to her lecture, and to correct her; he's got to be a teacher, he's got to be a scholar. Then the first people we produce have got to train others. They've got to return to their own institution and reach the point where they can start sharing this. And I am almost queasy about this. I almost think in our first institute we should make every institution send at least two people. That way, if one is wrong, the chances are the other one might be right. And if they disagree, they'll talk to their consultant. So you at least reduce the probability of incorrect input in the system at the outset.

The big thing is to get started without too many mistakes. There are going to be mistakes made all over the place. Sure there are going to be mistakes. We have to reduce the input of the mistakes. Now someone like Professor Roberts could consult with teachers in a radius of 100 miles who could simply come in, call upon him, he could visit them, they could come and visit him, and after the summer institute is over he could hold little Saturday morning workshops with them, keep their training up to date, add to what they are learning. This can be done across the country. I don't know if this has ever been done before; I don't know if we can find the bit of money it would take to do it. But I am convinced that I have learned one thing—universities and academies operate two ways. They go to foundations and get huge grants or they have no money, no people, no plan, nothing, and then they start stealing people from everybody else, and a great frantic race occurs, etc.

We have tried in this Association[5] to use the opposite approach. We have tried to say we'll go out and find thousands of people, and we're on our way. We have over a thousand already. We will deliver these people. We're not going to ask for money until we've got the people, the plans, what they want, what they need. We'll be able to name dollars and cents and figures and where they'll meet and what they plan to do, and what schools they will affect and how many undergraduates they've got, and when we've got all the people, then we'll ask for the money. But we are not going to try and get the money and then go out and scrounge around stealing people, and that's why the Law and Society Association exists. When we find enough people who are ready to go, then we'll try and find the funds to start the program. It is an ambitious program, it's very ambitious, I must admit, but I am firmly convinced that you can't introduce innovations in American teaching if you cannot simultaneously affect the kinds of things that are being done by the teachers in the existing positions today at the same time that you are affecting the kinds of training that the people coming into the profession are getting. You've got to do both simultaneously, and we're trying to do both simultaneously.

All I can say is that there is no guarantee about anything, but if there is interest, if there are people who want to do it, they don't even have to know anything about it, they have to have one thing really—and that is a firm conviction that it ought to be done. Now I am biased and prejudiced enough to think that anyone in the liberal arts/social science area today who doesn't think that law is an absolutely unbelievable institution in modern society, he is either blind, deaf or dumb, and I just can't imagine anyone not realizing this.

I am hardput, and I recognize other people have legitimate reasons for not being interested, but I am hardput to comprehend—and I have met some—the increasingly smaller proportion of American social scientists and humanities teachers who simply feel that the law is of no significance in modern society. This number is rapidly becoming almost extinct, and we can either move now or have an impasse, or we are going to be struggling, because the next five years is going to be so competitive that you can't possibly ever fill this need by training new people. We not only have to train new people, but we literally have to retrain a tremendous proportion of the people already in American college teaching, university and college level—humanities, social science, and in some cases even the physical sciences. So it is a big thing. And what I really want to know is what the people teaching at the undergraduate level feel at this point they need, and what kinds of capacities they've got. Would they try something with lawyer consultants? Is it possible to develop plans for a series of small colleges in a given geographical area to hire their own lawyer? They share him, you know, he goes around, he teaches one day at one school, the next day at another school. What's so sacred about having a specialist all on your own faculty? Why don't the colleges do what, as a matter of fact, elementary schools do all the time. They send a specialist around from school to school. They're talking about meeting this need in the sciences by sending physicists out from industry to teach in colleges and high schools. Why can't the universities do the same thing in the areas of law and the social sciences? Share the specialist—get three or four schools who will hire the same man and let him go from school to school. There are all kinds of ways to solve these problems, once you really think out the problems and also once you think that you not only will be trying to solve it by yourself, but you'll be trying to solve it with the assistance and help of an awful lot of other institutions of people within your own given areas.

That's all I want to say.

MASSEL—Shall we start with questions or reactions to Mr. Ball's statement?

FRANKINO*—I would like to give a reaction to Mr. Ball's statement.

MASSEL—If you want to give a reaction rather than ask a question, you'll have to come up here.

FRANKINO—Well it's a short reaction—As a law professor, where do I sign up?

BALL—He just fills out one of the green registration forms with the Law and Society Association. I am particularly interested in getting from law professors the names of the kinds of law students I was talking about who would also be interested in starting their social science training in the summer between their second and third year, because we can speed up their training process considerably, and they can have an awful lot of their social science training done up to the M.A. level by the time they finish their law degree. All of these things can be speeded up. You know education is so wasteful, and time right now can't be wasted, and motives can't be wasted, and interest at particular times in life careers is probably the thing that can be wasted least of all, so we've got to have as many kinds of programs as we find there are standard break points in life careers. Anytime someone is ready to make the change, we're ready too; we've got a program ready for that person. We've been trying to do it so far literally by developing programs tailored to individual needs. We are also convinced that almost every individual program we develop is a pattern. There are other people at the same breakpoint. So we can soon shift from playing with individuals to developing programs for groups of like individuals.

2. Area Planning and the Small Colleges

Unlike the Harvard conferees of 1954, the participants in this conference came in large part from disciplines other than law, and many were from smaller colleges that were interested in introducing law-society to

* Professor Steven P. Frankino, Catholic University Law School.

their undergraduate program within limited resources. This consideration is brought into focus by the following exchange, in which the Chairman, Mr. Massel, and Professors Victor G. Rosenblum of Northwestern, Thomas R. Peterson, O.P., of Providence College, and Sister Catherine Therese, C.S.J., of the College of St. Rose, Albany, N.Y., took part.

MASSEL—In the discussion of Wisconsin, and what was done there, as well as the discussions that we have heard about Northwestern and California and Denver, we have talked about major universities that have all sorts of resources right at their fingertips, that do not have to raise funds in order to be able to carry out any program that have people on law faculties, and people in political science faculties and sociology and other areas, that can work together in order to develop programs of this type. Have we begun to answer the question we typified as: What to do in a small women's college, considering the fact that there are many, many educational institutions in the country that do not have the resources of the University of Wisconsin or any of the other major universities, along the lines of giving them some affirmative help? Not in terms of the suggestion that they can get some occasional help from somebody who is willing to give them a slight amount of time here and there, for this is a problem which requires a considerable amount of investigation in order to see what may be done about taking some chances in taking some foundation grants for purposes of developing faculties and developing teaching materials, and developing programs which will make it possible for those institutions that do not have the resources to do the whole job by themselves.

SISTER CATHERINE THERESE—There is a great need for local centers where small colleges could share in common facilities, course materials, faculty instruction in interdisciplinary work in the social sciences, and from which they could possibly receive some financial assistance for introducing new programs of their own. As Professor Ball said, it is not enough if just one or two of the faculty of a small college are prepared by a meeting such as this. They can go back and be a minority of one, or two, and no one will listen to them.

MASSEL—Would it be desirable to recommend the establishment of an inter-university institution which would provide the broad interdisciplinary education for faculty members and potential teachers? Such an institute could employ a staff of people who ran seminars and helped individual colleges and universities in their program design. Perhaps it would be desirable to develop an organization which would stimulate and help to finance interdisciplinary research and the preparation of adequate teaching materials. Centers could be established at leading universities to provide aid to the small colleges in their vicinity. A university professor might lead faculty seminars at the colleges and help to design student seminars. A younger faculty member might give these interdisciplinary courses at two or three local colleges until they were prepared to give the courses with their own people.

SISTER CATHERINE THERESE—There are difficult budget problems to face in the small colleges. Some kind of stipend would seem to be needed, sufficient to replace a teacher who would take part even in a summer program. We've been more fortunate in getting grants for research and graduate study in the natural sciences than in the social sciences. Some of the sisters, for example, studied at UCLA in the nursing department and have received fellowships for their work. It seems to me when you look around that the social sciences are not as successful in getting the funds.

MASSEL—Are you suggesting that a program of the type we are discussing should include furnishing some financial aid for the colleges that are involved in the enterprise?

PETERSON—I would think so.

SISTER CATHERINE THERESE—It might hinge, in part, on whether you would plan this for the year-type program, or just for the summer session.

MASSEL—Would it be desirable to develop a program which would provide both year-long courses and summer sessions? Would it be desirable to arrange for a series of regional week-long conferences for faculty members, the program to cover the substance of this conference, plus a closer examination of one or two problems?

ROSENBLUM—Now that we are at a level of implementation I think our differences are getting much narrower. So when you are talking about the ways of getting it going, I think these are excellent proposals.

MASSEL—Apparently no university or college has the financial and personnel resources for such a venture. Would it be practicable to organize a group to promote the idea, to set up a more definitive program, and to attempt to arrange financing through the large foundations? Such a program would probably require a new inter-university organization which could take advantage of all the fine work that is going on right now at various major universities.

Such an institution probably would not engage directly in original research. It would encourage work at the major universities and would help to raise funds. However, its own efforts would be dedicated to the promotion of an educational program. The research projects that have been described at the conference are excellent. However, they do not fill the need for teaching materials in a broad course which covers the role of law in our society. Nor do they provide the type of teaching help needed at most universities and liberal arts colleges.

SISTER CATHERINE THERESE—We have many people studying and living at our colleges. They ought to have programs such as you suggest to interest them, and at which a member of every social science discipline taught at the college might be present.

ROSENBLUM—This is closely related to the organization that Harry Ball was talking about last night into which he is pouring in great facets of his energy. It would wind up as a section or a group assigned to work within the association.

MASSEL—But this is the problem I have with working within an association. I think Harry Ball's work with the sociologists has been excellent. I think he has made a great deal of headway. I think, however, that if you take the association I know best, the American Economic Association, and try to bring that forth, just forget it. I think the Political Science Association and the Philosophical Association would go along with this, but what I would be afraid of is if you start bringing associations in, you are either in the position of having to cover all of the associations or of taking the chance that if there's an association you haven't covered the members of that group will say "Why are we left out, this isn't our program."

So that I wonder whether if something of this type were considered it wouldn't be better to set it up on the basis of university and individual participation rather than association participation.

ROSENBLUM—In a sense the Law and Society Association is an association which is just getting started. I think that the major control comes from within a sprightly and interested new group. So I wish Harry were with us this morning; because he could answer all these questions.

MASSEL—I don't believe they are right but I think that the economists, for example, and this is true of many political scientists as well, do not hold the sociologists in very high regard. So that if it were focused on the sociologists it would be difficult to get the other economists greatly interested.

ROSENBLUM—Not necessarily today. I think I would keep that an open point; because Harry has been so careful to try to keep this from being narrowly conceived.

MASSEL—I know that. I don't mean this from a standpoint of sociologists, but rather in terms of the others. I believe that there would be less difficulty on this with sociologists than with almost any other group.

I would like to raise a question with you. People come to a conference of this type and it is very easy to get into the discussions. Very easy to go along with the discussion and even to be impressed by it and say this is the way. As a practical matter, if a program were started, what is your feeling about how much cooperation there would be on the part of the institutions? One of the reasons we are in this present state is because, as Dr. Arlt pointed out, programs of this type have to break through the vested interests. I think the vested intellectual interest is much harder to dislodge than the vested financial interest. How much cooperation could be developed from the institutions in the sense of really moving along with this. Obviously there can't be universal cooperation. If the program worked it would work because a handful of institutions went along with it and began to make some progress. But as you see it looking at colleges of your type, do you think that there would be substantial cooperation?

PETERSON—If it could be shown in some kind of a blocked out program that this will begin at such and such a time in this specific way, I think it would be put in. I think it would certainly be put in for example as a pilot program in the honors courses. If it were successful, I think it would be extended to the rest of the school. But there would have to be something definite and a definite schedule set up with difficulties answered. One of the big difficulties that was presented in a meeting before we came down here was: What can this program give us that we do not already have? I think I have the answer to that from these meetings that have been going on. I think that in our case, as in the case of pretty nearly every college, it's going to be a case of showing. Nobody is going to rush into this, no one is going to immediately accept it as something that is going to be taken without any question or without any difficulty. The going is going to be slow and from the very outset it is going to be a case of showing. But I think there would be cooperation if this could be done, and I think it can.[6]

CHAPTER IX
NEXT STEPS

This concluding chapter presents (1) the formal proposals of the conference, (2) a fuller formulation independently prepared by Mr. Mark S. Massel after the conference, (3) a postscript by the editor.

1. Recommendations of Conference

MASSEL*—I will undertake to report on the third (planning) group. It turned out that the third group was no longer interested in intellectual discussion or intellectual activities. We found ourselves in the third group as a collection of activists.

We started on the premise that the case for a Law-Society program had been made through the discussions we had in the last two and a half days, and that therefore there was no point in wasting any more time in trying to reaffirm and reestablish the case. The question was, "What do we do about it?" And we have a recommendation to make which the group agreed to unanimously. The recommendation was:

That some central institute, or some institution, be set up for the purpose of developing an effective program in this area;

That this institution should, on the one hand, work with the universities that have done work in the field already in order to get ideas and, on the other, to see what might be done about taking their materials for purposes of preparing additional materials;

That that institute should make available a series of programs to educational institutions that would be interested in cooperating;

That these programs would include setting up courses that might run for a full year, setting up conferences that might run several days or might run for a week;

That the purposes of this educational activity on the part of the institute would be to bring together people in the social sciences and the law—and there was some interest in extending this beyond the social sciences and including those people in the natural and physical sciences who would be interested—for purposes of developing faculty people

---

* Mark S. Massel, Brookings Institution, Conference Chairman.

who could give courses and conduct seminars in this area at their colleges and universities;

That the program should be developed in such a fashion that it not only had the flexibility with regard to the time—by providing courses for a year, for a summer, and discussions for a week—but also that the program should provide flexibility in helping to tailor programs which would be carried out at individual institutions. So, for example, an institution might well decide that it would set up three successive programs by quarters for an honors group in order to get started: A program in law and economics, a program in law and political science, and a program in law and sociology. That these courses would be taught by people coming from the social science departments, preferably with somebody who had a background in law. That in most instances it would be desirable to work the program out in such a fashion that there would be faculty seminars in the subjects in order, on the one hand, to develop people in the social sciences (and, if necessary, in the physical and natural sciences) who would have an understanding of the purposes and objectives of the law through discussion with legally-trained people, and that, on the other hand, the legally-trained people would develop an understanding of the social sciences, and, in some instances, the impact of the physical and of the natural sciences.

That, in addition, the program would be aimed at finding central areas in which there was a collection of small colleges that would cooperate, working out an arrangement through its own institutes and educational programs whereby men who were on the faculties of local law schools would undertake the task of running faculty seminars for the faculties within the area, and then cooperating with the faculties in the area in order to develop courses and seminars for the students. Illustrative of this was a situation in Los Angeles, where there are a number of small colleges that cannot afford to develop a program of this type but that might be helped considerably by a local program in the Los Angeles area. Now the basis of the discussion was that even though universities and colleges might like to participate in such a program no one university or college has the resources, in terms of funds and in terms of personnel, to be able to develop a program by itself. That it was most desirable therefore to find a way for channeling funds and resources to be used on a broader basis. That it was most desirable also to take advantage of the different experiments which would be developed in these various cooperating institutions; and that from that standpoint a program of this type required a considerable amount of effort and the development of an institutional framework to carry it through. In order to accomplish the total program it was felt that it would be desirable to develop preliminary plans for the entire program, probably to circulate the ideas about the preliminary plans among the people who had attended the conference, and others, in order to maintain interest, and then to see what could be done along the line of raising funds. That in any event it would be highly desirable to have some communications on the subject with the people who had attended the conference within a period of, say, six months, so that there would be no chance that interest would lag, and there would be no chance that there would be a dropping of the ideas and a dropping of the stimulation that this conference has produced.

That it might be desirable to go so far that even before the full program is implemented to have some follow-up discussions on a regional basis with the people who had attended the session, possibly bringing some others in, and looking for methods of cooperation with other groups and other organizations, including the National Science Foundation, the National Humanities Foundation, when it is set up, and the various charitable foundations who might help to supply funds.

2. Proposal for an Educational Program in Law in Society

MARK S. MASSEL

It is proposed that an institute should be organized to promote a clearer understanding of the roles of law and government in our society. The ultimate aim of the institute would be: to develop undergraduate courses; stimulate graduate departments in the social sciences to explore the many public policy issues which have legal consequences; and promote a clearer appreciation of the broad role of government and of the social sciences in the law schools.

Such an institute would be responsive to the demand of various colleges for a program which will give their students a deeper appreciation of the legal underpinnings of our society. At the same time, it would provide continuing encouragement and coordination for the teaching and research programs in public policy problems which are under way in various graduate and law schools.

Background

The increasing complexity of the problems of public policy creates a need for political and intellectual leaders who grasp the essential conditions for the effective operation of our democratic system. There is a steady increase of economic and political interdependence within our own borders and among nations. Dramatic changes have affected all nations: revolutionary technological advances on a broad scale; the unfolding of nuclear energy for war and peace; the increasing social awareness of poverty, an awareness which influences both the haves and the have-nots; the desire to move entire feudal or tribal societies into the twentieth century; and the growing role of government. A number of developments have had particular application in the United States: new concepts of civil rights; changes in the laws of trespass, of voting, and of consumer rights; the poverty program; and the increasing activities of government in research, development, purchasing, regulation of industry, improvement of natural resources, and consumer protection.

Many of these changes involve the new-found exercise of the rights of individuals and groups. We are witnessing a growing use of citizen action in a democratic manner to promote community solutions for pressing social problems. Slum dwellers have become aware of the legal bases for compelling housing improvements. Disenfranchised voters have instigated legal action to secure their constitutional rights. Minority groups have pressed for fair treatment. Law has become a stronger influence for social progress.

The advancing evolution of our democratic society requires a deep understanding of basic principles by all citizens. Those who need aid must appreciate the underlying rights which our legal system gives them as well as the limits which they must observe. During the course of many trying periods everyone must recognize the differences between permissible and illegal activity, between liberty and license, between the peaceful exercise of civil rights and mob rule. All of these emergent forces, whether they relate to the increasing role of government or the protection of the individual, cast a new emphasis on the leadership of people who understand the underlying legal attributes of our democratic system.

The education of political and intellectual leaders during these changing times casts a heavy burden on our colleges and universities. The proliferation of knowledge and discovery has stimulated more detailed, precise courses of study, courses which make for increasing specialization. Because of this specialization, considerations of the law have been confined largely to professional law schools. Yet, solutions for the many pressing public problems require people who grasp the fundamental interrelationships of the disciplines and appreciate our legal traditions. The physical and natural sciences have found a compelling need to formulate cross-overs. In much the same fashion, there exists a forceful necessity to relate law and the social sciences. A parallel requirement is the inter-relation of this group and the physical-natural science combination.

Our centers of learning must satisfy these needs to assure fruitful progress in the treatment of the substantial public policy issues. Unless they understand the framework of our legal system with its influence on personal liberties and the smooth functioning of the economy, many well-intentioned individuals may reach for "practical" authoritarian solutions which will injure the peaceful fabric of everyday life. Conversely, a mechanical application of legal principles can place severe limitations on solutions for these issues. Without an appreciation of the many changes in economic, social, and technological conditions, without an awareness of the analytical contributions of the various disciplines, many, if not most, of our lawyers—as legislators, government officials, judges, practitioners, and opinion leaders—may concentrate on outworn legal procedures and fail to cope with problems of substance. Similarly, unless we broaden their understanding, many social scientists will concentrate on narrowing technical fields which interest their own colleagues while they virtually ignore the vital public policy problems.

No single educational institution has the resources to make basic progress in this area. Courses must be devised. Teaching materials must be made available. Faculty personnel must be developed to give the courses while other faculty members need an effective introduction to this approach.

Nature of Undergraduate Courses

The specific designs of undergraduate courses would be developed through experimentation. The courses cannot be cast in a single mold. One school might have a course in Law in Society, given by a member of the law faculty. Another might center a course in the economics department, or political science, or sociology. The nature of the study would depend, in each instance, on the organization of the school and the interest of specific faculty members.

At this stage, however, the general objectives of such studies can be delineated in terms of the students' understanding of several features of our society: legal protection of the rights of the individual; influence of the structure of legal rights, duties, and liabilities on economic and social stability; administration of the legal system and its accommodation to change; developing role of government and the influence of its regulatory, purchasing, and fiscal policies on the legal system; relation between the legal procedures, the social sciences, and the humanities.

Obviously, such a course would center on an understanding of the institutional nature of law and government. It would avoid any pretense of law school education. While it might help students to understand when they require legal assistance, it would not provide any "black letter" law which would encourage them in the mistaken belief that they can provide their own legal advice.

Above all, the course would be aimed at the development of informed citizens. It would not attempt to provide specialized preparation for law school education.

Program

The proposed institute would be an inter-university organization. Most of its work would be farmed out to members of university and college faculties. It would carry on several types of activity.

1. Preparation of teaching materials. Many useful studies, as well as new work which is under way, would be assembled and worked into adequate publications for undergraduate study.

2. Development of faculties. Several methods would be followed.

a. Young teachers of social sciences and law would be given a year of postgraduate work designed to provide an appreciation of the roles of law and of government as well as an understanding of the relations between law and the social sciences. They would attend seminars and prosecute joint research in fields which require law and the social sciences.

b. Summer seminars would be organized for older faculty members.

c. Regional week-long seminars would be organized to introduce faculty members to the program.

d. Faculty seminars would be organized in a number of universities and colleges.

e. Instructors who are located in leading universities would be assigned to two or three smaller colleges in the region to conduct faculty seminars and undergraduate courses.

3. Promotion of research. The institute would provide continuing encouragement and coordination of research work which is undertaken jointly by teachers of law and of a social science. Conferences of these researchers would be held to compare findings and experience in joint research methods.

4. Joint committees of the learned societies. The institute would promote joint committees which would investigate problems of interest to the various disciplines. Aid would be offered to such existing committees as the joint committee on regulatory agencies of the American Association of Law Schools and the American Political Science Association.

5. Course experimentation. The institute would promote the development of specific courses. It would arrange for meetings of the course instructors and for publications describing their experiments and results.

The institute would be undertaken in response to a need which is felt in many educational institutions. The changing times have made many colleges aware of the necessity of providing improved preparation for citizenship. More and more law schools are trying to bring their courses closer to the requirements of modern government and private practice. Many educators share a belief that graduate students require a firmer understanding of modern public policy problems. A cooperative program sponsored by the institute would provide our centers of higher learning with much needed help.

3.   The Poverty Pocket

If there is, as the conference participants concluded without audible dissent, a decisive value to teaching undergraduates the role of law in society, there is a woefully distressed area in American higher education today. For a recent limited survey of university and college curricula suggests that a basic course on the legal system is offered at less than 4 percent of the nation's institutions of undergraduate instruction.[2] And no one contends that imparting significant knowledge about law in other liberal arts courses (as suggested at the conference) is a thing of the present. This too awaits a future when faculty personnel are trained for the task, teaching materials developed, and university administrations are willing and able to pay the price in course time, faculty man hours, and budget dollars.

As we reach for the moon and Mars, and dream about law in outer space or a "rule of law" in the world, one question remains unanswered to anyone's satisfaction: Does the educated American even faintly understand the role of law in his own national society?

How do his teachers themselves see law? As a phase of mechanics? As a mystery? Or as it is: that most dynamic social and moral system where fact and value meet.

If in social living the prime poverty is ignorance, perhaps the time has come for liberal arts educators to admit that here, at the hub of it all, is their own pocket of poverty.

Footnote References

PREFACE

[1] The following questions were posed in the preconference materials:

1. Is a basic college course in law now a must for an educated American? Do only the professional lawyers know where the "school prayer" decision came from and whether it must stay? How did the Supreme Court come to change its position on school integration? On right of indigents to counsel? On compelling state legislatures to redistrict? Why is the Court so concerned with "rights" of those accused of crime? Why is there anti-poverty legislation? Civil rights legislation?

2. Are lawyers equipped to handle their professional responsibilities without fuller cooperation with social scientists, philosophers, theologians? Is not law, truly understood, itself a social science?

3. Can social scientists find a common language in which to speak among themselves? With lawyers? Philosophers? Theologians?

4. Can positivist (behavior-oriented) and norm- (value-) oriented social scientists use "the law-society area" as a new, common field in which to attempt a reintegration of social science?

5. Can we exclude values (as "unscientific") from political science? From sociology? From law?

6. Can we stop the progressive splintering of social science (e.g., a suggested "new social science of organizations")? Should we try?

7. Can the undergraduate liberal arts curriculum find a place for the new theme of concentration—"Law-Society"? As a minor? As a major? Within a seminary curriculum (as Philosophy? Theology? Sociology?)?

8. Does the present theological dialogue have relevance to these educational problems in our pluralistic society? Is a "subjective" (individualized, emotional, equivocal) approach in the sciences from sociology to theology an inevitable reaction against the analytic (mathematical, positivist, univocal) approach?

[2] Author of *Competition and Monopoly:* (New York, Anchor Edition, 1964).

[3] A breakdown of conference participants shows 17 law faculty members, 42 from the other disciplines (anthropology 2, economics 2, history 4, philosophy 6, political science 10, sociology 15, theology 3), 5 from administration (3 Deans of Arts and Sciences, 1 Executive-Vice President, 1 Assistant to the President), 2 from government, and 5 from community organizations (Council of Graduate Schools in the United States, District of Columbia Bar Association, Legal Aid Society of the District of Columbia, Religion and Labor Council). In addition, several specialists in the fields of "Law and Poverty" and "Social Studies in Religious Education" participated in the workshops held on these subjects.

By contrast, 25 of the 31 eminent participants at the 1954 Harvard conference were lawyers, seven of whom were arguably bi-disciplinary (three in political science, one in history, one in rhetoric and oratory, one Dean of Humanities and Science, one Provost). The non-lawyers were one each from economics, industrial history, political science, and business, with two sociologists. The institutions represented were Harvard (9), Massachusetts Institute of Technology (3), Stanford (3), Chicago (2), Columbia (2), Amherst, Carnegie Institute of Technology, London School of Economics, Michigan, Princeton, Tulane, Washington University, Wisconsin and Yale, with one participant each from bench, bar and business.

[4] Berman, *On the Teaching of Law in the Liberal Arts Curriculum* (Brooklyn, Foundation Press, 1956). The Harvard conference led to the development of a slender literature on the subject that includes:

Appel, *Law as a Social Science in the Undergraduate Curriculum,* 10 J. LEGAL ED. 485 (1958); Beaney, *Teaching of Law Courses in the Liberal Arts College: A View*

209

from the College, 13 J. LEGAL ED. 55 (1960); Becker, *A Political Science-Law Course for the Liberal Arts Curriculum,* 16 J. LEGAL ED. 333 (1964); Berman, *Teaching Law Courses in Liberal Arts College: A Challenge to the Law Schools,* 13 J. LEGAL ED. 47 (1960); Eliot, *Law in the Liberal Arts Curriculum,* 9 J. LEGAL ED. 1 (1956); Hall, *Law and the Intellectuals,* 9 J. LEGAL ED. 8 (1956); Harum, *The Case for an Undergraduate Law Elective in Liberal Arts,* 12 J. LEGAL ED. 418 (1960); Weissman, *Law and Liberal Education,* 15 VAND. L. REV. 609 (1962); Wright, *Law as a University Discipline,* 14 U. of TORONTO L. J. 253 (1962).

INTRODUCTION

[1] The selections in this Part derive from the *Transcript,* pp. 1-13 (Section 1); 343-6 (Section 2); and 13-16 (Section 3).

[2] This movement coordinated with a comparable one in the Fine Arts and led to the passage by Congress of legislation establishing the Arts and Humanities Foundation which was signed by President Johnson on September 29, 1965.

[3] The legislation as passed (cf. n. 2, *supra*) appears to leave this conclusion intact.

CHAPTER I

[1] The selections in this chapter derive from the *Transcript,* pp. 62-79 (Section 1); 190-202 (Section 2); 203-211 (Section 3); 220-229 (Section 4); 40-61 (Section 5).

[2] New York, 1963.

[3] New York, 1932.

[4] This paper was translated for Professor Villey by Sister Mary Welling, O.P., Corpus Christi Monastery, Nairobi, Kenya.

[5] I.e., Professor Villey's.

[6] See Firth, *Elements of Social Organization* (Boston, 1963), pp. 36, 40 and 78.

[7] See Bidney, *The Concept of Freedom in Anthropology* (The Hague, 1963), pp. 11-13.

[8] See pp. 46-51, *infra.*

CHAPTER II

[1] The selections in this chapter derive from the *Transcript,* pp. 83-87 (Section 1); 88-96 (Section 2); 97-106 (Section 3); 107-112 (Section 4); 113-136 (Section 5).

[2] *Brown* v. *Board of Education of Topeka,* 347 U.S. 483 (1954) (footnote 11).

[3] *Lucas* v. *Colorado General Assembly,* 337 U.S. 713, 748 (1964).

[4] Dahl, *A Preface to Democratic Theory* (New York, 1964).

[5] Professor of sociology, Princeton University.

[6] The June 1965 newsletter of the Law and Society Association (which was only launched in 1964) advises that the Association has been officially incorporated, and that recruitment of membership has been extended from the American Sociological Association to the American Political Science Association (1965 meeting).

[7] Professor Philip Selznick; see *infra,* p. 51.

[8] Professor Robert G. Yegge; see *supra,* p. 42.

[9] The Russell Sage Foundation has granted the Law and Society Association a $54,000 grant for a three year experimental stage of the Law and Society Bulletin. (LSA Newsletter, June, 1965).

[10] Skolnick, *Justice Without Trial: Law Enforcement in Democratic Society* (New York, 1966).

[11] Berman, *Justice in the U.S.S.R., an Interpretation of Soviet Law* (New York, 1963). Revised ed. of *Justice in Russia* (Cambridge, 1950).

[12] Wasserstrom, *The Judicial Decision: Towards a Theory of Legal Justification* (Stanford, 1961).

[13] Massel, *Competition and Monopoly: Legal and Economic Issues* (New York, Anchor Paperback, 1964).

[14] Carlin, *Lawyers on Their Own* (New Brunswick, 1962).

CHAPTER III

[1] The selections in this chapter derive from the *Transcript,* pp. 137-150 (Section 1); 225-246, 259-283 (Section 2); 294-310, 247-258, 330-342, 366-369 (Section 3); 323-8 (Section 4).

[2] *Gibbons* v. *Ogden,* 6 Wheat. 131 (1820)

[3] Summers, "Law and the Undergraduate Curriculum," (mimeographed memorandum dated July 24, 1964).

[4] Law School Admission Test.

[5] See n. 4. to Preface, *supra,* p. 209.

[6] Berman, *The Nature and Functions of Law* (Brooklyn, 1958).

[7] Shepherd and Sher, *Law in Society: an Introduction to Freedom of Contract* (New York, 1960).

[8] Auerbach, Garrison, Hurst and Mermin, *The Legal Process* (San Francisco, 1961).

[9] In the latest edition only 200 of the 900 pages are principally devoted to workmen's compensation.

[10] Levi, *An Introduction to Legal Reasoning* (Chicago, 1949).

[11] Beveridge, *The Life of John Marshall* (New York, 1919).

[12] Bowen, *Yankee from Olympus* (Boston, 1944).

[13] Nizer, *My Life in Court* (New York, 1961).

[14] Auerbach, Hurst, etc., *op. cit.*

[15] *Wieman* v. *Updegraff,* 344 U.S. 183 (1952).

[16] *West Virginia State Board of Education* v. *Barnette,* 319 U.S. 624 (1943).

[17] Bedford, *The Faces of Justice* (London, 1961).

[18] Hall, *Theft, Law and Society* (Boston, 1935).

[19] Berman, *Justice in Russia* (Cambridge, 1950); *Justice in the U.S.S.R.* (New York, 1963) (revised edition of other book).

[20] Edgar S. Cahn; see *infra,* p. 119.

[21] Riesman, "Law and Sociology: Recruitment, Training and Colleagueship," 9 *Stanford L. Rev.* 643 (1957).

[22] Wilson, "Legal Education of Undergraduates," 17 *Reports of the American Bar Association* 439 (1894).

[23] Berle, *supra,* p. 6.

[24] Friedrich, *The Philosophy of Law in Historical Perspective* (Chicago, 1958).

[25] Sait, *Political Institutions* (New York, 1938).

[26] Bryce, *Studies in History and Jurisprudence* (Oxford, 1901).

[27] Holmes, *The Common Law* (Boston, 1881).

[28] Pound, *The Spirit of the Common Law* (Boston, 1921).

[29] Howe (ed.), *The Correspondence of Mr. Justice Holmes and Sir Frederick Pollock,* 1874-1932 (Cambridge, Mass., 1941).

[30] Cardozo, *The Nature of the Judicial Process* (New Haven, 1921).

[31] Cardozo, *The Growth of the Law* (New Haven, 1924).

[32] *Missouri Bar-Prentice Hall Survey, A Motivational Study of Public Attitudes and Law Office Management* (Englewood Cliffs, N. J., 1963). Copies were distributed largely to local bar associations.

[33] *Id.* at 41-43.

[34] *Id.* at 41.

[35] *Id.* at 37.

[36] The Institute of Continuing Legal Education in Ann Arbor, Michigan, sponsored by the University of Michigan Law School, Wayne State University Law School and the State Bar of Michigan, conducts a wide range of continuing legal education programs for lawyers. One of these is an "Annual Advocacy Institute." The 15th Institute, held March 20-21, 1964, was concerned with Medical Malpractice and was attended by approximately 2,000 lawyers drawn from something like 40 states.

[37] Dr. Charles G. Childs, III, Professor of Surgery and Chairman, Department of Surgery, The University of Michigan Medical School.

[38] *The Citizen in Court: Litigant-Witness-Juror-Judge* by Delmar Karlen, Professor of Law and Director, Institute of Judicial Administration, New York University Law School.

[39] Constitution of the U.S.S.R., December 5, 1936 (as amended), Article 130: "Every citizen of the U.S.S.R. is obliged to observe the Constitution of the Union of Soviet Socialist Republics, to execute the law, to maintain labor discipline, to have an honest attitude toward socialist duty, and to respect the rules of socialist community life."

[40] By and large the law, whether American, Anglo-Saxon or Soviet, probably is that one normally is not legally, but only morally, obligated to be a Good Samaritan, but if he undertakes to act he may be liable for negligence in acting. Post-World War II developments in France indicate that the duty to be a Good Samaritan is there becoming legal: a father-in-law who failed to extend a plank to his son-in-law who drowned in the icy canal was held both civilly and criminally liable. See Prosser, Handbook on the Law of Torts, 3rd ed. (St. Paul, 1964), pp. 334-346: and *Twentieth Century Comparative and Conflicts Law: Legal Essays in Honor of Hessel E. Yntema* (Leyden, 1961) edited by Kurt H. Nadelmann, Arthur T. Von Mehren and John N. Hazard for the Board of Editors of *The American Journal of Comparative Law.* See especially Dawson, "Rewards for the Rescue of Human Life," pp. 142-159, and Hazard, "Soviet Socialism and the Duty to Rescue," pp. 160-171.

[41] Henry M. Hart, Jr. and Albert M. Sacks, *The Legal Process: Basic Problems in the Making and Application of Law,*" (tentative edition, Cambridge, Mass., 1958).

[42] See latest edition, London, *The World of Law* (New York, 1960).

[43] Auerbach, Garrison, *op. cit.*

[44] Shepherd and Sher, *op. cit.*

[45] Berman, *The Nature and Functions of Law, op. cit.*

[46] Veblen, *The Higher Learning in America* (New York, 1918: Stanford reprint, 1954).

[47] Associate Dean Summer Marcus of the College of Business Administration of the University of Washington, wrote after the Conference of "the experience of our College in teaching law to undergraduates: Like other business schools, we require our undergraduates to take courses in business law. Four years ago, however, we revised the initial offering in this area to provide for our students an introduction to the legal process. The course is somewhat inappropriately entitled 'Legal Factors in the Business Environment,' but falls clearly within the ambit of the courses discussed at the Catholic University Conference. The text which is used is Berman's *The Nature and Functions of Law,* along with supplementary materials, which will be incorporated, in part, in a forthcoming revised edition of the book that is being co-edited by Professor William Greiner, a member of our staff. The two principal instructors in the course are Professor Greiner and Mr. Marvin Durning, both of whom are graduates of the Yale Law School, and who have done advanced work and taught in the field of economics, as well as that of law. In our graduate School of Business there is offered a field entitled Business and Its Environment, which is interdisciplinary in nature and which deals with materials in economics, law, and the behavioral sciences."

[48] See *supra*, p. 49.

CHAPTER IV

[1] The selections in this chapter derive from the *Transcript,* pp. 137-150 (Section 1); 225-246, 259-283 (Section 2); 294-310, 247-258, 330-342, 366-369 (Section 3); 323-328 (Section 4).

[2] Leclercq, *Du droit naturel à la sociologie* (Paris, Spes ed., 1960).

[3] Harrington, *The Other America: Poverty in the United States* (New York, 1962).

[4] Lewis, *Five Families* (New York, 1959).

[5] Lewis, *The Children of Sanchez* (New York, 1961).

[6] Goldstein and Katz, *The Family and the Law* (New York, 1965).

[7] Gellhorn, *Individual Freedom and Governmental Restraint* (Baton Rouge, 1957).

[8] *Infra,* p. 128.

[9] Woodward, *The Strange Career of Jim Crow* (New York, 1955).

[10] Litwack, *North of Slavery, the Negro in the Free States,* 1790-1860 (Chicago, 1961).

[11] Barkun, *Towards a Theoretical Framework for Decentralized Law,* Ph.D. Dissertation, Northwestern, 1964.

[12] Muir, *Primitive Government* (Baltimore (Penguin ed.), 1962).

[13] Frank, *Courts on Trial* (New York (Athenaeum reprint), 1963).

[14] Auerbach, Hurst, *et al., op. cit.*

[15] Professor Ball is presently at the University of Hawaii.

[16] *Colegrove* v. *Green,* 328 U.S. 549 (1946).

[17] *Baker* v. *Carr,* 369 U.S. 186 (1962).

[18] Kennedy, *Profiles in Courage* (New York, 1956).

[19] *Gideon* v. *Wainwright,* 372 U.S. 335 (1963).

[20] Since October 4, 1965 Mr. Justice Fortas of the United States Supreme Court.

CHAPTER V

[1] The selections in this chapter derive from *Transcript,* pp. 151-166 (Section 1); 406-458, 546-547 (Section 2).

[2] *Gideon* v. *Wainright,* 372 U.S. 335 (1963).

[3] See Botein, "Manhattan Bail Project: Its Impact on Criminology and the Criminal Process," 49 *Texas L. Rev.* 319 (1965).

[4] Criminal Justice Act of 1964, 88th Congress, 2nd Sess., Public Law 88-455, 78 Stat. 552.

[5] Cf. U.S. Department of Health, Education and Welfare, *Conference Proceedings on The Extension of Legal Services to the Poor* (1964).

[6] *Brotherhood of Railway Trainmen* v. *Virginia,* 377 U.S. 1 (1964).

[7] Cf. n. 2, *supra.*

[8] 369 U.S. 186 (1962).

[9] 347 U.S. 483 (1954).

[10] *HEW Conference, op. cit.,* pp. 13-14.

[11] Donnelly, Goldstein, and Schwartz, *Criminal Law: Problems for Decision on the Promulgation, Invocation and Administration of a Law of Crimes* (New York, 1962).

[12] See bibliography following this workshop.

[13] Mrs. Virginia Lehmann, a lawyer with extensive experience in coordinating with social workers, was prevented by a disabling accident from attending the workshop, as planned. She forwarded this relevant illustration: "The following is one example of cooperation between a lawyer and a social worker in the area of the law as a technique for helping people out of trouble:

"A young married man with several small children came to the lawyer because his paycheck was tied up by one of his creditors. The young couple were overwhelmed by multiple debts and it was useless to deal with the one creditor without dealing with all of the creditors on the basis of some workable plan. The lawyer suggested a wage earner's bankruptcy proceeding which would allow the young man to pay off his debts and at the same time free him from constant harrassment by one creditor or another—which might result in the loss of his job—while he was making his payments. The client was enthusiastic about the suggestion; he was then referred to the social worker.

"In consultation with the lawyer, the social worker helped the young man and his wife work out a budget together which would allow them enough for necessities and still leave a reasonable amount out of each pay check to turn over to the court for distribution to the creditors.

"With the plan made, the lawyer took all the necessary legal steps to initiate the wage earner's bankruptcy proceeding and to notify all the creditors. This, by the way, is a time-consuming and highly technical piece of work.

"Carrying through on the plan was a long drawn out process requiring self control and determination on the part of both the young man and his wife. The social worker stood by them throughout. She gave encouragment, helped them learn better buying habits, pointed out free or low-cost resources for health care and recreation which were available to them, suggested part-time work for the wife which would not interfere with adequate care and supervision of the children, and found out about night school courses so that the young man could equip himself for better paying and more satisfying work.

"The couple emerged from the ordeal debt free, with their self respect intact, and with increased capacity to handle their own affairs in the future. Neither the lawyer nor the social worker alone could have made this possible."

CHAPTER VI

[1] The selections in this chapter derive from the *Transcript*, pp. 355-361 (Section 1); 380-383, 390-395 (Section 2); 400-401, 517-519 (Section 3).

[2] The *licence en droit* compares roughly to a LL.B. or J.D. degree.

[3] *Méthode sociologique et Droit* (Strasbourg Conference) (Paris, 1958); *Droit, économie et sociologie* (Toulouse Conference) (Paris, 1959).

[4] *Supra*, pp. 9-21.

[5] Berman, *On the Teaching of Law in the Liberal Arts Curriculum, op. cit.*, p. 80.

[6] *Id.* at 131-132.

[7] *Id.* at 147.

[8] "Of the thirty one participants in the [1954 Harvard] conference, fourteen were law school professors, . . . seven were persons with law degrees who are college professors or educators in faculties other than law. . . . *Id.* at 3 (Professor Berman's Preface).

[9] See n. 3 to Preface, *supra*, p. 209.

[10] Cf. *supra*, p. 94.

[11] The Law and Society Association. See *supra*, p. 49.

[12] The course outlined here was subsequently given at Providence College in 1965-66, and is being repeated in 1966-67.

CHAPTER VII

[1] The selections in this chapter derive from the *Transcript*, pp. 459-514 (Section 1); 539-542 (Section 2).

[2] Maxwell, "Should Christians Press for Revision of Company Law?", 40 *U. of Detroit L. J.*, 1-165 (1962).

"Company Law: A Synthesis of Opinion," 40 *U. of Detroit L. J.* 439-509 (1963).

[3] Monsignor George Higgins, Executive Director, National Catholic Welfare Conference.

[4] Edward R. F. Sheehan, "Not Peace, but the Sword: The New Anguish of American Catholicism," *The Saturday Evening Post*, November 28, 1964.

[5] Gibson Winter, *Suburban Captivity of the Churches* (Garden City, N.Y., 1961).

[6] Gibson Winter, *The Metropolis as a New Creation* (New York, 1963).

[7] Edward Duff, S.J., "Property in the American Environment," *Social Order*, vol. 9, no. 1 (January, 1959), p. 2.

[8] Huizinga, *The Waning of the Middle Ages* (New York, 1954), p. 2.

[9] Todd, ed., *The Problems of Authority* (Baltimore, 1962).

[10] National Catholic Educational Association.

[11] Pope Paul VI, Encyclical *Ecclesiam Suam* (August 6, 1964), *The Pope Speaks*, vol. 10, no. 3 (1965), pp. 253-292, at p. 290 (Par. no. 113).

[12] Second Vatican Council, "Constitution on the Church," November 21, 1964, Par. 37.

CHAPTER VIII

[1] The selections in this chapter derive from the *Transcript*, pp. 371-378 (Section 1); 402, 528-534, 543-545 (Section 2).

[2] Berman, *On the Teaching of Law in the Liberal Arts Curriculum*, op. cit., pp. 143-145.

[3] *Transcript*, pp. 316-317.

[4] *Brown* v. *Board of Education of Topeka*, 347 U.S. 483 (1954)—the first desegregation case.

[5] I.e. The Law and Society Association. See *supra*, p. 49.

[6] See n. 12 to Chapter VI, *supra*, p. 215.

CHAPTER IX

[1] The selections in Section 1 of this chapter derive from the *Transcript*, pp. 546, 552-556.

[2] A survey compiled in the summer of 1964 by the chairman-designate of the 1965 A.A.L.S. Committee on Teaching Law Outside the Law Schools reports that of the approximately 2100 American universities and colleges only 80 as yet offer basic liberal arts courses on law. Summers, "Law and the Undergraduate Curriculum" (Mimeographed memorandum, dated July 24, 1964, p. 1). Professor Summers specifies that " 'basic courses about law,' as used here, refers to courses of the kind typically offered under one of the following titles: Law and Society, Legal Process, Elements of Law, Introduction to Law, The Nature and Functions of Law, Law and Social Control, Law and Its Administration, Law and the Modern State, Introduction to the Legal Order, Law and the Political Community." He adds that 40 other institutions "offer a course entitled Jurisprudence or The Judicial Process."

INDEX

Index

Abbott, Richard D., 79, 84-8, 93, 94, 97, 147-9, 150, 152
  "Fresh Start in Canada, A," 84-8
  "Undergraduate Law Department: Experiment in Canada, A," 147-9
Accounting and accountants, 27, 32, 91, 92
Accrediting agencies, xiv
Action Populaire, 168
Actuarial approach, xxii, 114, 116
Administration, the (Johnson) (*see also* United States Government), 2-3, 119, 137
Administrative law, 90, 92
Advocacy, 45, 129
African studies, xi
Agriculture, 14
Airlie House, 168
Aluminum Corporation of America (Alcoa), 35
American Council of Learned Societies, xiii
American Economic Association, 200
American Philosophical Association, 200
American Political Science Association, 200, 207
American studies, xi
American University, i, xiv, xv, 79, 88
Amherst College, 209
Anthropology and anthropologists, i, ix, xii, xvi, 26, 28, 29, 31, 95, 109-11, 164, 173
Antitrust, 32-3
Aquinas Institute of Philosophy and Theology (Chicago), 29, 58, 113, 159, 160, 163-4, 180
Aquinas, St. Thomas, xviii, 11, 15-21
  legal philosophy of, 11
  natural law in, 19, 164
Arbitration, xxiii
Archaeology, vii
Area planning, of law-society courses for small colleges, 197-201
Area studies, xi-xii
  institutes in, xi
  interdisciplinary activity in, xi
Arens, Richard, 27, 32, 57, 100-2, 104
  family problems as field for undergraduate instruction in law, 100-2

Aristotle, 11, 15-21, 98, 115
  Nicomachaean Ethics, 16, 19
  Politics, 19
Arlt, Gustave A., x-xii, xiii, xiv, 187, 200
  "Historical Survey of Interdisciplinary Studies," x-xii
Arts and Humanities Foundation, x, xiii, 210
Ashley, Very Rev. Benedict, O.P., 163
Association of American Law Schools, xviii, 195, 215
Atomic energy, viii, ix
Augustine, St., 20-1, 183
  Augustinian tradition, 17
  Rule of, 185

Ball, Harry V., 34-5, 46-51, 79, 89, 93-5, 107-9, 114-8, 150-2, 154-5, 193-7, 198, 199, 200
  "Law and Society Project at Wisconsin," 46-51
  "Need of Adaptability, The," 93-5
Barkman, Francis E., 79-84. 92
  "Understanding Law and Our Society," 79-84
Barkun, Michael, xx, 41, 64, 66, 109-11, 131
  anthropology as field for undergraduate instruction in law, 109-11
Barriers among social disciplines, viii, xv-xxiii
  need for breaking down, viii
  dialog concerning, xv-xxiii
Bazelon, Judge David, 161
Bedford, Sybille, 73
  Faces of Justice, The, 73
Behavioral sciences (*see also* Disciplines), xiii
Beitzinger, Henry, 28, 114, 150-1
Bellow, Gary, 129, 130. 132, 135, 137-8, 141-2
  bibliography for course in law and poverty (with Gerald M. Caplan), 138-41
  law and poverty workshop, chairman of, 129, 141-2
Bentham, Jeremy, 12, 14, 18
Beowulf, 119

219